New Zealand
Gardens
Open to Visit

Jillian and Denis Friar

Hodder Moa Beckett

*We dedicate this book to all
those kind people who offered us hospitality
on our journeying around New Zealand
and to our daughter and son-in-law,
Naomi and Robert Hall,
for caring so well for our children
Daniel (15), Joy (13) and Sarah (11)
in our absence.*

Front Cover:
Kimbolton Rhododendron Gardens, Rangitikei, North Island (page 130)
and Wrights Watergardens, South Auckland (page 53).

ISBN 1-86958-343-4

© 1996 J. & D. Friar / DENZART

Published in 1996 by Hodder Moa Beckett Publishers Limited
[a member of the Hodder Headline Group]
4 Whetu Place, Mairangi Bay, Auckland, New Zealand

Typeset by J. & D. Friar / DENZART, Auckland

Printed through Bookbuilders, Hong Kong

CONTENTS

ICON KEY

🐕	no dogs please
🚶‍🐕	dogs on leashes only
👫	supervised children only
👫	no children please
🚭	no smoking
♿	wheelchair access
♿	no wheelchair access
🚻	toilet available
🚻	no toilet available
⛱	picnickers welcome
☕	morning and afternoon teas available
🍽	lunches available

Map note: There are full-page maps at the beginning of each region to assist the traveller. The location of every garden is marked on these maps by a yellow numeral in a red rectangle. These correspond to the numeral at the top of each garden page.

INTRODUCTION

Denis and I are delighted to present this new edition of *New Zealand Gardens Open to Visit*. For the first time we are combining the North and South Islands into one book for ease of use by the traveller. We feature 255 gardens from throughout the country, including many new ones not included in our previous editions. The gardens cover a diversity of styles, sizes, terrain and ages. They range from smaller urban to large rural gardens; "medium" is defined as from one to four acres (0.4 to 1.6 hectares); less than an acre is "small", more than four acres is "large".

Unlike other garden guides, our book is accurately updated and comprises only gardens that are reliably open according to the times and conditions listed. The owners have paid for their gardens to be featured, ensuring a commitment to the visiting public, and reducing the retail price of the book. Each garden is professionally photographed, some owners choosing a double-page spread to do justice to their large or varied gardens. A location map enables visitors to find each garden readily, and regional maps assist in planning itineraries.

The gardens are arranged in approximate geographical regions, from north to south. As the climate varies, from subtropical in the far north to alpine in the high country and further down the South Island, so do the garden styles and content change as you travel through the country. New Zealand gardens display a huge range of flora, both native and introduced. Many of the gardens have nurseries attached, often specialising in plants that grow well in that particular region. For most an entrance fee is stated, but this is subject to change.

These gardens are mostly privately owned, so the privacy of the owners needs to be respected at all times. If a garden is open by appointment only, visitors must phone ahead to arrange a mutually convenient time. Those gardens that allow children to visit do so on condition that they are kept under strict supervision at all times. If morning or afternoon tea or lunch are by arrangement only, you will need to phone ahead. If there is a picnickers icon displayed, garden visitors are welcome to picnic, sometimes by arrangement.

If you visit a garden at a different time of year from when it was photographed, it may look different from its photo. Gardens are never static – they change with the seasons and years, so although one feature may have peaked, there is always something new to see.

As with the previous editions, I have endeavoured to describe each garden in neutral language, avoiding superlatives and "flowery" adjectives, in order to give the visitors an accurate idea of what to expect and to leave them free to form their own judgments and opinions. I have avoided excessive use of botanical names and have used Maori names with the plural the same as singular, eg nikau, ponga, rimu, tui. All garden owners have checked their text and map, but any improvements or suggestions are welcomed.

We spent many weeks travelling throughout the country gathering the material for this book. We trust you will enjoy the results and your subsequent visits to these gardens as much as we did. We should like to thank the garden owners for their hospitality towards us. Some offered us refreshments or meals and even put us up for the night. We are grateful for their kindness. Those we missed this time we hope to catch up with for the next edition in two years' time. If you, or anybody you know, would like to be included, or would like more information about it, please contact us as detailed over, on page 6. Happy visiting!

Jillian Friar

INVITATION

**Would you like your garden to be featured in the next edition of
New Zealand Gardens Open to Visit, to be published in 1998?**

**This book is produced to highlight glorious gardens that are open to visit
throughout New Zealand. If you would like to have your garden promoted
with a full-colour photograph, a location map and descriptive 200-word text,
then contact the authors or photocopy and send the form below.**

**There is a fee for each garden to be included in the book,
which helps to reduce the retail price.**

**Jillian and Denis Friar
11 Taioma Crescent
Te Atatu Peninsula
Auckland 1008
NEW ZEALAND**

**Phone: 6-4-9-834 3977
Fax: 6-4-9-834 3955
Mobile: 021 453 867**

I am interested in the 1998 edition of *New Zealand Gardens Open to Visit*.

Please contact me at the following address:

Name: ....

Address: ....

....

....

Phone/fax: ....

NORTH ISLAND

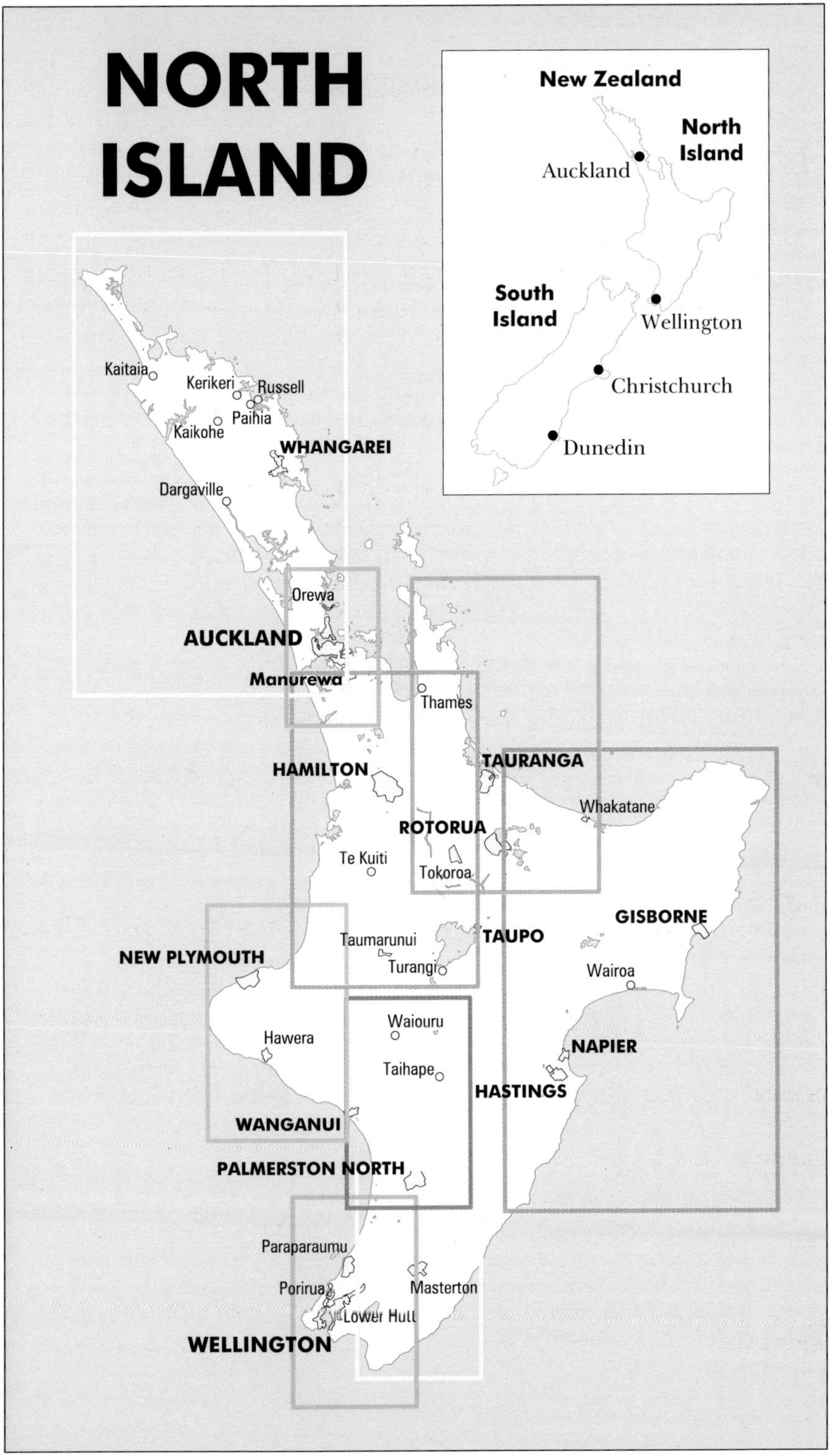

New Zealand

North Island

Auckland

South Island

Wellington

Christchurch

Dunedin

Kaitaia

Kerikeri · Russell
Paihia

Kaikohe

WHANGAREI

Dargaville

Orewa

AUCKLAND

Manurewa

Thames

TAURANGA

HAMILTON

Whakatane

ROTORUA

Te Kuiti

Tokoroa

GISBORNE

Taumarunui

TAUPO

NEW PLYMOUTH

Turangi

Wairoa

Waiouru

Hawera

NAPIER

Taihape

HASTINGS

WANGANUI

PALMERSTON NORTH

Paraparaumu

Porirua

Masterton

Lower Hutt

WELLINGTON

NORTHLAND

This northernmost region of New Zealand enjoys a balmy climate: warm, humid summers and very mild, frost-free winters, with a good rainfall. Tropical and subtropical species thrive under these conditions, and the citrus centre of the country is located here. The 18 gardens featured in this region extend from north of Auckland, just before Warkworth, up to the far north at Mangonui, 45 minutes drive from Kaitaia. This strip of land at the northern end of New Zealand is accessible by a sealed road right up to Cape Reinga at the very tip. It is very narrow in some portions, only four kilometres at one point where both the west and east coasts are visible simultaneously. Ninety Mile Beach borders the Tasman Sea, while the South Pacific Ocean lies to the east.

The southernmost garden, the Old Shearing Shed, provides a teahouse for refreshments in a peaceful garden setting with a play area for children, eight minutes south of Warkworth, just off the highway. Next is a display garden, Wellsford Wholesale Plants, then Mooney Farm Gardens and Rosalie's Retreat are further gardens in rural settings. East of Whangarei is the Country Cottage Teahouse, where refreshments are available in a rambling cottage garden. The Kamo gardens, Parikiore, not far west of Whangarei, feature over 40 palms, particularly our native nikau, and further north, Waimate North Gardens include a native bush backdrop.

Northland's Bay of Islands was the first area settled in New Zealand, and still features buildings and trees planted in the early 19th century. The garden surrounding the 1833 Treaty House at Waitangi is being restored, with magnificent views out over the Bay of Islands. The water's edge garden at Pompallier in Russell has also now been restored as the Edwardian garden it once was, planted in 1880 in front of the restored historic printery built in 1841. The New Zealand Historic Places Trust is gradually restoring its buildings and gardens to replicas of the originals, with Kemp House at Kerikeri the most recent of its achievements. Kemp House is notable for being the oldest wooden building in New Zealand, having been built as a mission house in 1821, and the adjacent Stone Store is the oldest stone building, built in 1832.

Kerikeri also features Wharepuke Subtropical Gardens and Nursery, Ngatipa with its lavender enfilade and Gardeners' Bookshop, and Daffodil World with dahlias as well as four million daffodils. Just north at Waipapa is Liddington Garden with its central stream and bog garden and Kerikeri Flora featuring many different lavenders and herbs. A further seven kilometres north is the turn-off to Redheugh, a subtropical garden offering self-contained quality accommodation. Twenty minutes north of Kerikeri are Taraire Water Gardens with waterlily ponds and a Japanese garden in a native bush setting.

The northernmost garden is at Butler Point opposite the historic township of Mangonui. The garden surrounds a restored historic house built around 1846, and features a huge old pohutukawa grove. Added attractions at Butler Point are a Maori pa site and a small whaling museum. On the isthmus leading up to Cape Reinga at Houhora Heads is the Wagener Settlers Museum, with adjacent historic 1860 Wagener/Subritzky home and garden. Pohutukawa feature throughout the coastline of the far north, with their magnificent red blooms flowering at the end of the year, giving them the name "The New Zealand Christmas Tree".

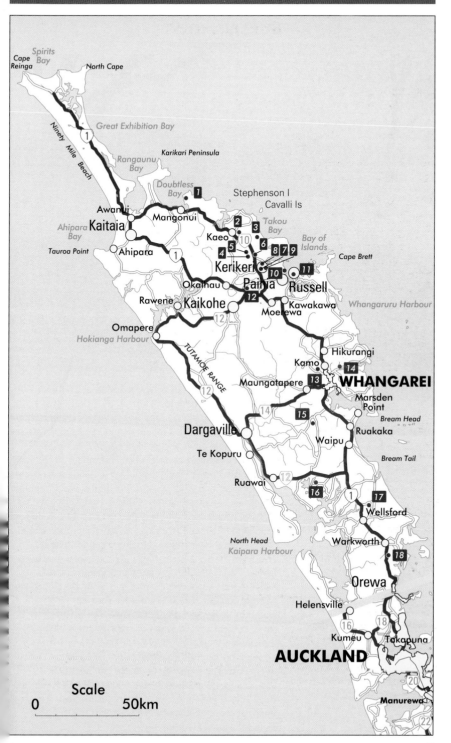

Cape Reinga
Spirits Bay
North Cape
Ninety Mile Beach
Great Exhibition Bay
Rangaunu Bay
Karikari Peninsula
Doubtless Bay
Stephenson I
Cavalli Is
Awanui
Ahipara Bay
Kaitaia
Mangonui
Takou Bay
Bay of Islands
Ahipara
Kaeo
Cape Brett
Tauroa Point
Kerikeri
Paihia
Russell
Whangaruru Harbour
Okaihau
Rawene
Kaikohe
Kawakawa
Moerewa
Omapere
Hokianga Harbour
TUTAMOE RANGE
Hikurangi
Kamo
WHANGAREI
Maungatapere
Marsden Point
Bream Head
Dargaville
Waipu
Ruakaka
Te Kopuru
Bream Tail
Ruawai
Wellsford
North Head
Kaipara Harbour
Warkworth
Orewa
Helensville
Kumeu
Takapuna
AUCKLAND
Manurewa

9

BUTLER POINT
Mangonui

Owners:
Lindo and Laetitia Ferguson

Address: Hihi Rd, Mangonui, R D 1
Directions: 27km north of Kaeo turn
off SH 10 at Hihi Rd. Travel 6km to
Marchant Rd leading to Butler Point
Phone: 0-9-406 0006
Fax: 0-9-406 0006
Open: All year, daily, by appointment
Groups: By appointment
Fee: $5 per adult for garden and
grounds; $7.50 includes Butler House
and whaling museum
Size: Large – 4ha (10 acres) including
smaller (1 acre) house garden
Terrain: Garden flat, grounds hilly
Nursery: Pohutukawa, hoheria, agave
Historic house: Open by appointment;
small whaling museum adjacent
Attraction: Maori pa site nearby

 self-serve facilities

Butler Point takes its name from Captain William Butler, who built his home on its shores in the 1840s and is now buried in an attractive cemetery among mature pohutukawa. This magnificent pohutukawa grove features a 700-year-old giant, recorded in *Great Trees of New Zealand* as having a trunk girth of 10.5 metres. A secluded cottage garden surrounds the old house, with many natives such as cordylines, arthropodiums, and *Elingamite johnsonii*, as well as exotics. Captain Butler's legacy includes a superb magnolia, which guards the cottage and is underplanted with freesias, polyanthus, primroses and ferns. A pond is surrounded by huge gunneras and a variety of irises and daylilies. The orchards, which feature citrus, peaches, a macadamia plantation and a picturesque shelter for picnics, are being developed with new olive and fig trees. The garden provides pleasure whatever the season. Masses of hydrangeas flower in summer, with a mixture of old and new roses blooming into winter, including the old pale pink "Cecile Brunner" growing beside fluffy blue ageratum and delicate mauve thalictrum. The formality of colour combinations is balanced by the exciting foliage which is used to delineate the garden. Geraniums and agapanthus brighten the impressive ponga fence which separates Butler House from Mangonui Harbour.

TARAIRE WATER GARDENS
Kaeo

Owner:
Aubrey Westgate

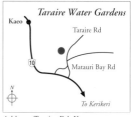

Taraire Water Gardens

Kaeo · Taraire Rd · Matauri Bay Rd · To Kerikeri

Address: Taraire Rd, Kaeo
Postal: c/o Post Office, Kaeo
Directions: 20 minutes north of
Kerikeri. Turn right off SH 10 into
Matauri Bay Rd. Take second road on
left into Taraire Rd. Taraire Water
Gardens on left
Phone: 0-9-405 0466
Open: All year, daily, 10am–4pm
Groups: As above
Fee: $6 per adult, $3 per child under
12 years, $5 per senior citizen and
groups of 10 or more $5 each
Size: Large – 3.2ha (8 acres)
Terrain: Flat and hilly

walking paths or 4-Wheel Drive

Aubrey has created three levels of water areas in a native bush setting over the past six years. The Taraire water gardens were dug out from an extensive bush swamp with a 12-tonne digger, then beautified with a wide selection of plants from native poroporo and ferns, to orchids, begonias, fuchsias and foxgloves. The walk down through native forest to the water gardens is an experience in itself, with totara, rimu, tawa, kahikatea, rewarewa, miro and fine specimens of the taraire, a once sought-after tree. Kiwi live in the rata and a giant bunya or burr can be viewed. Massive vines, ponga tree ferns and nikau palms give a tropical air which Aubrey has encouraged by planting banana palms. Huge rock formations add interest and a bog garden in the bush is planted with gunneras, papyrus, hostas, irises and Chatham Island forget-me-nots. The ponds feature a fish hatchery and many waterlilies including deep blue tropical varieties. A Japanese garden features a weeping white cherry blossom tree as the focal point of an island in one of the ponds. Aubrey has planted a white garden solely with white lilies and other white flowering plants. A replica English bridge leads to the Misty Pond where a fountain creates continuous mist.

REDHEUGH
Waipapa

Owners:
Maureen and John Elliott

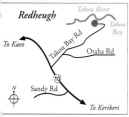

Address: Takou Bay Rd, Kerikeri
Postal: P O Box 55, Waipapa
Directions: Take SH 10 north of
Waipapa for 7km. Turn right into
Takou Bay Rd. Keep left and
continue 7km to end of road to
garden
Phone: 0-9-407 8065
Fax: 0-9-407 8065
Open: 1 November to 31 March,
daily, by appointment
Groups: By appointment, as above
Fee: $5 per adult
Size: Large – 2ha (5 acres)
Terrain: Different levels
Accommodation: Magic Cottage –
quality self-contained cottage
available

 mainly

Redheugh is an nine-year-old garden with subtropical and Mediterranean atmosphere. It features old logs, rocks and timber that John enjoys recycling to provide structures such as the pergolas and archways throughout. A paved patio is adorned by a rose pergola that echoes the curve of the unusual roofline. Maureen likes to paint pictures with plants, preferring interesting shapes and colours, especially purples and reds and the strong colours of cannas that make vibrant splashes of colour against the lush green of the tropical foliage. Vireya rhododendrons flower virtually year-round and alstromerias are another favourite of Maureen's. She likes the garden best in summer when the perennials are joined by the tropicals such as hibiscus, datura and climbers including petrea, bougainvillea and passionfruits. The garden slopes down to the water's edge, where goldfish ponds are covered in waterlilies and planted with various water plants and bog plants. As well as the many ponga, Redheugh features other natives including pohutukawa, totara, manuka, cabbage trees and big native flaxes. Maureen also likes fruit in the garden such as persimmons, loquats and citrus. Ducks shelter in the shade of the trees and guinea fowl strut across the lawns. Redheugh is bounded by the Takou River, which provides a peaceful backdrop.

LIDDINGTON GARDEN
Waipapa

Owners:
Sue and Malcolm Liddington

Address: Waipapa West Rd, Kerikeri
Postal: P O Box 1, Waipapa, Kerikeri
Directions: Take SH 10 north to
Waipapa. Then take second road on
left into Waipapa West Rd. Travel
1km to garden on left
Phone: 0-9-407 9738
Mobile: 025 860 844
Fax: 0-9-407 6430
Open: All year, daily, 10am–3pm, by
appointment
Groups: By appointment, as above
Children: Welcome – playground and
Wendy House available
Fee: $3 per adult
Size: Large – 4ha (10 acres) including
walks through mandarin block
Terrain: Rolling
Nursery: Plants from garden for sale

🚶   🐕   👩👨   😁

♿ mostly

Shelter trees were planted a decade ago and Liddington Garden was developed over the past six years, gradually reclaiming the land from the gorse, except for the native areas where bush walks are being built to enable visitors to see kowhai, rimu and other native trees in their natural setting. Special features of this garden include a tropical area, rose section, perennial borders, terraced banks, rocks and the crazy pathing that is gradually linking the whole garden. The sound of water pervades the garden as a natural stream runs into a lily pond. Gunneras and other water garden plants feature here, with flaxes, taro and ponga, making this bog garden a restful part in contrast with the more colourful areas. Sue groups her perennials in pinks, whites, blues, lilacs and lemon, the pastels highlit with crimson roses. The formal design of the rose area contrasts with the herbaceous borders. Sue is mad on pansies and violas and loves the foxgloves, daisies and Queen Anne's lace, as well as her favourite roses of all kinds. Native hebes are another summer feature while the deciduous exotics provide autumn colour. The warm climate allows colour throughout the year, with camellias and early azaleas flowering in late winter. Ducks on the pond, bantam hens and fantail pigeons are added attractions.

KERIKERI FLORA
Kerikeri

Owners:
Julia Geljon and Wendy Hamilton-Gates

Address: Ness Rd, Waipapa
Postal: Ness Rd, R D 2, Kerikeri
Directions: Take SH 10 north of
Kerikeri. Turn left into Waipapa West
Rd & travel 1km. Continue another
1km along Ness Rd to garden on left
Phone: 0-9-407 9066
Fax: 0-9-407 9066
Open: All year, daily, 9am–5pm
Groups: By appointment
Fee: No charge; group talks charged
Size: Medium – 0.5ha (1¼ acres)
Terrain: Flat
Nursery: Lavenders, herbs, daisies,
natives, perennials
Workshops: Herb workshops for
groups of 10 – 12 by arrangement
Talks: Talks on lavenders, herbs, plant
propagation, etc by arrangement

gravel & grass paths

Kerikeri Flora was developed as part of the plant nursery around a cowshed converted into Julia and Wendy's living space. The cottage garden was begun five years ago, with the lavender specialty developed over the past two years. As to be expected, their favourite plants are lavenders, with herbs and daisies. The focal point of the garden is the lavender patch comprising two mounds of lavenders of many different species and varieties, all labelled with attractive wooden signage. In spring the European *stoechas* lavenders bloom, their colourful bracts making them an increasingly popular garden addition, either as individual bushes, clipped into hedges, trained as standards, or in pots. The traditional English *angustifolia* lavenders flower in the summertime, their flower spikes valued for their lasting perfume. Julia plans to establish a commercial planting of lavenders for oil and other products. Daisies and herbs complement the lavenders and fruit trees contribute to the potager. Native and exotic trees feature throughout the garden and shrubs are underplanted with perennials. Roses climb a pergola, adding to the summer colour and abutilons flower into the autumn. The pond provides a water feature for the garden. Julia and Wendy hold herb workshops and gives talks on lavenders, herbs, plant propagation and related topics to interested groups, by prior arrangement.

DAFFODIL WORLD
Kerikeri

Owners:
Ralph and Pamela Richardson

Address: SH 10, R D 2, Kerikeri
Directions: Travel north of Kerikeri, on SH 10, to corner of Kapiro Rd. Garden on right
Phone: 09-407 8227
Fax: 09-407 6227
Open: August to September for daffodils; mid-January to March for dahlias; daily, 10am–4pm
Groups: By appointment
Fee: Gold coin
Size: Large – 8ha (20 acres) including small (½ acre) home garden
Terrain: Flat
Nursery: catalogue available; mail-order daffodil bulbs sent February/March; dahlia tubers delivered October; cut flowers in season; other flowering plants by arrangement

 by arrangement

16

Six hectares of daffodils create a spectacular spring display, with four million bulbs of a thousand different varieties. Five hundred are exhibited indoors for six weeks, with 180 at any one time. The range of colour and type of daffodil or narcissus is vast, from long-stemmed cut-flower varieties, through show flowers, to shorter garden daffodils, classified horticulturally into 12 divisions. Colours range through all shades of yellow to pinks, with many variations, from *Narcissus* "Fleurimont" with large yellow perianth, a yellow cup with red edges, to *N.* "Shirley Ann", a white daffodil with a white cup and frilly pink edge. The display shed is backed by yellow conifers, with yellow gleditsias and *Robinia pseudoacacia* "Frisia" trees complemented with copper beeches and lots of magnolias. Eight waterlily ponds are edged with sparaxis and other bulbs, and lavender hedging will line the driveway. Azaleas and rhododendrons precede the 40 new roses and Asiatic and oriental lilies, both cut flowers and bulbs being sold. Half an acre of dahlias flowers in summer, with an indoor dahlia display. Freesias brighten the borders in winter, with named camellias. A macadamia nut grove and orchard also feature. New iris stock is bought in, to accompany the bouquets of daffodils. A mail-order catalogue offers daffodil, lilium, iris, freesia and gladioli bulbs.

NGATIPA
Kerikeri

Owners:
Sue and Allan McLeod

Address: Kerikeri Rd, Kerikeri
Directions: Travel 1 km from Kerikeri township on Kerikeri Rd. Ngatipa garden on left
Phone: 0-9-407 9564
Open: Wednesday to Saturday, 10am–4pm; other times by appointment
Closed: July
Groups: By appointment
Fee: No charge
Size: Large – 2ha (5 acres)
Terrain: Flat
Shop: The Gardeners' Bookshop in a garden

Established on a dairy farm in 1932, Ngatipa is sheltered to the south by a massive stand of eucalyptus which creates a temperate micro-climate for the garden. Many of the exotic trees were planted around the colonial homestead in the 1930s, including two pin oaks, jacaranda, Italian cypress, Norfolk Island pine, *Magnolia campbellii* and Lawsoniana lining the curving driveway. The mature trees are underplanted with camellias and shrubs to provide seasonal colour. A stand of poplars, planted in the 1970s to shelter a block of mandarins, now frames the Lavandula Enfilade, transformed by Sue in 1994. This formal lavender garden contains 22 varieties of lavender, mostly summer-flowering English *angustifolia*, and companion grey-foliaged plants. Sue has also transformed an orchard shed into The Gardeners' Bookshop where she sells Touchwood Gardening books and lavender products. Teas can be taken under the historic trees that are a haven for native pigeons and tui. Other attractions include a petanque court and the resident donkeys, Dulcie and Carmen. A home orchard features several varieties of citrus, persimmon, nashi and macadamia nuts, making this two-hectare lifestyle property a diverse garden to visit.

WHAREPUKE SUBTROPICAL GARDENS AND NURSERY
Kerikeri

Owner:
Robin Booth

Address: Stone Store Hill, Kerikeri
Postal: 190 Kerikeri Rd, Kerikeri
Directions: Turn off SH 10 to
Kerikeri. Travel along Kerikeri Rd,
through the town, towards the Stone
Store. Wharepuke Subtropical
Gardens are halfway down hill on left
Phone: 0-9-407 8933
Fax: 0-9-407 8933
Open: 3 January to 24 December,
Tuesday to Saturday 9am–5pm;
Sunday 10am–4pm
Groups: By appointment
Fee: $5 per adult refundable against
purchase
Size: Medium – 0.5ha (1¼ acres)
Terrain: Sloping, without steps
Nursery: Wide range of subtropical
plants
Attraction: Exhibitions of crafts

 sloping metal paths

Wharepuke, meaning "house on the hill", is a subtropical and dry climate garden featuring various unusual and exotic plants, with a representative collection of natives also being established. Although the planting at Wharepuke was begun only in 1993, it includes mature plants transferred from Robin's previous nursery and garden. The prominent species are aloes and bromeliads which are Robin's favourites, along with tropical and subtropical fruiting plants, other large-leafed plants and anything out of the ordinary. In late spring the alstromerias and *Heliconia subulata* come into flower, followed by amaranthus in summer, when the arids are in leaf and the Brazilian fern trees (*Schizolobium parahybum*) and other subtropical foliaged plants feature. The aloes then flower in autumn. A sunken garden is under development which will eventually be roofed in, to provide a year-round tropical feature. Also being developed are fern and bromeliad areas, a children's playground and a shop area which will display changing exhibitions of crafts and plants. The entrance to this family property is marked by a pair of Dragon trees (*Dracaena draco*) and a stone pillar with a sculptural stone sign made by Robin's brother Chris. Plans are afoot to incorporate a sculpture park adjacent to the nursery, with a lake as the focal point.

KEMP HOUSE
Kerikeri

Owner:
NZ Historic Places Trust

Address: Kerikeri Rd, Kerikeri
Directions: Travel 1km from Kerikeri township on Kerikeri Rd. Kemp House on left
Phone: 0-9-407 9236
Fax: 0-9-407 9236
Open: All year, daily, 8am–5pm
Groups: As above
Fee: $5 per adult
Size: Medium – 0.8ha (2 acres)
Terrain: Flat
House: Historic Kemp House open for viewing, as above

 across road at tearooms

Built in 1821 as a mission house, Kemp House is notable for being the oldest wooden building in New Zealand. And the Stone Store built in 1832 adjacent is the oldest stone building. The garden surrounding Kemp House was established in 1822 by the Reverend Samuel Butler who lived there for a decade. The Kemp family then resided there until 1974, when Kemp House was gifted to the Historic Places Trust. The historic garden is unique in that it has been under continuous cultivation for 174 years and still reflects the balanced formality of the Georgian period. The flower beds themselves were filled in the cottage garden style, proudly displaying the industriousness of the resident missionaries. This is still evident today, even to the well-stocked vegetable garden and orchard. A mature wisteria adorns the verandah with its mauve flowers in spring and heritage roses bloom from many periods, especially the turn of the century. Colourful annuals such as candytuft, larkspur, nigella, poppies, violas and alyssum provide summer colour, arranged in the fashion of the early 19th century, and a jacaranda tree and *Magnolia grandiflora* blossom. Old-fashioned perennials including alstromerias, *Stachys lanata*, pink phlox, irises, cannas and Japanese anemones continue the colour into autumn.

TREATY HOUSE GARDEN
Paihia

Owner:
Waitangi National Trust Board
Manager: Tim Jackson

Address: Waitangi National Reserve,
Paihia
Postal: P O Box 48, Bay of Islands
Directions: Travel north of Paihia,
crossing Waitangi River on to
National Reserve. Park at Visitor
Centre and walk up to Treaty House
Phone: 0-9-402 7437
Fax: 0-9-402 8303
Open: Daily except Christmas Day;
9am–5pm
Groups: As above
Fee: $7 per adult; includes access to
Treaty House and grounds
Size: Small garden around house;
total reserve – 506ha (1,265 acres)
Terrain: Mostly flat
Nursery: perennials, salvia, fuchsia,
impatiens, heliotropium, pohutukawa
Shop: High-quality souvenirs

The garden surrounding the Waitangi Treaty House is set in an extensive reserve, gifted to the nation in 1932 and redesigned in 1977. This semi-formal cottage garden features colourful annuals summer and winter, the mild, frost-free climate allowing cineraria and impatiens to flourish during winter. Clipped hedges of *Buxus sempervirens* "Suffruticosa" separate beds of old English plants, with perennials and a   so complemented by native ferns. A surviving cutting from the first rose planted in New Zealand grows along the fence behind the historic Treaty House, built in 1833. Red "Dublin Bay" roses climb a picket fence beyond the back courtyard herb garden, where fragrant *Heliotropium arborescens*, rosemary and other herbs feature within a brick-edged square, with pelargoniums and foxgloves in an adjacent bed. Daphne, fuchsia and bougainvillea are among favourites with visitors. Curved beds border the expansive lawn, with panoramic views of the Bay of Islands towards Russell. An oak and Norfolk Island pine, planted in 1836, grow beside indigenous species, including cabbage trees and pohutukawa with their spectacular red blossoms in summer. A large pale pink camellia, planted by the Busby family in the 19th century, grows alongside the native bush track to the Treaty House. A boardwalk leads through mangrove forest to Haruru Falls.

Treaty House

POMPALLIER
Russell

Owner:
NZ Historic Places Trust

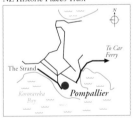

Address: The Strand, Russell
Directions: Take car ferry to Russell
or passenger ferry from Paihia.
Pompallier at left end of The Strand
on sea front
Phone: 0-9-403 7861
Fax: 0-9-403 7861
Open: All year, daily, 10am–5pm,
Closed: Christmas Day and Good
Friday
Groups: As above
Fee: $5 per adult, NZ Historic Places
Trust members free
Size: Medium – 1ha (2½ acres)
Terrain: Flat and hilly
Tours: Guided tours of Pompallier
available by arrangement

 to flat areas

Pompallier House was built in 1841, but the garden was not established until 1880, when Jane Mair laid it out in a form that survives in the restored garden today. The garden shed has been reconstructed, the orchard restored using 19th-century cultivars, and the original Marist chapel site can be seen. From 1905 until the mid 1930s, the Edwardian garden was immaculately maintained by the Stephenson family. Henry Stephenson affixed a brass plate misspelt "Pompalier" to the imposing front gate, erected by Jane Mair's brother, Hamlyn Greenway, and now restored, misspelling intact. The flagpole is back in its original position, and the tennis court which graced the front lawn is under restoration. Shell pathways once more lead from the karaka and acmena at the entrance to box-edged beds of old-fashioned flowers, some from original plants, such as aquilegias, dianthus, poinsettias, gerberas, *Cordyline rubra*, pearl bush and Poor Knights lily, planted in 1927. Heritage roses include "Anna Maria de Montravel", "Cecile Brunner", "Safrano", "Perle d'Or" and a yellow banksia. High elaeagnus hedges were planted for windbreaks and protection from roving cattle. Original palms, snowball trees, camellias and old cultivars of bulbs feature, with "Ham-and-egg" daffodils, ixias and sparaxis in spring, South African bulbs, crinums, *Dietes grandiflora* and gladioli in summer, and Japanese anemones at Easter.

WAIMATE NORTH GARDENS
Waimate North

Owners:
Mike Nesbit and Suzette Neeley

Waimate North Gardens

Address: Waikaramu Rd, Waimate North
Postal: R D 2, Kaikohe
Directions: From Kawakawa travel north-west on SH 1 towards Ohaewai. Turn right into Old Bay Rd, then take left fork into Waikaramu Rd. Garden 1km on left
Phone: 0-9-405 9861
Mobile: 025 960 155
Fax: 0-9-405 9861
Open: Garden: open late August to end May, daily, by appointment; Nursery: open October and April
Groups: As above
Fee: $3 per adult
Size: Medium – 2ha (5 acres)
Terrain: Flat to rolling
Nursery: Flowering shrubs to forest

mostly

by arrangement

This woodland garden has been developed out of a gorse-infested peat swamp since 1988. Although he specialises in forestry, Mike likes fragrant plants, so there are a lot of old roses, "Atlas" magnolia, *M. stellata* and port wine michelia. Other large deciduous trees include quite a few acers, fraxinus, liriodendrons, claret ash, robinias and ulma varieties – both deciduous and evergreen. Hardwoods include different species of eucalypts, grevilleas and cypress. QE II native bush is reached across farmland, through flaxes following a stream up through a forestry block to the path being established through Northland podocarps featuring taraire, rimu, totara, puriri and kauri. Four ponds are home to ducks and ducklings, while a shady lathe house is covered in clematis in spring and roses in summer. The garden is planted in whites, pinks and reds with old roses including the white Waimate rose and blue irises. Various spring bulbs including daffodils are followed by white and purple wisteria blossoming at the same time as the waratah. Summer sees daisies flowering with Louisiana irises and cannas. Suzette is increasing the lush subtropical look by planting palms, bamboos and Australian natives in the valley behind the house.

PARIKIORE GARDENS
Kamo

Owners:
Wayne and Lynne Clarke

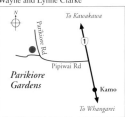

Address: Pakiore Rd, Kamo
Postal: R D 6, Whangarei
Directions: Take SH 1 north of
Whangarei to Kamo. Continue 1km
north, then turn left into Pipiwai Rd.
Take first right into Parikiore Rd.
Garden immediately on left, on corner
Phone: 0-9-435 2993
Open: August to May, 10am–4pm,
daily, other times by appointment
Groups: As above
Fee: $3 per adult; group concession
Size: Large – over 2ha (5½ acres)
including 2 acres native bush
Terrain: Sloping and terraced
Nursery: Palms, ferns, cuttings from
garden, cut flowers eg carnations,
alstromerias, roses, freesias, gladioli,
callas for sale

Parikiore are diverse gardens, developed over the last decade, with older established trees. A new garden has been added to the top of this terraced property recently, with a new walk through almost a hectare of native bush. Nikau palms have native orchids and epiphytes growing on them and the northern rata climb more mature nikau. Other natives include ferns, taraire, puriri, totara, karaka, kohekohe and kauri with clematis climbing through them. Other climbers adorning the trees include stephanotis and more than nine different coloured wisterias. Groundcover of native arthropodiums enhances the bush in early summer. Wayne's favourites are his 40 palms and 50 prunus, while Lynne prefers the camellias. Four waterlily ponds feature eight varieties of lilies and two bog gardens include primulas, lobelias, irises and other bog plants. Forty camellias, acers, magnolias and rhododendrons, including vireyas, feature in spring, followed by 250 roses in summer, with daylilies and Asiatic lilies. There are patio and miniature rose beds with floribundas and teas in the new top garden. Deciduous trees include a huge liquidambar and deep red *Nyssa sylvatica*. Proteas and leucadendrons in the new garden predominate in winter.

COUNTRY GARDEN TEAHOUSE
Whangarei

Owners:
Minnie and Terry Mora

Address: Main Ngunguru Rd,
Glenbervie
Postal: P O Box 7017, Tikipunga
Directions: 10km east of Whangarei,
on Ngunguru–Tutukaka Highway,
Kiripaka Rd, Glenbervie. Country
Garden Teahouse on right
Phone: 0-9-437 5127
Fax: 0-9-437 5163
Open: October to April, daily,
10am–4pm
Groups: By appointment
Fee: $3 per adult
Size: Medium – 1.4ha (3½ acres)
Terrain: Flat
Nursery: Perennials, flaxes, shrubs,
bulbs

This rambling cottage garden has grown since 1985 from bare paddock. Minnie began growing foliage, then developed the garden from 1989. It now features pinks, mauves, blues, whites and blending colours with many perennials and a few annuals spot-planted through the garden. Spring bulbs and new foliage growth are followed by the summer flowers, with many lilium and dahlias. A more formal area features Rosa "Wedding Day" over an archway, with further roses underplanted with pansies and alyssum. A scoria pathway encircles a statue and leads through more rose bowers to a mustard-coloured gazebo high on a stone-walled mound. Further stone walls surround the garden, with a grove of conifers and various exotics providing autumn colour, such as maples, robinia, weeping copper beech, golden beech, spotted elm and idesia. There is a lot of statuary, including native birds and animals, stalking through the under-growth. Water features include curved bridges, a fountain made from an old trunk and a waterfall over rocks. Minnie has also built a stumpery with a row of ivy covered stumps and driftwood. Other features of interest include a windmill, a telephone box, a rockery, an oriental area, an ivy walk and a New Zealand corner with Minnie's native-bird figures. Minnie serves Devonshire tea and light lunches from her Teahouse.

ROSALIE'S RETREAT
Waiotira

Owners:
Rosalie and Lloyd McCullough

Rosalie's Retreat

Address: Waiotira Rd, R D 1,
Waiotira
Directions: Take SH 1 north from
Kaiwaka to Oakleigh. Turn left
towards Paparoa. Take Waiotira Rd to
left. Travel 2km to garden on left (3rd
property). Or take SH 1 south from
Whangarei to Oakleigh, then as above
Phone: 0-9-432 2134
Open: All year, daily, by appointment
Groups: By appointment, as above
Fee: $3 per adult
Size: Medium – 1ha (2½ acres)
Terrain: Easy rolling

 mostly

Rosalie has been planting her garden for 25 years now, adding a new area over the past five years. She began with the now mature trees and has developed diverse areas of different species flowering through the seasons. In the spring rhododendrons are accompanied by different types of lychnis, cinerarias and blue cynoglossum. Summer perennials, including a lot of penstemons complement the roses, daisies, Louisiana bog irises, bougainvillea and dahlias which continue into autumn. Deciduous trees such as oaks and she-oaks colour up, contrasting with conifers, gums, bottlebrushes and natives including pohutukawa, kauri, rimu, nikau, pittosporums, cabbage trees and ponga tree ferns. The flame vine *Pyrostegia venusta* provides winter colour along with camellias. Two goldfish ponds run into each other and are surrounded by grasses, papyrus and conifers. A fern garden under the trees is coloured with impatiens and a Japanese garden features bonsai. The new area of two circular lawn and garden beds is curbed and bordered by *Alchemilla mollis* and lychnis with penstemons and other perennials. Special features include a dry waterfall, alpine garden, bromeliad shade house, conifer beds, bamboo, statuary and hypertufa pots made by Rosalie. Fred, the sulphur-crested cockatoo, is an added attraction.

MOONEY FARM GARDENS
Maungaturoto

Owners:
Shirley and Ted Mooney

Address: Mooney Rd, R D 1,
Maungaturoto
Directions: 73km south of Whangarei.
From Auckland take SH 1 north to
turn-off to Dargaville. Turn left into
SH 12 and travel to Maungaturoto.
Continue to Ford Rd. Turn left and
travel 4km, veering right to Mooney
Rd. Garden at end of road
Phone: 0-9-431 8249
Freephone: 0800 575 044
Fax: 0-9-431 8249
Open: 1 November to 30 April, daily,
by appointment
Groups: By appointment, as above
Fee: $4 per adult over 15 years
Size: Large – 2ha (5 acres)
Terrain: Gentle slopes

    & to toilet

   by arrangement

Mooney Farm Gardens include sweeping lawns, formal beds and lily ponds, set in 320 hectares of farmland. Over the past four to twelve years, the garden has been established, predominantly in natives which are the Mooneys' favourites. Native hebes feature around the two water gardens, and a pohutukawa hedge and arthropodiums flower in summer. A rockery has been created with limestone boulders and an enclosed rose garden features over 300 roses, including the dark red "Deep Secret". There are also miniature rosebeds and other raised garden beds built up with compost and sheep manure. The heavy clay and limestone base requires lots of Epsom salts to counteract its alkalinity. A camellia bed is edged with alyssum and other colourful beds are bordered with both white and purple alyssum and with impatiens. Dianthus and purple ageratum encircle a golden-foliaged gleditsia tree and pots of impatiens decorate the verandah. Shirley mass plants annuals for summer colour, which is offset by the green lawns.
The park features specimen *Magnolia grandiflora* and pohutukawa, and seats are strategically placed for viewing the rural landscape and are colourfully planted round with dahlias and marigolds. Bougainvillea climb the fenceline and hibiscus provide a tropical touch.

WELLSFORD WHOLESALE PLANTS
Wellsford

Owner:
Maggie Roberts

Address: Lower Silver Hill Rd,
Wellsford
Postal: P O Box 215, Wellsford
Directions: Take SH 1 north of
Wellsford through Te Hana. Turn
right into Mangawhai Coastal Rd.
Then take first right into Lower Silver
Hill Rd. Garden is second property on
left
Phone: 0-9-423 8882
Fax: 0-9-423 8882
Open: All year, daily, by appointment
Groups: By appointment, as above
Fee: $3 per adult, refundable against
plant purchase
Size: Medium – 0,4ha (1 acre)
Terrain: Terraced
Nursery: Perennials, shrubs, trees,
miniature roses; at wholesale prices

Over the past two years Maggie has been transforming a paddock into a rambling display garden, terracing and planting it with perennials, roses and shrubs and establishing a pond for water supply. Maggie colour coordinates the garden, grouping peaches through to apricots in one area, pinks and whites in another, and blues and yellows together. Beside the summer house is a large shade garden in greys and whites. Lots of spring colour comes from foxgloves, aquilegias, echiums and most cottagey plants. In summer, the roses – mainly miniature and patio – hollyhocks and lilies continue the colour. Deciduous trees colour up in the autumn, then the camellias provide winter colour, with the groundcovers that flower all year. Waterlilies are being established in the pond and a bog garden is expanding into the adjacent cow paddock. Maples, flowering cherries and magnolias planted behind the pool will reflect in the water. Natives including many hebes are being interplanted with the exotics. A big variety of shrubs and large range of perennials seen by the visitor strolling through the garden can be bought at the nursery. The plants for sale have been grown outdoors, so are well hardened up.

THE OLD SHEARING SHED
Warkworth

Owners:
Laurie and Paul Broomhall

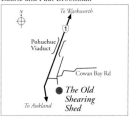

Address: Cowan Bay Rd, Pohuehue
Postal: P O Box 358, Warkworth
Directions: Turn off SH 1 about 15 minutes north of Orewa, or 8 minutes south of Warkworth, at top of Pohuehue Viaduct into Cowan Bay Rd. The Old Shearing Shed is just round the corner
Phone: 0-9-425 8500
Open: All year, daily, 10am–4.30pm
Groups: Groups 10 or more, by appointment
Fee: No charge
Size: Medium – 0.4ha (1 acre)
Terrain: Sloping
Shop: Teahouse with collectables and antiques, especially vintage farm tools, for sale; home-made produce, some local crafts

The Old Shearing Shed is a tearooms set amid a colourful garden where outdoor tables and chairs combine with a children's play area made out of timber and lawns set with beds of cottage plants. Original old trees, camellias and lawn provided the backbone of the garden when the Broomhalls began developing it in 1989. A spectacular old puriri, some young kauri and other natives attract birdlife, including native pigeons, tui and shining cuckoos. A row of Norfolk Island pines and gums has been underplanted with magnolias, and a flowering cherry blossoms in spring. Old-fashioned roses bloom in the summer, with bright yellow daisies for contrast. A rose-covered archway features, with a rose arbour and pond to be developed. All colours of the rainbow are used, one colour setting off the next. There is a long perennial border and a whole bank of grevilleas. Old outdoor garden accessories and an old wheelbarrow surrounded by perennials are complemented by the collectables and antiques for sale inside the tearooms. The Broomhalls specialise in tools collected from local farms, such as the hanes and swingle bars displayed on the walls. An aviary of fantail pigeons and a dovecote are added attractions, particularly with young children. Laurie serves Devonshire teas and lunches from her tearoom.

AUCKLAND

South of Warkworth is Auckland with its 21 featured gardens, Touchwood Bookshop and Mike's Garden Tours. The gardens are spread from Helensville in the north-west down to Bombay in the south. Auckland boasts the largest population in New Zealand, enjoying a warm, consistent climate, which favours the growth of subtropical plants. Summers are sunny and warm with light rain. Winters are mild, with twice as much rain as in summer, but little frost. Being sited on an isthmus, Auckland's climate is influenced by the maritime conditions, resulting in changeable weather. Much of Auckland is built on volcanic soil with a lot of clay in parts.

Northernmost in Helensville is Greenlaw, followed at Whenuapai by Briar Cottage, where roses feature in the garden surrounding the teahouse. At the end of the north-western motorway is the Kumeu garden, at Floriade Villa, specially designed for garden weddings. The Swanson garden, Tranquil Glen, is very diverse, and West Lynn Gardens feature a Butterfly House. In Epsom is the Eden Garden, established in an abandoned quarry, with camellias predominating. Two Historic Places Trust gardens in Auckland are Highwic in Epsom and Ewelme Cottage in Parnell. The Hills' garden at St Heliers is landscaped into a series of rooms on a steep site. Cottonwood, a Panmure garden on the Tamaki Estuary, features established trees sheltering sweeping lawns, camellias and roses, in contrast to Waikare, an exposed Bucklands Beach garden with breathtaking views over the harbour, where azaleas and camellias are also favourites. A garden at Mangere East, Quarter Acre Paradise, is designed to be an inspiration to all backyard New Zealand gardeners, with masses of colour and a huge conservatory.

We include two gardens from Whitford, each over a hectare: Quails Croft, on a clifftop, provides harbour views, while Haunui Farm is in the shelter of century-old trees. Both have roses and perennials, while at Takanini there is a camellia specialist, Camellia Haven. Atarangi at Papakura features roses and natives, and Roseville at Ramarama specialises in Trevor Griffiths roses. Towards Waiuku are Wrights Watergardens with 30 waterlily ponds and four lotus ponds. Then at Waiuku is the Ploughman's Garden and Nursery specialising in lavender. At Pukekohe are the two southernmost gardens, Joy Plants specialising in bulbs and perennials and Forget Me Knot Gardens specialising in New Zealand natives, with tearooms overlooking extensive ponds.

Plants flower for much longer periods in Auckland than further south because of the mild conditions, with spring beginning early and autumn extending into winter. The area is well known for its grapes and citrus. Most of the gardens featured are also in the biennial Trinity Gardens Festival that attracts thousands of visitors. Other botanical features of Auckland include public gardens such as the Domain in the centre of Auckland with its Winter Gardens, the Regional Botanical Gardens beside the southern motorway at Manurewa, Albert Park opposite the University above the city and Old Government House in the University grounds, and Cornwall Park, an extensive rural park set in the heart of Auckland surrounding One Tree Hill. The Waitakere Ranges, to the west of Auckland, offer many walking tracks through native bush, and the Hunua Ranges east of Auckland provide bush walks for experienced trampers. Wenderholm, north of Auckland, is an attractive scenic reserve.

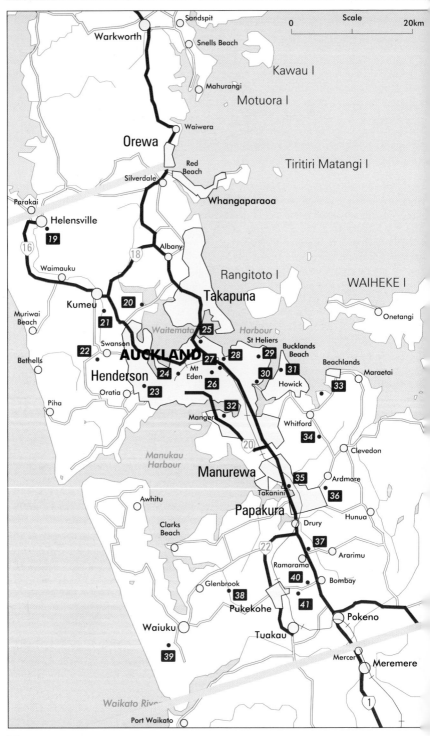

Scale
0   20km

Sandspit
Warkworth
Snells Beach
Mahurangi
Kawau I
Motuora I
Waiwera
Orewa
Red Beach
Silverdale
Tiritiri Matangi I
Whangaparaoa
Parakai
Helensville
19
Albany
16
Waimauku
18
Rangitoto I
Kumeu
20
Takapuna
WAIHEKE I
Muriwai Beach
21
Onetangi
Swanson
22
Waitemata
25
Harbour
St Heliers
Bucklands Beach
Bethells
AUCKLAND
27
28
29
Beachlands
Maraetai
Henderson
24
Mt Eden
30
Howick
33
Oratia
23
26
31
Piha
32
Whitford
Mangere
Manukau Harbour
34
Clevedon
Manurewa
35
Ardmore
Awhitu
Takanini
36
Papakura
Hunua
Clarks Beach
Drury
20
37
Ararimu
22
Ramarama
Glenbrook
40
Bombay
38
41
Pukekohe
Pokeno
Waiuku
Tuakau
39
Mercer
Meremere
Waikato River
1
Port Waikato

GREENLAW
Helensville

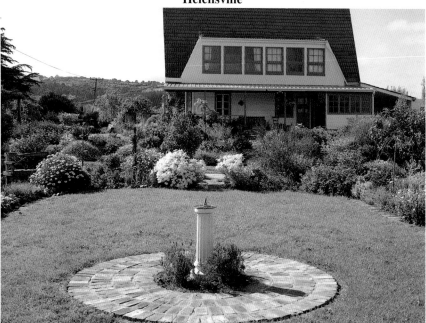

Owners:
Raywin and Wayne Cruickshank

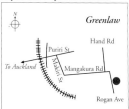

Address: 29 Rogan Ave, Helensville
Directions: Take Northwestern
Motorway (SH 16) from Auckland to
Helensville. Cross overhead railway
bridge and turn right into Puriri St.
Take first right into Makiri St.
Continue into Mangakura Rd and
travel about 1km, with 300m on
metal. Then turn right into Rogan
Ave, cross railway line and continue
to garden, second property on left
Phone: 0-9-420 8951
Mobile: 025 943 877
Open: October to May; by appointment
Groups: By appointment, as above
Fee: $3 per adult
Size: Medium – 0.4ha (1 acre)
Terrain: Flat
Nursery: Perennials from garden and
hand-crafted wooden seats for sale

by arrangement

Greenlaw is surrounded by countryside, the cattle
pastureland creating a peaceful rural atmosphere.
Beginning just with lawn round the house, Raywin sat
down and designed the garden areas she has developed
over the past five years. It is planned in garden rooms,
softened with self-seeding flowering plants. A new sunken
garden provides a semi-formal air, planted with cream
roses and lavender. Raywin's favourites are the perennials
and roses such as "Souvenir de Malmaison" and "Albertine"
that adorn the verandah. From there the sunken garden
edged with brick and featuring a sun-dial can be seen
across the re-sited driveway, hidden from view by a haha.
Raywin's terracotta pots harmonise with the brickwork
and unify the garden, a specialty being the urn sculpted
by Christchurch potter Peter Burelli. A yellow and blue
garden follows a long curving path dominated by a nine-
metre pergola covered in yellow roses and blue wisteria.
Blue echiums also add height. Spring is a time of cherry
blossom, bulbs, magnolias, lots of lavenders and forget-
me nots. The perennials, roses and daisies take over in
summer, then the silver birches and gleditsias feature
in autumn while roses continue along with the tall blue
salvias and perennial lobelias. Natives include pittosporums,
flaxes and hebes, but Raywin can't wait for the exotics
and evergreens to mature.

BRIAR COTTAGE
Whenuapai

Managers:
James and Christine Elkins

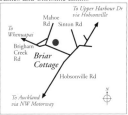

Address: 164 Brigham Creek Rd, Whenuapai
Directions: Take Northwestern Motorway (SH 16) out of Auckland. Turn right at end into Hobsonville Rd. Take third left into Brigham Creek Rd. Cottage on right
Phone: 0-9-416 7369
Open: All year; 10am– 4pm from Thursday to Sunday; other times by appointment (increasing over summer)
Groups: As above; booking for tearooms for groups 10 or more
Fee: $2 per adult
Size: Medium – 1.2ha (3 acres)
Terrain: Mostly flat
Tearooms: Book for functions

Briar roses appropriately climb through the trees around Briar Cottage and its gardens. The tearooms are surrounded by semi-formal gardens where old roses predominate. From beds of purple lavender, orange calendula and herbs around the paved area of chairs and tables, visitors can see rose- and wisteria-covered archways, and a row of standard miniature red and pink roses that line the fishpond. Specimens of weeping pale pink roses and silver pears are complemented by elegant red and white standard roses on the lawn. Yellow pansies encircle a golden rose, and further roses climb the archways of a statue-lined laburnum walk at the far end of the garden. Box edging formalises the rosebeds, and a rose walkway leads to an old ivy-clad fireplace, now transformed into "Owl's House". A cherry tree walk is underplanted with cynoglossum and dwarf agapanthus. Nearby, a dovecote housing fantail doves is surrounded with blues and greens, such as love-in-a-mist and rosemary. Statuary adorns perennial beds of petunias, pelargoniums, delphiniums, salvias, penstemons and naturalised bulbs in spring. In the adjoining manor garden yet more roses abound, covering the fences that divide it into rooms, with "Wedding Day" climbing a peach tree. The gardens are a lovely setting for weddings and other functions, or just for relaxing over lunch or a cuppa.

FLORIADE VILLA
Kumeu

Owners:
Lesley and John Brady

Floriade Villa

Address: 200 Taupaki Rd, R D 2,
Henderson
Directions: 20 – 25 minutes from
Auckland city. Take Northwestern
Motorway (SH 16) from Auckland to
northern end. Turn left into Kumeu
Rd. Turn left into Taupaki Rd. Travel
2.8km to garden on right
Phone: 0-9-412 8520
Open: Daily, by appointment
Groups: As above
Fee: $4 per adult, including
Devonshire tea
Size: Medium – 0.4ha (1 acre)
Terrain: Flat
For sale: Floriade Fruity Jam

 Devonshire by arrangement

The Bradys' 1904 villa was moved from Devonport 18 years ago, but Lesley has only developed the garden over the past four years. She has designed it specifically as a venue for weddings, other functions and garden parties. Structures such as trellis pergolas, archways, ponds and bridges divide the garden into rooms and a semi-circle of poplars underplanted with a white garden is a favourite spot for wedding photography. Weddings often take place under a walk-through white archway. Lesley is fond of lavender and pansies. She likes old-fashioned perennials like mignonettes and old roses, "Albertine", "Utersen" and "Wedding Day" featuring in the garden. Roses in pinks to creams include "Parade", "Alberic Barbier" and "Peace". Two rock-edged ponds are planted around with ponga, "Green Goddess" lilies, and giant ajuga. Lesley has planted her garden in mauves and pinks, such as the semi-circle of "Marshwood" lavender with toning pansies in the centre. She uses a mixture of annuals for underplanting to tone in with bridesmaids' dresses and has been influenced by floral art work in her design of the garden. Autumn features rhus trees, *Gleditsia* "Sunburst" and weeping trees such as *Gleditsia* "Emerald Cascade" and maples.

TRANQUIL GLEN GARDENS
Swanson

Owners:
John and Janice Curtis

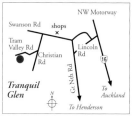

Address: 30 Tram Valley Rd, Swanson
Directions: Take Northwestern
Motorway (SH 16) out of Auckland.
Exit at Henderson into Lincoln Rd.
Turn right into Swanson Rd, travel
past Swanson shops, turn left into
Christian Rd and right into Tram
Valley Rd. Travel along unsealed road
to Tranquil Glen on left
Phone: 0-9-833 9869
Open: 1 September to end May, by
appointment
Groups: By appointment
Fee: $5 per adult
Size: Medium – 1ha (2½ acres)
Terrain: Undulating
Nursery: Plants from garden
Attractions: Taxidermy studio open

   limited

  by arrangement

Tranquil Glen features diverse gardens developed over the past decade to provide colour and interest throughout the year. Early spring brings camellias, bulbs, cherry blossom and 27 different magnolias into flower. Grevilleas, warratahs, proteas and red-hot pokers lining the driveway attract native birds, and tui are drawn to a flax garden of seven different varieties, from pink to black and variegated. Aviaries and dovecotes also ensure birds fly throughout the gardens. A woodland area features a bromeliad walk, with epiphytic orchids and staghorns. Summer turns on the colour, with beds of gazanias and nasturtiums bordering the sweeping lawns. Marigolds edge a bed of various conifers. Groundcover includes two ivy "lawns", one variegated. A paulownia shades the silver garden, where clematis covers a ponga archway. Another clematis climbs a brick archway into the Diana garden, her statue overlooking standard miniature roses and succulent beds separated by shell pathways within silvery teucrium hedging. An octagonal garden flowers pink, white and blue, with scoria paths bordered by "Barnsley" lavatera, David Austin roses and larkspurs, with lobelias beneath. Pandorea climbs a trellis, and a circular "window" reveals Japanese irises around a wishing well beyond, by an arched bridge leading to a glazed gazebo encircled with pelargoniums.

WEST LYNN GARDENS
New Lynn

Owner:
West Lynn Gardens Society

Address: 73 Parker Ave, New Lynn
Directions: Take Great North Rd towards New Lynn. Turn into Titirangi Rd. Turn left into Parker Ave. Gardens on right
Phone: 0-9-827 7045
Open: All year, daily except Christmas Day; 10am– 4pm
Groups: By appointment
Fee: $1 per adult; 50 cents per child over 5 years
Size: Large – nearly 2ha (4½ acres)
Terrain: Flat and sloping
Nursery: Plants and creepers $3 – $5
Attractions: Butterfly House open October to April
Fuctions: Available for garden weddings and photography

  by arrangement

West Lynn Gardens were established by Jack Clark, founder of Eden Gardens, with a continuous band of hard-working volunteer helpers, and opened to the public in 1983. The predominant species are camellias, magnolias, conifers and New Zealand conifers attracting plenty of birdlife which feed on the Taiwan cherry and other favourite flowers. Special features of the garden include a native area with unusual plants, a tropical area with bananas, bromeliads and palms, and a walk-in butterfly house. Monarchs and some native butterflies feature from October until April when they are released. The size of the building and the number of varieties of butterflies are being increased. Other special areas include a gazebo with garden seats in the centre of the garden, small ponds, a dry stream bed and a developing cacti garden. West Lynn is an all-seasons garden displaying bulbs and blossoms during spring, perennials over summer, vireyas and autumn foliage, then conifers and camellias in winter. The gardens are popular for garden weddings and photography. Visitors can join an endowment scheme, by selecting a tree in memory of a loved one for $350. The West Lynn Gardens Society was formed in 1992, annual membership is $10; or life membership is $50.

MIKE'S GARDEN AND SCENIC TOURS
Auckland Central

Operator:
Mike Maran
Address: 3 Edith St, Pt Chevalier
Directions: Mini Coach will collect
you from your Auckland accommo-
dation
Phone: 0-9-846 5350
Mobile: 025 784 779
Fax: 0-9-846 7183
Open: Depart daily at 9am or 1.30pm
Groups: Licensed for up to 9 people;
minimum of 2 people
Fee: $49–$89 per person for ½ day or
day tours; entry fees to gardens are
included in tour price
Size: Various
Terrain: Varies
Tours: 6 different tours available
1 Auckland City Highlights
   (9am–2.30pm) $49 per person
2 Waitakere Ranges Tour
   (1.30pm–5pm) $55 per person
3 Auckland's Botanical Treasures
   (9am–5pm day tour) $89 per
   person excluding lunch cost
4 Regional Botanical Gardens
   (3.5 hrs) $49 per person
5 Private City Gardens Tour
   (3.5 hrs) $55 per person
6 Country Gardens Tour
   (3.5 hrs) $60 per person

 included in fee

With his extensive horticultural background, Mike is the ideal garden guide. He escorts garden tours around Auckland, personally providing a commentary on the gardens visited. Mike collects you from your accommodation either morning or afternoon, in his air-conditioned mini coach, then takes you around private and public gardens, showing you the sights of Auckland. Tours last three to four hours, or a full day tour can be arranged to combine the city and country tours or take in the Waitakere Gardens Tour. Mike's Tours operate in all weather, with umbrellas supplied and all paths are asphalt. Each of the two or three private gardens visited has its own character, whether terraced, bush, English style, country estate, Spanish, Japanese, bonsai, or small city garden. Mike also visits Auckland's public gardens as part of the City Tour itinerary. These include the Parnell Rose Gardens, the Savage Memorial Gardens overlooking the Waitemata harbour, Cornwall Park studded with plantations of native trees leading up to One Tree Hill, the Domain and Wintergardens with rare native ferns and tropical flowers, or the Regional Botanical Gardens. The Waitakere Ranges garden tour features New Zealand native forest with its mature kauri trees and panoramic views of Auckland.

TOUCHWOOD BOOKS
Auckland City

Owners:
Peter and Diane Arthur
Manager: Julie Fowlie

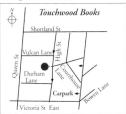

Address: 35 High St, Auckland City
Directions: Central city, parallel to
Queen St. Turn east into Shortland St.
Turn first right into High St (one way
street). Shop on right
Phone: 0-9-379 2733
Fax: 0-9-379 2373
Open: All year, Monday to Friday,
10am–5.30pm;
Saturday 10.30am–2.30pm
Groups: As above
Fee: No charge
Size: Indoors
Terrain: Flat
Shop: Home of Touchwood Books –
10,000 different titles in stock, 2,000
second-hand, probably biggest
collection in world of garden books,
for mail order and retail

At Touchwood Books you have access to over ten thousand different books relating to gardening topics. In addition, the bookshop provides the biggest mail-order service for gardening books in the southern hemisphere, including two thousand second-hand books. Subjects range from garden design to hydroponics to viticulture, with everything horticulturally related in between! There is a section on New Zealand gardens and natives and practical books are also popular. Customers of all nationalities frequent the shop, which has gained quite a reputation in the two years it's been opened, as a bookshop run by gardeners for gardeners. An oasis in the city, it is located off-street, along a marble corridor which adds to its quiet atmosphere. A large window provides natural light and a view of pigeons and sparrows in the city. Fresh flowers from the staffs' gardens adorn the table that is provided, with chairs, for customers to use for relaxing while browsing. Soft classical music enhances the atmosphere. Customers can join the Touchwood Bookclub for only $10 per year. This entitles them to three catalogues a year, specials, free searches on the 2.6 million titles of Touchwood Books' database and access to the huge range of titles in stock on almost any garden associated topic.

EDEN GARDEN
Epsom

Owner:
The Eden Garden Society Inc

Address: 24 Omana Ave, Epsom, Auckland
Directions: From the city, take Gillies Ave exit from Southern Motorway. Turn right into Gillies Ave, then take second on right up Albury Ave. Turn left into Mountain Rd, then right into Omana Ave. Eden Garden at end
Phone: 0-9-638 8395
Fax: 0-9-638 7685
Open: All year, daily, 9am–4.30pm
Café: Open 10am– 4pm
Groups: As above; refreshments by arrangement
Fee: $3 per adult; $2 per senior citizen; members free
Size: Large – 2.2ha (5½ acres)
Terrain: Flat and hilly
Wheelchair: Available

Eden Garden, once an abandoned quarry on the slopes of Mt Eden, has been transformed since 1964 into a "Garden of Eden". It is developed and maintained by volunteer workers, members of the Eden Garden Society. Camellias, rhododendrons, azaleas and vireyas predominate, with many areas underplanted with ferns, hostas and clivia. The camellias are complemented in spring by cherry blossom, magnolias, *Cedrella sinesis* and a variety of maples. Bromeliads have naturalised in a glade which features a 13.5m waterfall and a rock surround. New Zealand natives are emphasised on the slopes; rewarewa is replacing pines, pohutukawa are regenerating, and ponga, kowhai, nikau palms, cabbage trees and flaxes encourage birdlife, which include tui, waxeyes and native pigeons. Higher up in the garden there are views to Rangitoto Island and the steeper slopes are being landscaped to accommodate more arid plantings, with yuccas and agaves naturalising on the scoria base. Leucadendrons, grevillea and protea also flourish in these drier conditions, making a striking contrast to the sheltered woodland below. The original English-style plantings with statuary are being supplemented by subtropicals, such as hibiscus, giant strelitzia, palms and cycads, appropriate for Auckland's climate.

HIGHWIC
Epsom

Owners:
NZ Historic Places Trust and
Auckland City Council.

Address: 40 Gillies Ave, Epsom,
Auckland. Entrance Mortimer Pass
Directions: Opposite Southern
Motorway exit. Turn left into Gillies
Ave, then first right into Mortimer
Pass. Entrance on right
Phone: 0-9-524 5729
Fax: 0-9-524 5575
Open: Daily, except Good Friday
and Christmas Day; garden and house
10.30am–noon and 1pm–4.30pm
Groups: As above
Fee: $3.50 per adult, $1 per child,
group discounts, NZ Historic Places
Trust members free
Size: Medium – over 1ha (about
3 acres)
Terrain: Mainly flat
Functions: Bookings for catered
functions and special events

Highwic homestead was built in revived Gothic style in 1862, when it was surrounded by farmland. Trees around the homestead were planted at that time, including old, once fashionable, pines underplanted with clivias. The Norfolk Island pines that dominate the croquet lawn and front entrance are home to magpies. Beyond, huge mature camellias line a pathway down to the drive, with ivy and South African bulbs underneath. The original layout of the Victorian garden is still in evidence, the house and grounds having remained in the Buckland family until 1978. An old orchard borders Gillies Ave, with tall echiums above the corner of the original wooden fence overlooking a sea of commercial buildings beyond. Some of the garden design at Highwic is quite formal, especially a hedged, circular garden with narrow, curving pathways around rosebeds. Other formally edged beds contain old-fashioned perennials and annuals. Native species include ferns, palms, a cabbage tree, and a large totara on the edge of the lawn underplanted with a silver and white border. A fern house features many further varieties of indigenous ferns. A rock walkway leads past a bank of agapanthus, once a sophisticated rockery, under ivy-clad trees, past belladonna lilies down to the driveway by the original stables. A marquee on the tennis court caters for functions.

EWELME COTTAGE
Parnell

Owner:
Auckland City Council – leased to
NZ Historic Places Trust.

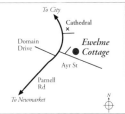

To City

Cathedral
×

Domain
Drive

Ewelme
Cottage

Ayr St

Parnell
Rd

To Newmarket

N

Address: 14 Ayr St, Parnell, Auckland
Directions: Off Parnell Rd, turn into
Ayr St. Garden on left
Phone: 0-9-379 0202
Open: Every day except Good Friday
and Christmas Day; 10.30am–noon
and 1pm–4.30pm
Groups: Ring beforehand
Fee: $2.50 per adult, 50c per child,
NZ Historic Places Trust members
free
Restrictions: No parking on site
Size: Small – 0.1ha (¼ acre)
Terrain: Level, dropping to bushed
gully

Ewelme Cottage has been gardened since 1863, when the house was built for Rev Vicesimus Lush and his family. A large oak, planted in 1866, dominates the garden, dwarfing adjacent pohutukawa and *Magnolia grandiflora*. An old banksia rose climbing up the verandah was planted around 1885. Two camellias are also original, planted in the 1890s, while other trees were planted in the 1920s. The main garden is behind the house, and framed views out to the Hauraki Gulf before the trees grew up. The beds are arranged in crescents and their borders edged in box. Here are many early roses, with original bergenia joined by other sympathetic plantings gleaned from old catalogues. These include dahlias, cosmos, delphiniums, scabiosa, achillea, species geraniums, *Centaurea montana*, and hellebores. A pomegranate at the verandah steps was planted 20 years ago. A summer house, near the oak, was built in 1981. Massive clumps of original crinum and dietes flourish beneath the oak, and the path to the woodland area beyond is bordered with clivias. At the base of the woodland is a gully filled with mixed species of trees, including totara, bay and myrtle. At the roadside of the cottage is a shady area featuring giant billbergias, daphnes, hebes, agapanthus and lace-cap hydrangeas.

HILLS' GARDEN
St Heliers

Owners:
Ada and Gordon Hill

Hills' Garden

Address: 54 The Parade, St Heliers, Auckland
Directions: Off Tamaki Drive, turn into The Parade. Garden on left
Phone: 0-9-575 8577
Open: All year, by appointment
Groups: By appointment
Fee: $4 per adult
Size: Small – 0.13ha (⅓ acre)
Terrain: Steep with steps

 limited

Landscape designer Gordon Hill planned his steep garden carefully seven years before he and Ada moved there in 1960. Back then it was covered in noxious weeds, but forethought resulted in pathways and taps being in the right places 30 years later! The southerly aspect exposes this garden to various climatic conditions, so Gordon designed a series of garden rooms linked by connecting paths, planted in different styles accordingly. Free-laid rock walls terrace the steep slope, the heavy clay loam suiting natives, including pohutukawa, *Entela arborescens*, and the climber *Tecomanthe speciosa*, complemented by deciduous magnolias, acers, malus and avocado in the orchard area. Early spring brings camellias and bulbs into flower, followed by azaleas, rhododendrons and then roses in summer, including four miniature climbers. *Philadelphus coronarius* flourish, as do ground-covers such as brachycome. At the top of the garden Gordon has designed a studio to blend in, with "Wedding Day" roses over it and orchids nearby. Other features include a small rockery, a wisteria-covered pergola, and a shaped fish pond below the house, fountain-fed from an upper pool and planted with hostas, fuchsias, irises, and *Primula obconica*. Autumn features a massive vitis vine above the front windows.

COTTONWOOD
Panmure

Owners:
Judy and Tony Laity

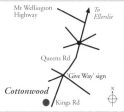

Address: 87 Kings Rd, Panmure, Auckland
Directions: Exit Southern Motorway at Ellerslie if travelling south, or at Mt Wellington if travelling north. After roundabout, continue along Queens Rd to "Give Way" sign, then take Kings Rd. Garden on right
Phone: 0-9-527 7381
Fax: 0-9-527 7381
Open: All year, by appointment
Groups: By appointment
Fee: $5 per adult
Size: Medium – 1.2ha (3 acres)
Terrain: Flat
Nursery: Plants from garden

  by arrangement

Cottonwood is named after the century-old tree in the garden, protected along with oaks, pohutukawa, titoki, totara, puriri, a *Magnolia grandiflora*, a *Ginkgo biloba*, and many established trees planted by Judy's parents in the early twenties. Since 1980 the garden has been landscaped, with beds enlarged and developed, some around trees, many featuring epiphytes. Sweeping lawns separate the beds, which are grouped according to colour – blue and grey, red and yellow, a blue bed and a white bed. Judy's favourites are the blue-flowering and textured plants. She loves changing the colour combinations with the seasons and the passing of years. Situated on the western bank of the Tamaki River, this rambling garden offers views of the estuary through the trees, especially at high tide, from the river walk through the agapanthus and established native ferns. Lilies self-seed and spring bulbs multiply under the trees, where a glade of clivias and a variety of camellias flower under the canopy, which also favours vireyas and azaleas. Many shrub roses bloom throughout the summer, Tony's favourite being the old China "Mutabilis" which changes colour as it flowers continually, from buff to pink to crimson. The rose garden features a central summer house where visitors can sit and view the river and boat jetty, and enjoy the tranquillity of Cottonwood.

WAIKARE
Bucklands Beach

Owners:
Doreen and Tony Priestley

Address: 43 Takutai Ave, Bucklands Beach, Auckland
Directions: Off Bucklands Beach Rd
Phone: 0-9-534 6310
Fax: 0-9-534 6310
Open: All year, by appointment
Groups: By appointment, as above
Fee: $3 per adult
Restrictions: Children 12 years and over only;
parking on road only available
Size: Small – 0.1ha (¼ acre)
Terrain: Sloping with steps
Nursery: A few seedlings from garden
Art: Doreen's watercolours of flowers for sale

 under 12 years   limited

by arrangement

A panoramic ocean view is built into this city garden, with many seats strategically placed and railway-sleeper steps leading down to a semi-circular bricked lookout over the toetoe-topped cliff above the boat harbour. In summer a sea of blue agapanthus on one side with a bank of nasturtiums on the other complement the flaxes, Mt Cook daisies and loads of hydrangeas. Tony is establishing native orchids in the ponga walls, and a native fernery is a special feature. Extensive use has been made of wind-hardy plants, such as proteas, in this clifftop garden over the past decade. Many crucibles hold succulents in the bricked rock garden. Underplanting is being developed down the side of the house, with clivias, bromeliads, fuchsias, and Doreen's many favourite azaleas, creating a continuous walk round the property. The predominant colourings tend to be whites and lavenders, with jasmine, Queen Anne's lace, cinerarias, foxgloves and irises in the spring, then roses when the summer colour emerges. In winter Tony's camellias feature, his favourites including flame-red *C. reticulata* "Dr Clifford Parks", pale pink *C. japonica* "Desire", and white anemone-like "Maui". This seasonal variety of flowers with many other perennials helps to inspire Doreen in her watercolour paintings of flowers, which she sells from home.

QUARTER ACRE PARADISE
Mangere East

Owners:
Dale Harvey and John Newton

Address: 23 Vine St, Mangere East
Directions: Take Mt Wellington or
Otahuhu exits from Motorway.
Follow signs toward airport. From
Mangere/Massey Rd, take Vine St
near Hospital & King's College
Phone: 0-9-276 4827 (office); or
0-9-276 1600 (florist shop)
Fax: 0-9-276 4025 or 0-9-276 1600
Open: All year, by appointment;
Garden: 10am–4pm; Florist Shop:
Monday to Friday 8.30am–5pm
Groups: By appointment
Fee: $5 per adult
Size: Small – 0.14ha (over ¼ acre)
Terrain: Flat
Nursery: Specialists in perennial and
annual seed; landscape and garden
consultants
Shop: Florist

🐕 👫 groups only 🦽 limited
🚶 ⚳ 🍽 by arrangement

Quarter Acre Paradise is designed to be an inspiration
to all backyard New Zealand gardeners, to encourage
the greening of our country into a garden paradise. Dale is
an international garden expert and media personality who
revels in colour and abundance. His specialty is annuals
for all seasons. He loves the fleeting colour massed into
borders and corridors, creating different displays each
season. John specialises in design and artistry. His florist
shop, located within the focal point of the garden – a huge
6-metre-high conservatory – provides a startling subtropical
atmosphere. The conservatory opens to a woods walk,
then a central lawn encircled with roses, bulbs, annuals
and hardy perennials, including colourful North American
specimens, with shrub borders. A cut-flower meadow
supplies John's florist shop, and a pond features a cascade.
A wide range of spring bulbs gives way to begonias, lilies
and masses of summer flowers. Then autumn foliage mixes
with late-season colour, followed by continuing displays
throughout winter in the conservatory. Exotic trees from
almost every continent provide shade, with cypress and
karaka windbreaks. The skyline features other natives,
including totara and titoki, underplanted with shrubs and
ferns. Grapevines, ornamentals, citrus and other fruit trees
were planted by Dale's forebears over three generations.

Dale Harvey

QUAILS CROFT
Whitford

Owners:
Susanne and David Lee

Address: 397 Clifton Rd, Whitford, Auckland
Directions: From Southern Motorway, take Otara turn-off to East Tamaki Rd, turning right into Ormiston Rd, then to end of Sandstone Rd. Turn left into Whitford Park Rd, right into Whitford-Maraetai Rd, then left into Clifton Rd. Garden on left
Phone: 0-9-530 8741
Open: October to February, daily, by appointment
Groups: By appointment
Fee: $5 per adult
Size: Medium – over 1ha (about 3 acres)
Terrain: Mostly flat, with steps between levels

Quails Croft was named after the quail that roamed the garden up to a decade ago. This old-English-style romantic garden is sited on a clifftop, providing wonderful harbour views. The impressive wrought-iron gates set the scene. At the top of the drive, a curve of piceas greets visitors, and "Claire Jacquier" roses climb the verandah posts with prostrate junipers at their feet. The garden has been planted since 1973 on the oldest site in Whitford. It features expansive lawns with pergolas covered in old, modern and David Austin roses, over 300 altogether. A lavender border leads down to a paved area under a horizontal elm and a loggia, with views to Rangitoto Island framed through roses. Further seating in the summer house and under cherry trees provides panoramic views. Susanne loves her 80 maples, which give autumn colour and rise above perennial borders. Spring colours are mainly pinks, creams, whites and blues, featuring clematis and standard wisterias, azaleas, rhododendrons and magnolias. A yellow and white garden surrounds a fish pond with a hedge of the golden David Austin rose "Graham Thomas". A native bush walk, a further pond and a bog garden are in the course of formation.

HAUNUI FARM
Whitford

Owners:
Carolyn and Ron Chitty

Address: Whitford Park Rd, R D,
Manurewa
Directions: From the north, take
Manurewa exit. Turn left then first
right into Stratford Rd. Turn left into
Alfriston Rd, then left again into
Whitford Park Rd. Second driveway
on left. From the south, take Takinini/
Manurewa exit, then as above
Phone: 0-9-530 8013 or 0-9-530 8736
Fax: 0-9-530 8690
Open: All year, by appointment
Groups: By appointment, as above
Fee: $3 per adult, with discount for
busloads
Size: Medium – over 1ha (3 acres)
Terrain: Varying – undulating
Nursery: "Horsh" (sawdust-based
horse manure) for sale
Stables: Stallions from thoroughbred
horse stud can be viewed by prior
arrangement

 by arrangement

Although Haunui means "Big Wind", native bush underplanted with clivias provides shelter for this extensive garden. Huge puriri, rimu, kanuka and three large monkey-puzzle trees nearly a century old, and now interplanted with rhododendrons and camellias, attract birdlife. The camellias provide winter colour and thrive in Whitford clay, enriched with large amounts of "horsh". Carolyn has planted gradually over the past decade, gardens within gardens reclaimed from the lawn, one bed established before another is begun. She likes a quiet garden with areas of lawn and extensive use of whites, creams, greys and greens to soften the brighter colours. Carolyn changes the colours with the seasons, mixing creams and pinks or reds and yellows. Spring blossom on malus and prunus sets off large-leafed foliage, contrasting with feathery ferns. A wide range of perennials is used, with simple cottagey annuals that re-seed. Summer features the roses, hybrids such as "Pot o' Gold" in a mixed bed edged with fibrous begonias. Climbers on the house include rich red "Dublin Bay" and pale salmon-pink "Compassion" intertwined with clematis. Further roses can be seen around the staff quarters. The driveway is lined with agapanthus, a variety of New Zealand ornamentals, nandinas and flax, with an *Acmena smithii* (Australian willow) by the gate.

49

CAMELLIA HAVEN
Takanini

Owner:
Neville Haydon

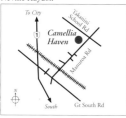

Address: 80 Manuroa Rd, Takanini
Postal: P O Box 537, Papakura
Directions: Take Takanini exit off
Southern Motorway. Travel south
down Great South Rd 400 metres,
turn left into Manuroa Rd. Camellia
Haven on left, on corner of Manuroa
Rd and Takanini School Rd
Phone: 0-9-298 7392
Open: March to October, daily,
except Good Friday and Anzac Day
(25 April); 8.30am–4.30pm;
other times by appointment
Groups: By appointment
Fee: No charge
Size: Small – 0.3ha (¾ acre)
Terrain: Flat
Nursery: Camellia specialist

A specialist camellia display garden at Camellia Haven is attached to the only exclusive camellia nursery in New Zealand. Several hundred camellias demonstrate the different growth habits and ways of growing camellias, including varieties for espaliering, growing over archways or in tubs. Camellia blooms range from a tiny 1cm diameter to very large 12.5cm. Neville finds the smaller and slower-growing camellias are in demand for today's city gardens. Plant form is a vital consideration for permanent planting. The more compact varieties fit well into a landscaped urban garden, and the deep green, shiny foliage is a striking feature throughout the year. Camellia Haven displays a selection of the small-leafed hybrids with miniature blooms, from the dwarf "Baby Bear" to the tall "Cinnamon Cindy". The flowering season begins in March with *Camellia sasanqua*, which are particularly suited for use as screening hedges or as specimens. A few japonicas and hybrids such as Camellia Haven's own seedling "Takanini" also bloom early, but the main flowering period is from June to October. A continuous display of camellia blossoms is maintained in the shop from May to October. Neville is continually testing new varieties produced in New Zealand and overseas. A few of the best of these are offered as new releases each year.

ATARANGI
Papakura

Owners:
Wendy and Neville Guy

Address: 85 Awanui Rise, R D 2, Papakura
Directions: From Papakura, travel along Clevedon Rd. Turn right into Heard Rd, left into Ohiwa Rd, right into Awanui Rise, then right down private road, Awaiti Heights
Phone: 0-9-298 3238
Mobile: 025 758 977
Open: All year, daily, by appointment; weekends and public holidays 10am–7pm during daylight saving; 10am–4pm autumn and winter
Groups: As above
Fee: $3 per adult; group discount
Size: Medium – 0.8ha (2 acres)
Terrain: Flat and steep
Nursery: Miniature rose "Atarangi", climbing roses from local breeder Doug Grant; selection of perennials

    partial

by arrangement

Developed since 1986, an extensive rose garden looking over Manukau harbour at Atarangi now features over 600 old and new roses. Beyond is a native area with two kauri, 10 different pohutukawa, ferns, hebes and massed arthropodiums. Indigenous trees attracting tui and native pigeons are underplanted with rhododendrons, kalmias and hostas. Below is a pond developed from swamp, with flaxes and ducks. A rock garden in the gully above is under construction with a waterfall and stream. A collection of over 30 vireyas forms a walk, with maturing ponga bordered by mollis azaleas. An extensive perennial garden with a thyme walkway emphasises collections of salvias, penstemons and aquilegias, planted among camellias, magnolias and shade trees. A pink terrace features azaleas and camellias in varying shades of pink, and *Camellia sasanqua* line the boundary. A wilderness area is home to quail, pheasants and eastern rosella. Above the house, a U-shaped grove of specimen trees, with a border of shrubs and perennials, is being developed for outdoor eating. An orchard grows along the fenceline, and a conifer garden with companion plants separates the property from the driveway. Future plans include the establishment of a walled garden above the roses and a sunken garden beside it. Atarangi, meaning "new beginning", is living up to its name.

ROSEVILLE
Ramarama

Owners:
Wendy and Dudley Johnson

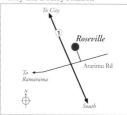

Address: Ararimu Rd, Ramarama
Postal: R D 3, Drury
Directions: Turn off Southern
Motorway at Ramarama exit. Turn
left into Ararimu Rd. Roseville on
corner
Phone: 0-9-294 8674
Mobile: 025 997 869
Fax: 0-9-294 8674
Open: October to December;
weekends; 10am–5pm;
other times by appointment
Groups: As above
Fee: No charge
Size: medium – 1.5ha (3¾ acres)
Terrain: Flat
Nursery: Extensive range of old
roses, David Austin English roses,
ramblers and hybrid musks; orders
taken for any roses from Trevor
Griffiths' comprehensive catalogue

Wendy has "inherited" her love and extensive knowledge of roses from her father Trevor Griffiths. She will give a two-hour guided tour round the display garden, with its formal raised beds radiating round a circular central bed featuring a silver pear edged with erigeron. Companion planting accompanies the roses, including borders of *Stachys lanata*, violets, violas, daisies, poppies, foxgloves, hebes and Queen Anne's lace. The Johnsons are agents for Trevor Griffiths Roses, who are sole New Zealand agents for David Austin English roses. They specialise in roses of yesteryear, the older roses being in the red and purple colour range, with whites. Roseville is designed with separate colour beds, from white through to pink to salmon/yellow, with matching companion planting. Collections of all 21 families of old roses include three recurrent mosses. Musk roses are used as hedges and climbers, with silvery teucrium and lavender hedging also featuring in the rose arbour. Ramblers range from the popular peachy "Albertine", two varieties of "Wedding Day", and the small, purplish "Veilchenblau", to the lesser known "Francois" roses and apricot "Filipes Treasure Trove" – a prolific grower. Special roses include the oldest known rose, soft pink "Sancta", and the green China rose "Viridiflora".

WRIGHTS WATERGARDENS
Patumahoe

Owners:
Dael and Malcolm Wright

Wrights Watergardens

Address: Mauku Rd, Patumahoe
Postal: R D 3, Pukekohe
Directions: From Southern Motorway, take Drury exit and travel towards Waiuku. Turn first left into Ostrich Rd. Travel to Patumahoe. Continue 1.5km on Mauku Rd to garden on right
Phone: 0-9-236 3642
Mobile: 021 623 636
Fax: 0-9-236 3642
Open: November to April, 10am–4.30pm; other times by appointment
Groups: By appointment preferred
Fee: $4 per adult
Size: Large – over 2ha (6 acres)
Terrain: Easy walking on 2 levels
Nursery: Waterlily plants, lotus plants, some aquatics & garden plants
Shop: Cut waterlilies, dried lotus pods, waterlily pots, crafts, film, cold drinks, icecream. by arrangement

mostly

Over the past three years the Wrights have developed 30 waterlily ponds and another four lotus ponds. They specialise in tropical waterlilies which have long stems, making them suitable for the cut flower market. As well as the usual whites, yellows and pinks, the tropical varieties include purples and blues. A 10-metre waterfall provides a magnificent backdrop to the garden, which has been developed on three levels. There are two entrances, one at the top, where the shop is sited, then pathways lead down past the bridal area, petanque pitch, rock garden, love-swing, lookout beneath an umbrella, to the ponds below. Diverse plantings range from a cactus garden to a shady garden featuring hostas, astilbes, ferns and vireyas. Perennials predominate in the waterfall gardens with dahlias a summer feature along the banks. The waterfall once ran a flax mill, which was dismantled in 1869, then the area was quarried until 20 years ago. The rock face from the quarry is still impressive today. Many of the 80 varieties of hardy and tropical waterlilies are scented. The spectacular lotus flowers are also scented, their petals falling in about three days, leaving the seedpod exposed. Most of the lotus seed at Wrights is not fertile, but the pods make interesting dried displays. It is advisable to allow at least an hour to see the gardens. There is seating throughout and sun umbrellas are available for use.

53

THE PLOUGHMAN'S GARDEN AND NURSERY
Waiuku

Owners:
The Carter Family

Ploughman's Garden & Nursery

Address: Duff Rd, R D 2, Waiuku
Directions: Travel to Waiuku township, then turn left into Otaua Rd. Take Whiriwhiri Rd to right, then Duff Rd to left. Ploughman's Garden at end on right
Phone: 0-9-235 9739
Fax: 0-9-235 2659
Open: All year, Wednesday to Sunday, 10am–5pm; Monday and Tuesday by appointment
Groups: Phone ahead
Fee: Tour parties, $3 per head
Size: Medium – 1.2ha (3 acres)
Terrain: Flat
Nursery: Lavender and rosemary specialists; conifers, herbs, shrubs and a few perennials
Art: Colin's pottery and sculpture for sale

   mainly

The Ploughman's Garden and Nursery began in 1990 with a herb garden that expanded into lavender and rosemary specialities until now there are 34 varieties of rosemary and 164 lavender varieties, including 20 English, 12 Australian and another 25 lavenders coming from USA. Mass planting of lavender provides spectacular colour from August till January as the European *L. stoechas* varieties flower, with their long attractive bracts; then the traditional English *L. angustifolia* spiky varieties take over from mid November until March. The green *L. viridis* is a good foil for the more colourful varieties, from the very blue *L. angustifolia* "Hidcote" and "Blue Mountain" through all the purples to the pink "Rosea". Fernleaf lavenders also feature. The sizes range from dwarf species to 1.8m seven-year-old *L. dentata* bushes. Standardised versions are clipped for city courtyards. The Carters mix colours in true cottage style; irises, ageratum, statice and white daisies abound. Roses flow over archways and a great range of perennials add variety. Californian poppies contrast beautifully with the lavender beds, and pansies self-seed. One hundred different conifers are grown, with maples, mulberries and persimmons providing autumn colour. Water gardens feature a water wheel and pump, with waterlily ponds and a bridge. A Tuscan garden is being developed to exhibit Colin's pottery and sculpture.

JOY PLANTS
Pukekohe East

Owners:
Terry, Pam, and son Lindsey Hatch

Joy Plants

Address: Runciman Rd, R D 2,
Pukekohe East
Directions: Take Motorway south of
Auckland to Bombay. Turn right into
Mill Rd and travel 4km towards
Pukekohe. Turn right into Runciman
Rd. Garden is second property on right
Phone: 0-9-238 9129
Fax: 0-9-238 9129
Open: All year, except Sundays and
public holidays; 9am–5pm, or
other times by appointment
Groups: By appointment
Fee: No charge
Size: Medium – 1.2ha (3 acres)
Terrain: Undulating to steep
Nursery: Large range perennials,
NZ native trees, shrubs, vireya
rhododendrons; bulb specialists

  partial

hot water available for ☕ 🏓

Joy Plants Garden and Nursery is a family business,
with Pam, Terry and their son Lindsey having
collected rare and unusual plants over the past 23 years
as well as breeding new plants. Joy Plants specialises in
bulbs and perennials with many varieties grown in their
wilderness garden, from subtropicals to alpines. A range
of native trees with extensive underplantings of rare and
unusual perennials and shrubs predominate, with a large
range of South African bulbs. Natives such as taraire,
kauri and rimu trees combine with exotics including
various nuts such as pecan, walnut and macadamia.
Spring brings the cherries and magnolias into blossom
as well as the spring bulbs and perennials in the small
rock garden and cottage garden. Late spring sees the
flowering of alstromerias including some of the Hatches'
own hybrids. A good range of summer perennials are
followed by amaryllis and nerine bulbs, with
Metrosideros or pohutukawa flowering at Christmas.
Various autumn bulbs bloom including oxalis species in
containers, followed by lachenalias, moraea and ixia in
winter. The large wilderness area attracts much birdlife
including native pigeons and other indigenous birds.
A stream flows through the garden with a bog area under
development.

FORGET ME KNOT GARDENS
Pukekohe

Owners:
Ross and Colleen Baker

Forget Me Knot Gardens

Address: Golding Rd, Pukekohe
Postal: P O Box 558, Pukekohe
Directions: Take Motorway south of
Auckland to Bombay. Turn right into
Mill Rd and travel 7km towards
Pukekohe. Turn left into Golding Rd.
Travel 700m to garden on left
Phone: 0-9-238 3980
Mobile: 025 774 623
Fax: 0-9-238 1649
Open: All year, daily, except Christmas
Day; 9am–9.30pm or dark
Groups: As above
Fee: No charge
Size: Medium – 1.2ha (3 acres)
Terrain: Terraced
Nursery: NZ natives eg arthropodiums,
putawetaweta, kauri, corokia, karaka,
totara; gunnera, carex, quercus,
canariensis ivy

Devonshire

by arrangement

Over the past four years the Bakers have developed
a bull paddock and swamp area into Forget me Knot
Gardens. Now they are terraced around waterlily and
duck ponds, surrounded with marginal water plants and
Ross' favourite bog plants such as gunneras, hostas, ferns,
arums, cannas and black taro. Visitors can enjoy Devonshire
teas under the shade of umbrellas at the many wine-
coloured tables and chairs under trees, or in the tearooms
and courtyard overlooking the ponds. Nearby are stone
walls and an aviary of lorikeets and budgies. Pathways
lead down the terraced banks to the ponds where a boat
lies moored beside a jetty beneath a weeping willow.
Bridges cross the stream and a pergola is covered in
a wonga-wonga vine in summer. Other climbers such
as clematis ramble over structures in spring. Exotic trees
include frangipani, fraxinus, prunus, maples and jacaranda,
with natives predominating such as kauri, putawetaweta,
ponga, many varieties of ferns, arthropodiums and lots
of hebes. A stand of mature pines shelters the extensive
nursery. Perennials include penstemons and many varieties
of fuchsias. *Hypericum* "Rose of Sharon" creates a yellow
border in summer. Many other shrubs are grown and sold.

THE COROMANDEL PENINSULA
AND THE BAY OF PLENTY

We feature 17 gardens from the Coromandel and Bay of Plenty region, south of Auckland. On the way to the Coromandel is Valhalla Country Garden at Ngatea, with a nursery specialising in old roses, unusual perennials and climbers. The Coromandel Peninsula has a warm climate with greater-than-average rainfall, favouring moisture-loving plants. Two of the three gardens in this area are situated around the Tairua area on the east coast, with Harmony Gardens towards Coromandel itself on the west of the peninsula. Trees, subtropical specimens, rhododendrons and herbs are the predominant features. Easterley specialises in garden pottery and Colenso is a welcome refreshment stop amid flowering herbs. Harmony Gardens are sited beside a river amid native bush. The rugged indigenous forest has largely regenerated to cover the effects of early gold mining and kauri logging.

South of the Coromandel Peninsula on the east coast is the Bay of Plenty, with its abundant sunshine and popular beaches. The Bay of Plenty gardens stretch from the coast, which is drier, to inland areas, both experiencing warm summers and cool winters with frosts, and only very occasionally some snow.

At Katikati is Katikati Bird Gardens, a sanctuary for birds. The two Tauranga gardens are Siesta Orchard at Te Puna, south of Katikati, a cottage garden with raised beds adjacent to an orchard, and Glenmyst at Welcome Bay, a terraced garden providing wonderful views across to Mt Maunganui. Further down the coast, inland from Whakatane, at Waimana is My Garden set in rolling farmland.

At Ngongotaha, north of Rotorua, is Janian's Way, featuring irises and south of Ngongotaha is Rhodohill, a rhododendron specialist. There are two gardens along Dansey Road towards Mamaku: Avonlea Cottage Garden, displaying mainly roses, and Kahilani Farm Garden, featuring a woodland garden of natives underplanted with rhododendrons. Off State Highway 5 into Rotorua is the Goodwins' garden with colonial-style structures, archways, rose pergolas and gazebo. In Rotorua City itself are the indoor Orchid Gardens, with unique water organ. Out towards the airport, at Lynmore, is another small urban garden, the Garden Art Gallery then beyond within the Lake Okareka Scenic Reserve is Glade House, with spectacular views down over the lake. Finally, Tikitere Gardens are out past the airport on the road towards Whakatane, where there is space for their 12 hectares of parkland.

Rotorua City also provides Government Gardens around the historic Bath House, and Tauranga has rose gardens and a begonia house to visit at Robbins Park, as well as The Strand gardens. The Rotorua area is volcanic, with underground thermal activity causing spectacular geysers, steaming mineral pools and boiling mud pools. Many attractive lakes incorporate surrounding scenic reserves, including Lakes Okataina, Tarawera, Okareka, Rotomahana, Rotoiti, and Rotorua itself and the Blue and Green Lakes. Walkways provide access to these natural beautiful areas, as well as to the exotic Whakarewarewa Forest with its magnificent Redwood Grove.

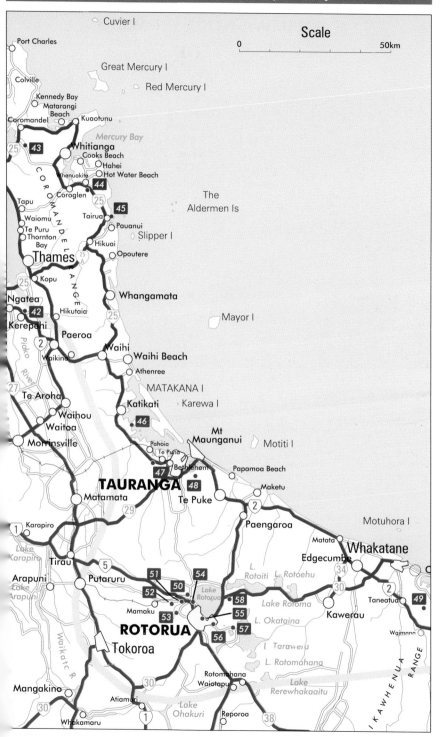

Scale

0   50km

Cuvier I

Port Charles
Colville
Great Mercury I
Red Mercury I
Kennedy Bay
Matarangi Beach
Coromandel
Kuaotunu
43
25
Mercury Bay
Whitianga
Cooks Beach
Hahei
Whenuakite
Hot Water Beach
44
Coroglen
25
Tapu
Tairua
45
The Aldermen Is
Waiomu
Te Puru
Pauanui
Thornton Bay
Slipper I
Hikuai
Thames
Opoutere
25
Kopu
Whangamata
25
Ngatea
42
Mayor I
Hikutaia
Kerepehi
Paeroa
2
Waikino
Waihi
27
Waihi Beach
Te Aroha
Athenree
MATAKANA I
Waihou
Katikati
Karewa I
Waitoa
46
Morrinsville
Mt Maunganui
Pahoia
Te Puna
Motiti I
TAURANGA
Bethlehem
47
Papamoa Beach
Matamata
48
Te Puke
Maketu
29
1
Karapiro
2
Paengaroa
Motuhora I
Lake Karapiro
Tirau
Matata
Edgecumbe
Whakatane
Arapuni
5
Putaruru
51
54
L. Rotoiti
L. Rotoehu
34
2
Lake Arapuni
52
50
Lake Rotorua
Lake Rotoma
30
Taneatua
49
Mamaku
58
Kawerau
ROTORUA
53
55
L. Okataina
57
Waimana
Tokoroa
56
L. Tarawera
I KAWHENUA RANGE
L. Rotomahana
Mangakino
Rotomahana
Lake Rerewhakaaitu
Waiotapu
Atiamuri
30
Reporoa
30
Whakamaru
1
Lake Ohakuri
38

VALHALLA COUNTRY GARDEN
Ngatea

Owners:
Anna and Peter Monrad

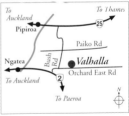

Address: 65 Orchard East Rd, R D 2, Ngatea
Directions: 10km from Thames. Take the Thames turn-off from SH 1. Travel past Pipiroa and turn right into Bush Rd. Turn left into Orchard East Rd. Garden on left. Or take SH 2 from Paeroa, towards Ngatea. Turn right into Bush Rd, then right again into Orchard East Rd. Garden on left
Phone: 0-7-867 7344
Open: All year, Friday to Tuesday, 10am–4pm
Groups: By appointment
Fee: No charge
Size: Medium – 0.4ha (1 acre)
Terrain: Flat
Nursery: Specialists in old roses, unusual perennials, climbers
Shop: exclusive range of garden fabric ideas, kneelers, tool boxes, garden books, etc

Started five years ago, Valhalla Country Garden features Anna's favourite old-fashioned roses complemented by cottage plants. Tea-tree fences, seats and arches, constructed by Peter, divide the garden into rooms, with old brick walkways and circular beds. Features include two rosemary circles; a circular edible garden planted by Kit, a Danish relation, and filled with red currants, raspberries, strawberries and blueberries; Jenny's Scottish garden planted by a daughter-in-law with Scottish plants; and Nana's Memory garden with a statue from Anna's maternal grandmother encircled with white alyssum. One garden planted in blues and pinks, with "Cecile Brunner" roses climbing an archway, is separated by lawn from another garden in yellow, white, orange and cream. Spring bulbs and roses are accompanied by unusual perennials as well as all the cottage favourites including campanulas, penstemons, catmint, salvias, geraniums, irises and foxgloves. A more formal garden with an arbour walk and secret rooms is being developed on another acre, with a small cottage for selling garden accessories. Although Valhalla is primarily a spring and summer garden, Anna plans to establish a winter garden featuring unusual trees and shrubs.

HARMONY GARDENS
Coromandel

Custodian:
Grant Eyre

Address: 309 Rd, Coromandel
Directions: Travel 4km south from
Coromandel towards Thames, then
turn left up 309 Rd towards
Whitianga. Travel 1.6km to Harmony
Gardens on left
Phone: 0-7-866 8835
Fax: 0-7-866 8835
Open: October to Easter, daily,
10am–4pm; other times by
appointment
Groups: As above
Fee: $5 per adult
Size: Medium – 0.7ha (under 2 acres)
Terrain: Undulating
Music: Annual concert at end of
January

mostly

Harmony Gardens is, just as its name suggests, a harmonious paradise. Originally developed in 1980 from a jungle of manuka, gorse and blackberry, this garden was gradually established and carefully landscaped to create an uncluttered, peaceful atmosphere. Mass plantings achieve overall beauty in the garden. Walkways enable the visitor to capture each new scene from the path around to the Waiau River, which flows by the garden, its banks lined with South African *Aristea*. Features include a waterfall tinkling into a lily pond; three bridges, one an expansive arch leading into a silver birch grove; three ferneries; some rare natives, such as dwarf totara and manuka; and some fairly rare hostas. Spring bulbs, including 2,500 daffodils and 150 Dutch irises, are complemented with about 200 azaleas. A wonderful display of 295 rhododendrons follows, featuring group plantings of "Lem's Cameo". Then in summer vireya rhododendrons, lilies, hydrangeas, dahlias, agapanthus, Japanese irises, and many more perennials take over. Matching benches are strategically placed throughout the garden, allowing the atmosphere of beauty and tranquillity to be absorbed beneath the many native and exotic trees. Meditative music wafts through the valley, and a concert for charity is an annual event in summer. Grant is further developing the garden since change of ownership in 1996.

COLENSO
Tairua

Owners:
Ruth and Andy Pettitt

Address: Main Rd, Whenuakite,
R D 1, Tairua
Directions: On left of main highway
to Whitianga, 10 minutes north of
Tairua. About 2km before the turn-off
to Hot Water Beach and Hahei.
Colenso on left
Phone: 0-7-866 3725
Fax: 0-7-866 3759
Open: All year, daily, 10am–5pm
Groups: By appointment
Fee: No charge
Size: Small – 0.2ha (½ acre)
Terrain: Flat
Shop: Café and country shop –
hand-made goods eg pot-pourri, local
honey, soap, Colenso preserves;
agent for Touchwood Books
Wayside stall: Tree-ripened fruit and
produce

Named after the botanist William Colenso, the
Colenso herb garden was created from part of an
orchard in 1988. Now featuring a knot garden behind the
café and country shop, Colenso is a welcome stop for
travellers. Through a jasmine-covered archway, the front
garden features standard rosemary and *Lavandula dentata*
edged with pansies. A dovecote is surrounded by fragrant
herbs such as santolina, with beds of lavender, borage,
lychnis and scented pelargoniums, and roses flourish
throughout. Another archway, this time covered in
banksia, leads into the brightly coloured knot garden,
with triangles of calendulas edged with box and borders
of aquilegias and cornflowers. Ruth loves a riot of colour,
the more the better. Roses climb up the trelliswork above
the fence, accompanying the other old roses throughout
the garden, which is framed by 20-year-old trees. A new
sunflower and lavender patch features a central pergola.
Ruth grows mixed herbs – medicinal, culinary, herbs for
dyeing, drying and perfume. Her favourites are the
lavenders and rosemary which grow in abundance at
Colenso. She has also established a parterre of herbs as
a working garden for teas served in the garden, or in the
café which is warmed by a lovely old coal range in
winter. Ruth serves orchard fresh juice, Devonshire teas
or light lunches, with picnic lunches by arrangement.

EASTERLEY
Tairua

Owners:
Pat and David Boyes

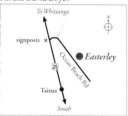

Address: 44 Ocean Beach Rd, Tairua
Postal: P O Box 52, Tairua
Directions: Off main road, 1km north of Tairua. Signposted both from north and south
Phone: 0-7-864 8526
Open: All year, daily, dawn to dusk
Groups: As above
Fee: No charge
Size: Medium – 0.8ha (2 acres)
Terrain: Hilly
Shop: Cottage Craft Shop selling only New Zealand-made pottery and craft
Art: Courtyard of garden sculptures

Sited on the east coast of the Coromandel Peninsula, this bush garden has been developed over the past two decades. The steep driveway was hacked out with pick and shovel and designed for walking up, so everything can be seen at eye level. The two massive pots David made to flank the drive entrance give an intimation of what lies beyond. Sculptures by local artists feature throughout the garden, and a sculptural courtyard displays one-off pieces, made by local potters, in front of the three-roomed craft shop, with work such as that of John Sweden, Norma Nell, and the Boyes' son, Bill Roberts. Small ponds and a stream meander through the garden, and wide walkways with sleeper steps lead down to a very dark "monster" pool. A pottery fountain is surrounded by ferns, which abound in this woodland garden; it also features many native trees blending with introduced ones. The predominant colour is green, with early bulbs beginning to flower in winter; then, as the days warm up, the greenery offers coolness and shade as the banana like "traveller's palms" flourish, giving a subtropical feel to the garden. A small rose garden provides spring and summer colour, then autumn colours up the maple trees. Vegetable terraces and fruit trees add variety, and bird cages complement the native birds, including the large numbers of wood pigeons.

KATIKATI BIRD GARDENS
Katikati

Owners:
Chrissie and Peter Looker

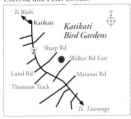

Address: Walker Rd East, R D 2,
Katikati
Directions: Off SH 2, 30km north of
Tauranga or 6km south of Katikati.
Turn into Walker Rd East. Katikati
Bird Gardens on left
Phone: 0-7-549 0912
Open: All year, daily, except July,
weekends only in August; re-opening
daily from August holidays
Groups: As above
Fee: $5 per adult; $2.50 per school
child; $1.50 per pre-schooler
Size: Large – 4.8ha (12 acres)
Terrain: Undulating
Nursery: Cottage plants
Shop: Café and craft shop

 by arrangement for groups

This bird sanctuary was established in 1974, with almost five hectares of English-style gardens and a series of lakes reclaimed from swamplands. In 1991 Chrissie and Peter took over, revamping the gardens and developing new areas. They have also introduced a larger selection of birds, which now includes approximately 65 different species. Peacocks, pheasants, ducks and a large range of many other birds roam the extensive lawns that slope down to the waterlily ponds. These are edged with bog plants, arum and taro lilies, irises, arthropodiums, hostas and gunnera. Chrissie chooses the softer colours, using brighter ones for impact only. She groups scarlet cannas with chrysanthemums and dahlias of similar intensity. The aviaries by the ponds house the rarer birds, including injured birds like harrier hawks for Bird Rescue. Endangered species such as weka and brown teal are bred here too. Springtime ushers in magnificent magnolias, flowering cherries, masses of bulbs, banks of azaleas and rhododendrons. Then the lilies come into their own in summer, along with hibiscus and David Austin roses, as well as an abundant variety of perennials. Natives abound and English trees provide autumn colour, with a large gleditsia shading the table and chairs in front of the teahouse. Masses of camellia hedges brighten the winter. A café provides delicious lunches.

SIESTA ORCHARD
Tauranga

Owners:
Colleen and Stewart Thwaites

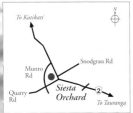

Address: 6 Quarry Rd, Te Puna,
R D 6, Tauranga
Directions: Off SH 2, 12km north of
Tauranga or 23km south of Katikati.
Turn west into Quarry Rd. Garden
immediately on right
Phone: 0-7-552 5888
Open: All year, Wednesday to Sunday
Groups: By appointment
Fee: $2 per adult
Size: Medium – 0.4ha (1 acre)
Terrain: Sloping
Shop: Studio – dried flowers and
arrangements for sale

  limited

A cottage garden developed over the past decade on
bare land is now a series of pretty beds under
established trees. The lower part was planted first, and the
upper slopes have been developed since 1990. Colleen
works with raised beds for convenience, using ponga,
rocks, and half-rounds for edging, perennials spilling over
the sides, with mown grass between beds. Annuals such
as helichrysum are grown for use as dried flowers, which
Colleen arranges in her studio. A shade house contains an
orchid collection, and some flourish outside too. Colleen
uses lots of white between hotter colours, planting phlox
in the borders, with alyssum, daisies, and hostas. In spring
the softer colours emerge, with foxgloves, azaleas and
cottage garden flowers such as pansies under the *Magnolia
campbellii* and three kowhai. Then the hot colours come
out in summer, with dahlias, roses and summer-flowering
perennials under the shade trees, while tuberous begonias
blaze in the summer house. Autumn bulbs are complemented
with deciduous foliage, including the lovely male idesia.
Then camellias take over in winter. There is a sprinkling
of natives throughout the garden, including groups of
ferns. Walks through the adjoining Siesta Orchards can be
arranged. These are mainly citrus and kiwifruit. The family
enterprise was named from a combination of family initials.

GLENMYST GARDEN
Tauranga

Owners:
Gwynn and Fred Glentworth

Address: 157 Waikite Rd, Welcome
Bay, R D 5, Tauranga
Directions: 8 minutes from Tauranga
City, take Welcome Bay Rd at
roundabout. Turn right into Waikite
Rd and travel 1.5km to garden on left
Phone: 0-7-544 2707
Open: September to May; Monday to
Thursday 11am–4pm, Saturday
1pm–5pm, Sunday by appointment
1pm–5pm
Groups: By appointment
Fee: $3 per adult
Size: Medium – 0.7ha (nearly 2 acres)
Terrain: Flat to sloping
Nursery: Occasional perennials,
shrubs, etc
Special occasions: Ideal for wedding
photos, etc

 flat areas

Glenmyst Garden was developed in response to the
heat of Tauranga. In order to provide shelter for
plants on the sloping field, the Glentworths planted trees
to form a canopy for shade and to filter the sun. In this
way they have created a micro-climate in which
succulents, crown-of-thorns (*Euphorbia milii*), and
subtropicals thrive along with perennials and a variety of
shrubs. Several small ponds have been established within
a rockery, connected by native ground cover and thyme-
covered steps. Two larger pools feature Egyptian and
Asian lotus waterlilies. Terraced beds edged with ponga,
ferns and tumbling plants create layers of colour, with
lawn between the borders. Early spring ushers in the
pinks and whites of flowering cherries with lilac, pink and
white wisteria. Unusual bulbs, such as deep maroon cobra
lilies (*Arisaema speciosum*), feature with yellow
daffodils, red tulips and a large variety of thornless cacti
providing hot colours. Summer brings many lilies and
unusual perennials into flower with masses of colour, then
autumn colours up the maples, cherries, oak, and other
deciduous foliage. Varieties of banana palms, tree ferns
and conifers add a cool, restful feel in contrast to the
colourful poinsettias, exotic rhododendrons and Japanese
irises. Magnificent harbour views to Mt Maunganui can
be seen throughout the seasonal changes of this garden.

MY GARDEN
Waimana

Owners:
Dianne and Barry Yeoman

Address: Fraser Rd, SH 2, Waimana Gorge
Postal: P O Box 78, Waimana
Directions: Turn off SH 2 into Fraser Rd. Travel 3km over 6 cattle stops to garden at end of road
Phone: 0-7-312 3254
Open: 1 October to 31 March, daily, 10am–5pm, by appointment
Groups: By appointment, as above
Fee: $3 per adult; groups of 10 or more $2 per head
Size: Small – 0.8ha (½ acre)
Terrain: Flat

 by arrangement

Dianne has created her garden over the past 23 years, beginning with a bare paddock and achieving a series of garden rooms separated by archways covered in climbing roses and clematis. Outdoor seating is sited under various pergolas looking out to the rural scenery. Dianne has designed her garden to incorporate the surrounding farm-land and bush and feels the green valley sets off all the colours of her flowers, obviating the need to coordinate them. A ponga house is 19 years old, planted round with 50 different hostas, and crytomerias are limbed up so they can be underplanted with more of Dianne's favourite hostas. She also loves roses, with more than 170 different varieties. Chatham Island forget-me-nots are a feature in spring with many other perennials and *Romneya coulteri* in late summer. Dianne is also keen on tuberous begonias that add to the colour in February. A small water garden surrounds a pond and an arched bridge leads to a wishing well with the David Austin rose "Graham Thomas" climbing over the roof. There are over 200 potted plants throughout Dianne's garden. An added attraction is the large aviary and dovecotes housing fantail pigeons. My Garden won third prize as the "Best Rural Garden" in the Whakatane Garden Competition, in both 1994 and 1995.

JANIAN'S WAY
Ngongotaha

Owners:
Ian and Jan Hossack

Address: 28 Bruce St, Ngongotaha
Directions: Travel north about 10km
from Rotorua to Ngongotaha
township. Turn left into Hood Street,
then second right into Bruce St.
Janian's Way on left
Phone: 0-7-357 2074 evenings and
weekends
Open: All year, daily, by appointment
Groups: By appointment, as above
Fee: Donation – gold coin
Size: Small – 0.08ha (⅕ acre)
Terrain: Flat and terraced
Nursery: Iris rhizomes in season,
dianthus, perennials and cuttings
from garden

   flat areas

  by arrangement

Although Jan and Ian have lived here for about three decades, it is only since 1986 that they have intensively planted their suburban garden. Irises are Jan's favourites, and the garden includes many species. The front garden is flat with beds of irises, standard roses and perennials. Behind the house are more irises, roses, poppies and a rockery. Down the terraced hillside is an old cherry tree underplanted with beds of perennials, hostas and begonias. Several small pools surrounded by irises and hostas feature large and dwarf waterlilies. A dovecote erected in 1991 is home to free-flight fantail pigeons and ring-neck doves. In early spring the dwarf bearded irises bloom, then intermediate and tall beardeds, along with roses, lavender, lilies and perennials, including peonies and Chatham Island forget-me-nots. A collector's corner features trilliums, iris species and many treasures. Spring also ushers in tulips galore in red and gold, with daffodils and a growing collection of crocuses and hyacinths. These are followed by rhododendrons and azaleas. Autumn is crocus time again, and winter sees the beauty of irises extended to their eternal grey foliage. Natives include a red kaka-beak on the front fence, native clematis and ponga. Jan likes climbers such as hybrid clematis and hoyas, and plans to build a gazebo featuring climbing roses and clematis.

AVONLEA COTTAGE GARDEN
Mamaku

Avonlea

Owners:
Christina and Ramon Humphreys

Address: Dansey Rd, R D 2, Mamaku
Directions: Take Fairy Springs Rd north of Rotorua. Turn left into SH 5, then left again into Dansey Rd. Travel 1km along Dansey Rd to gardens on right
Phone: 0-7-357 5095
Fax: 0-7-357 5095
Open: All year, Wednesday to Friday 1pm–5pm, weekends 10am–5pm
Groups: Other times by appointment
Fee: $3 per adult for garden walk, refundable on purchase from nursery
Size: Small – 0.3ha (¾ acre)
Terrain: Slight slope
Nursery: Roses, perennials, shrubs, trees
Shop: Wooden garden furniture for sale

  limited

Avonlea Cottage Gardens were established in 1991 on a former sheep paddock, with hilltop vistas across a valley. Conifers and English trees were planted, then the garden planned. The rose specialist nursery features grass walkways, creating a soft look, with neat ponga-edged beds and totara-post rose pergolas, such as one covered in "Wedding Day". Christina loves old roses, including "Stanwell Perpetual" and "Old Blush", and David Austin varieties like "Heritage", as well as modern roses such as "Julia's Rose". Salmon pinks and reds predominate, but Christina grows all colours, including the pale lemon Austin rose "Windrush". Low, clipped honeysuckle hedges add to the cottagey look, as do many perennials. At 360 metres above sea level, spring arrives late because of the altitude. Bulbs, flowering cherries, kaka-beaks, white honesty and daisies bloom throughout. Summer brings more daisies, foxgloves, mimulas and delphiniums into flower, with pyrethrum effective in keeping the giant Savoy cabbages spray free. Other features are "Earl of Avonlea", a majestic 26-point red stag, and "Madam Twinkle" the deer, with pet fawns, lambs and Siamese cats. A planned walkway winding down through the deer farm, stream, bush and woodland areas will enhance the "Anne of Green Gables" atmosphere from which Avonlea takes its name.

KAHILANI FARM GARDEN
Mamaku

Owners:
Yvonne and David Medlicott

Address: 691 Dansey Rd, Mamaku
Postal: P O Box 296, Rotorua
Directions: Turn off SH 5 into
Dansey Rd, travel 6.8km towards
Mamaku. Kahilani Farm Garden on
left, drive through gully for 1km
Phone: 0-7-332 5662 or
0-7-347 9168 (business)
Mobile: 025 990 690
Fax: 0-7-332 5662
Open: 15 September to 15 December,
daily, 10am–6pm; other times by
appointment
Groups: As above
Fee: $2.50 per adult, $2 senior citizen
Size: Medium – over 1 ha (3 acres)
Terrain: Flat to undulating
Nursery: Some plants from garden

  by arrangement

A kilometre's drive through a spectacular gully of natural rock formations leads to the woodland garden of Kahilani, meaning "Beautiful Companions", referring to the Labrador breeding kennels. Inspired by Pukeiti, the Medlicotts have underplanted the plentiful indigenous bush with rhododendrons since 1989. Mature tawa and ponga are interspersed with young rimu and regenerating tree fuchsias; cabbage trees, ferns and other natives remain, attracting native birdlife. A collection of almost 1,000 named rhododendron varieties, both hybrids and species, now thrive in filtered light under the woodland canopy. These peak in October and November with azaleas and camellias underplanted with primulas, hostas, trilliums, Chatham Island forget-me-nots, cardiocrinums and meconopsis, complemented by pieris, kalmia and conifers. Spring begins in late July with the thousands of daffodils and bluebells throughout the garden and lining the driveway. Wide ponga-lined walkways intersect plant beds. In August camellias and the earliest rhodos flower, later ones continuing into summer with many and varied shrubs. Autumn colours the foliage of larches, maples, liquidambars, golden elms and prunus. A romantic cottage garden around the house features roses, perennials and annuals. Plans include a damp area, a native bush walk and further rhododendrons.

RHODOHILL
Rotorua

Owners:
David and Ailsa Stewart

Address: Paradise Valley Rd, R D 2, Rotorua
Directions: Turn left into SH 5, then left again into Valley Rd. Follow this loop road round Mt Ngongotaha to Trout Springs. Garden beyond on left
Phone: 0-7-348 9010
Fax: 0-7-348 9041
Open: Garden: October and November; Wednesday to Sunday 10am–5pm. Nursery: March to Christmas; hours as above
Groups: As above
Fee: $3 per adult
Size: Medium – 1.6ha (4 acres)
Terrain: Hilly
Toilet: At Trout Springs 1km away
Nursery: Specialising in rhododendrons, azaleas, hostas, magnolias, Japanese maples, camellias
Catalogue: Mail order throughout NZ

    limited

Rhodohill began as a hobby when rhododendrons were collected from Europe and the USA and planted on the hill. The Stewarts took over the garden and nursery in 1983 and have developed it into a mature woodland garden, until there are over 800 rhododendrons, from tree varieties down to the dwarf species in the rockery. Rhodohill is essentially a spring garden, the soft colourings of the rhododendrons complemented by over 300 camellias and hostas. A 50-metre arched laburnum tunnel, in flower mid November, forms Gothic windows through which the garden slopes below can be viewed, different levels being connected by sweeping pathways. Conifers and exotic trees harmonise with ponga and many smaller ferns planted underneath along the sheltered walkways beside the lawns. Japanese umbrella pine (*Sciadopitys verticillata*), dawn redwood (*Metasequoia glyptostroboides*), drimys, michelia, and weeping copper beech form a canopy over shrubs including viburnums, pieris and kalmias, underplanted with shade-loving perennials such as trilliums, cardiocrinum, rhodohypoxis, anemones, daylilies and astilbes. Now that shelter trees are established, providing cool overhead shade, the plan is to expand further on up the hill. As well as Rhodohill, Paradise Valley also features a trout hatchery, trout springs and wildlife park nearby.

GOODWINS
Kawaha Point

Owners:
Eric and Jean Goodwin

Address: 82 Grand Vue Rd, Rotorua
Directions: From Rotorua City, take
road north towards Ngongotaha.
Turn right into Kawaha Pt Rd, then
left into Koutu Rd. Turn right into
Grand Vue Rd. Garden on right
Phone: 0-7-347 6888
Open: September to May, by
appointment
Groups: By appointment, as above
Fee: $2 per adult
Size: Small – 0.15ha (⅓ acre)
Terrain: Flat

  by arrangement,
hot water available

Although the Goodwins are both octogenarians, they are actively involved in their urban garden, which Eric developed from a bare paddock 15 years ago. Colonial style structures and statuary harmonise with the house architecture, with rose archways and pergolas, a gazebo covered in "Dublin Bay" and "Wedding Day" and a pond and fountain area planted with aquatics. A cool area features fuchsias, hostas, ferns, gunneras, irises, lilies and astilbes. With his background as a florist, Eric likes to make a picture with plants, grouping together whites and pinks, with reds and yellows together in other areas. Eric uses pots extensively, with freesias and tulips in spring, then lilies and annuals in summer, followed by potted chrysanthemums in autumn. Goodwins is a shrub garden with open spaces, many hybrid and reticulata camellias featuring in spring, with rhododendrons, wisteria, clematis, weeping cherries and echiums for height. Eric also grows many irises – Japanese, water and beardeds. Over 200 begonias flower in February accompanied by raised beds of perennials and Eric's favourite roses and delphiniums. In autumn hanging baskets provide colour, adding to the dahlias and potted chrysanthemums. The garden is planted for a continuity of colour through the seasons.

THE ORCHID GARDENS
Rotorua

Manager:
Garth Padman

Address: Hinemaru St, Rotorua
Directions: Travel along Hinemoa St,
turn left into Hinemaru St
Phone: 0-7-347 6699
Fax: 0-7-346 3600
Open: Daily, 8.30am–5.30pm
Groups: As above
Fee: $9.00 per adult, $3 per child
under 15; group discounts
Size: Indoors
Terrain: Ramps and steps
Nursery: Orchids
Shop: Souvenirs
Attractions: Water organ, unique in
NZ, provides display of colour from
700 water jets choreographed to
music on the hour;
Microworld of insects
Restaurant: Open 8.30am–5.30pm

The Orchid Gardens display exotic orchids and tropical plants in their "natural" environment. Being fully enclosed, this is an all-season, all-weather attraction, with different orchid species flowering each season. The gardens were redesigned in 1988, incorporating exotic birds such as sulphur-crested cockatoos, lorikeets and golden pheasants. A viewing platform is edged with moss-covered totara and rimu railings from the hospital which was sited here in 1895. Visitors can look out over a waterfall surrounded by ferns, palms and cycads into a large goldfish pond. Other tropical plants, such as crotons, anthuriums, epiphytic bromeliads and tillandsias growing on ponga, complement palms and native ferns. Colourful impaties, tuberous begonias and perennials thrive amid luxuriant tropical foliage. Tiny New Zealand orchids grow on rocks and ponga tree ferns with elusive Australian green tree frogs throughout the complex. Pure white and pink *Phalaenopsis* or moth orchids with their arching sprays are popular in wedding bouquets. Other orchid species include *Cattleya*, spidery *Brassia*, *Odontoglossum*, *Oncidium*, *Cypripedium* or slipper orchids, *Epidendrum* (such as the crucifix orchid), birdlike *Masdevallia*, and *Cymbidium*, which can tolerate cooler conditions than the 12 to 16 degrees celsius maintained in the Orchid House by thermal energy.

THE GARDEN ART GALLERY
Rotorua

Owners:
Jeanette and Graeme Blackburn

Address: 60 Lynmore Ave, Lynmore, Rotorua
Directions: 5km from Rotorua, turn off Te Ngae Rd, right into Tarawera Rd. Then take second on left to Lynmore Ave. Garden on left
Phone: 0-7-345 9660
Open: By appointment, all year; afternoons preferred
Groups: By appointment
Fee: $3 per adult
Size: Small – 0.13ha (⅓ acre)
Terrain: Flat with low terraces
Art Gallery: Jeanette's detailed wildlife and landscape paintings, limited edition prints, calendars, cards and placemats for sale; commissions taken

This award-winning urban garden of only 1,350 square metres gives an illusion of space. This is created by its division into rooms with trellis, allowing glimpses into adjoining garden rooms and providing framework for climbers such as wisteria, an espaliered apple, wonga-wonga and grapevine. Graeme gardens and constructs to Jeanette's careful design, while she paints representational works from nature. Prior to 1987 this was a typical back vege garden and old orchard. Three plums remain, underplanted now with arthropodiums, ferns, hostas and gunneras around the bridged goldfish pond in one corner of the garden. Visitors can look out from the swinging chair in the gazebo, to the delphiniums, lupins and geums under the robinia, which offers summer shade. Deciduous trees allow winter sun through, as does the grape arbour, which lets the fragrance of violets growing beneath waft up. Dovecotes add interest, and a rose arbour is a favourite, Graeme going for the old intense pink "Zéphirine Drouhin" climber and Jeanette opting for "Wedding Day" which tumbles over the archway. Graeme uses plenty of orange in his typical cottage-garden rainbow of colours, with calendulas and pansies brightening the base of the sun-dial, for instance. Jeanette sells her work from her adjoining gallery. She is the first New Zealand artist to feature on Bradford Exchange plates.

GLADE HOUSE
Rotorua

Owners:
Annette and Ron Marsden

Address: Millar Rd, Lake Okareka,
R D 5, Rotorua
Directions: Travel 3km from Rotorua.
Turn right into Tarawera Rd, continue
into Loop Rd, veer left into Millar
Rd, continuing for 3km into Reserve
Phone: 0-7-362 8542
Fax: 0-7-362 8542
Open: All year, by appointment
Groups: By appointment, as above
Fee: $3 per adult
Size: Small – about 0.3ha (less than
acre), plus 2ha (5 acres) bush walks
Terrain: Steep drive, but flat garden
Toilet: Available at Okataina
Walkway further up Millar Rd
Nursery: Some plants from garden
Accommodation: B&B available at
Glade House Lodge

by arrangement

Glade House is a Lockwood home set in the middle of a glade surrounded by native bush, on a plateau within Lake Okataina Scenic Reserve. A sweeping croquet lawn is bordered by raised beds full of bulbs, annuals and perennials, edged with ponga walls. Since 1990 the Marsdens have introduced cherries, maples, camellias and old-fashioned roses into the garden. Annette likes to colour-block the planting, providing patches of warmth against the impressive green backdrop. The indigenous bush, including titoki, rewarewa, kowhai, kawakawa, red kaka-beak, and mamaku tree ferns attracts native birds, such as pigeons, bellbirds and tui. The cliff-top view down to Lake Okareka is a special feature from the Lodge behind the house, 105 metres above the lake or 510 metres above sea level. The high altitude means that spring comes late, with camellias, bulbs, cherries, and clematis followed by azaleas and rhododendrons. Summer brings more bulbs, a variety of perennials, and roses including "Iceberg" and "Ispahan", with climbers such as "Wedding Day" scrambling up trees after the clematis. Close planting helps to conserve moisture as there is no water available for watering. The Marsdens plan to blend the garden into the bush more, and rimu and kohekohe are already starting to appear round the borders of their garden.

TIKITERE GARDENS
Rotorua

Owner:
Bill Robinson

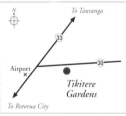

Address: SH 30, Rotorua
Postal: P O Box 819, Rotorua
Directions: Travel east out of Rotorua
along SH 33. Past the airport turn
right into SH 30. Travel 1km to
Tikitere Gardens on right; 13km from
Rotorua
Phone: 0-7-345 5036
Fax: 0-7-345 5036
Open: Daily; summer 8am–6pm;
winter 9am–5pm
Groups: As above
Fee: $5 per adult
Size: Large – 12ha (30 acres)
Terrain: Flat to rolling
Nursery: Rhododendrons, hostas,
azaleas, maples, *Hemerocallis*, iris,
camellias, perennials
Shop: Craft shop and tearooms
pending

These extensive gardens, developed since 1987 from a boysenberry farm, incorporate a natural stream and established trees. Tikitere means "precious waters", referring to the dominant feature, the Waiohena Stream, walled in stone by local craftsmen. Bog plants including hostas and primulas are planted along the stream, with hellebores under a silver birch plantation featuring in winter. Bridges cross the stream, which is lined by maples, with cherry trees in the more established areas. Azaleas, both mollis and evergreen, and rhododendrons cover the slopes beyond the stream banks, with gums, laburnums and other woodland trees behind, surrounded by farmland. A waterfall is a focal point, with lavenders and azaleas edging the banks. A driveway winds throughout the garden, following the contours of the stream. The predominant colour is yellow, with Japanese and many other varieties of iris, *Hemerocallis* (daylilies) and astilbes flowering in summer in a bog area under the canopy of trees. Oaks and liquidambars add to the autumn foliage, complemented by natives including kauri and totara. Magnolias, camellias and prunus blossom in spring, followed by tree peonies and dogwoods. *Fothergilla* shrubs also flower in spring, the foliage a brilliant red in autumn. Imported and rare plants are displayed, and many sold in the adjacent nursery.

THE WAIKATO AND KING COUNTRY

A total of 18 gardens are featured from the Waikato and King Country regions. The Waikato is one of the most fertile areas in the country, being renowned for its dairy pasture. The volcanically rich soil and abundant rainfall contribute to its fertility. Hamilton, the only city in the Waikato, is about an hour and a half's drive south of Auckland on State Highway 1.

The Waikato gardens featured stretch from Gordonton to Cambridge. Taitua Arboretum, with its glorious autumn colour, is sited north of Hamilton, while two gardens are located at Gordonton; one, Willow Glen, with extensive indoor gardens, and the other, with historic trees and camellias, being developed around the historic home of Woodlands. Flora Vale, a two-acre garden towards Morrinsville, has an oriental flavour, and Naumai, just south of Waitoa, is the same size and features raised perennial beds of different colours.

A smaller rural garden north of Waharoa is Garden of Joy, featuring three water gardens among immaculate flower beds, while Carolyn Gardens at Matamata although a new garden has already won local awards. West of Matamata is Tui Grange, set in a farmscape over-looking the Waikato countryside. Near Cambridge is Farnaharpy, a 10-year-old garden with adjacent milking shed. South of Hamilton are two gardens at Tamahere, Seven Oaks, an English cottage garden under huge old oaks, and Gails of Tamahere, which features dried flowers. The Poplars at Matangi features a large lake and thousands of daffodils with an exhibition nursery.

The Waikato gardens feature a range of plants and trees, all thriving in this fertile region. Hamilton Gardens, formerly known as the Rose Gardens, feature in Hamilton itself on the banks of the Waikato River. This expansive public garden complex includes individual gardens such as the extensive rose gardens, a Chinese garden, an old-fashioned English flower garden, a herb garden, and a huge kitchen garden.

South of Waikato is the King Country, a hilly, rugged region, with increasingly cooler temperatures closer to National Park and the Central Plateau. The six King Country gardens stretch from Te Kuiti down past Taumarunui to Manunui in the south. This area has a high rainfall, being a higher-altitude climate. The three gardens around the Te Kuiti district are a diverse group. The Birches focuses on fuchsias, Tapuwae grows many rhododendrons and Aramatai has roses and a large rockery. The McKenzies' garden in Taumarunui is a floral artist's domain, with roses and other suitable flowering plants and trees. Thirty kilometres west of Taumarunui is Wicky's Garden, an extensive 40-hectare woodland garden featuring whole hillsides of rhododendrons, trees and lakes. The southernmost King Country garden, Crowhill at Manunui, is a neat urban garden with mixed beds.

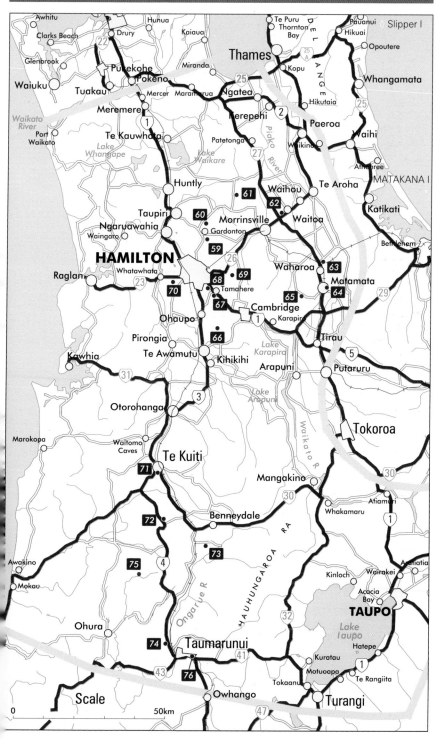

Scale

0   50km

WILLOW GLEN GARDENS
Gordonton

Owners:
Cindy and Del Henley

Address: Gordonton Rd, R D 1,
Hamilton
Directions: 11.6km north of
Hamilton, turn right into Gordonton
Rd. Garden after Taylor Rd on right.
Or 14.7km south from Taupiri, turn
left off SH 1 into Gordonton Rd.
Garden after Piako Rd on left
Phone: 0-7-824-3691
Fax: 0-7-824 3691
Open: All year, daily, 10am to dark
Groups: By appointment
Fee: $5 per adult
Size: Medium – 1ha (2½ acres)
Terrain: Flat and hilly
Shop: Gardening gifts
Accommodation: Homestay available

   mostly

   by arrangement

These unique botanical gardens and hot houses were established over the last decade by New Zealand gardening "guru" Eion Scarrow and his wife, Ann, as educational gardens. They demonstrate many facets of horticulture, including a rustic stone-edged water garden and many specialist gardens with different types of plantings. These include a conifer section with a rare weeping picea, a fuchsia glade, rhododendron garden, camellia collection and newly established rose garden, set amid meandering paths and lush lawns. Indoor display houses are a special feature. Known locally as "The Guru's Temple", an octagonal Mist House contains a 10-metre-high "Bromeliad Tree" with orchids and other aerial plants clinging to beams and ponga walls. Varieties of ferns, native orchids and cymbidiums thrive in the cool of the adjoining shade house. A 33-metre-long tropical house features a large cacti display and other succulents, hoyas, vireya rhododendrons and a vast array of exotic plants and tropical creepers. Cindy and Del, the present owners of Willow Glen, have added a teahouse overlooking the gardens, petanque courts, toilets and more parking areas. The extensive indoor displays, camellias, rhododendrons and the many perennial and annual plantings provide interest to visitors all year round. Homestay accommodation is available, by arrangement.

WOODLANDS
Gordonton

Owner:
Waikato District Council,
administered by Woodlands Trust

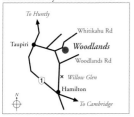

Address: Whitikahu Rd, Gordonton
Postal: P O Box 53, Gordonton
Directions: 9km north of Hamilton,
along Gordonton Rd, turn right into
Whitikahu Rd. Or travel south of
Taupiri from SH 1 into Gordonton Rd
on left, then turn second left into
Whitikahu Rd. Garden on right
Phone: 0-7-824 3687
Fax: 0-7-824 3986
Open: 10am–4pm, Sundays all year,
public holidays except Christmas Day,
other times by appointment
Groups: By appointment; ample
parking for buses
Fee: $4 per adult
Size: Large – 2ha (5 acres),
full reserve 6.5ha (16¼ acres)
Terrain: Flat with gully
Historic Home: Functions catered for

Woodlands is a Waikato District Council Historic Reserve, once part of a 98,000ha estate. In 1983 a 120ha block was gifted by Irene Riddell to the Presbyterian Support Services. They in turn gifted the 6.5ha Historic Reserve to the then Waikato County Council. The Woodlands Trust, formed in 1989 to manage the property, has restored the charming 1875 homestead and extensive garden using turn-of-the-century-style planting. The garden features wide vistas across expansive lawns, a cricket oval and a croquet green, which is framed by massive 120-year-old English ornamental trees, underplanted with this country's most significant collection of old camellias, shipped from England in 1876. Walkways wind through the woodland area beneath *Liriodendron tulipifera*, American ash, Chinese junipers, planes, elms, lindens, and other historically important trees including New Zealand's largest *Eucalyptus fastigata*. The pathways lead to the moat-like pond, with its Monet-style bridges and gazebo as focal point on the far side. The colour coordinated garden at Woodlands is vast, and development continues, a recent addition being the formal garden in front of the marquee. With all-weather paths and the feature camellias, this garden is worthy of winter visiting.

81

FLORA VALE
Morrinsville

Owners:
Doug and Irene Clarke

Address: Tainui Rd, Hoe-o-Tainui,
R D 3, Morrinsville
Directions: 25km from Morrinsville,
take Tahuna Rd to Hoe-o-Tainui. Turn
left into Tainui Rd. Travel 3km
Phone: 0-7-887 7859
Fax: 0-7-887 7859
Open: Spring to early summer best,
but open till autumn, by appointment
Groups: By appointment, as above
Fee: $3 per adult
Size: Medium – 0.8ha (2 acres)
Terrain: Mostly flat
Nursery: Occasionally from garden
Accommodation: Homestays
available; also small self-contained
house for 5 people, with meals
provided on request

   mostly

  by arrangement

Flora Vale is a dairy farm garden with a difference. An oriental flavour pervades this rural garden with its areas within areas. Trips to Japan have inspired the development of a new Japanese garden, with ponds spanned by an arched bridge, a bamboo gate and bamboo fencing. Japanese maples abound throughout the garden. Mature trees, planted three decades ago, create woodland settings for walks through underplantings of shade-loving species, including masses of purple and white honesty. A large selection of camellias begins flowering in autumn with sasanquas, continuing through winter and into spring. Ponds edged with damp-loving plants, such as hostas and primulas, feature a water wheel and fountain. The colourful driveway is bordered by drifts of forget-me-nots in spring, with aquilegias under cedrelas. Ivy, clematis and roses, such as the old Gallica "Anais Segales", are trained up established trees, and wisteria climbs a massive archway of banksia. A wide variety of perennials are planted in groups for impact, with large clumps of "Black Dragon" grass and Tasmanian grass with black ends. Beyond the house is a fernery underplanted with hostas, and a conifer area. These and the evergreen natives are a good balance for all the deciduous trees, including *Davidia involucrata*, Judas trees, idesia, elms and aesculus.

82

NAUMAI
Waitoa

Owners:
Pauline and Bruce Luxton

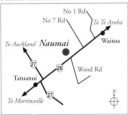

Address: SH 26, Waitoa
Postal: Main Rd, R D, Waitoa
Directions: On SH 26, 1.5km east of
intersection with SH 27. Garden on
left of highway, across disused
railway line
Phone: 0-7-887 1800
Open: By appointment
Groups: By appointment, as above
Fee: $4 per adult
Size: Medium – 0.8ha (2 acres)
Terrain: Flat
Nursery: Selection of perennials from
garden

 by arrangement

Naumai means "welcome", a fitting name for this spacious country garden around an old homestead. Pauline and Bruce are third-generation Luxtons, having developed the garden from 1980. A disused railway line borders this level garden with its grass tennis court, front herbaceous border of whites and pinks, pool enclosed with plantings and brick walls behind. *Cupressus sempervirens* "Swane's Golden" and other conifers grow by the pool area, with a white garden nearby appropriately featuring a white statue of "Pauline Bonaparte". Pauline has colour coordinated separate raised beds of white, pink, blue and yellow. But the focal point is a large bed of mixed perennials surrounding a sun-dial in a box-edged paved circle. Here pastels mix with white and silver in a sea of pattern, with foxgloves towering over mignonettes, aquilegias, nicotianas, penstemons, artemisias and old roses, with forget-me-nots and annuals scrambling round their feet. Hundreds of spring bulbs, daffodils and irises are joined by cherry blossom and azaleas. Following the rhododendrons are 200 roses, some climbing over archways and a ponga pergola. A dahlia bed complements the range of perennials and colourful annuals. Autumn foliage gives way to 50 camellias which brighten the winter months. A native corner is being established and a corner of *Proteaceae* supplies flowers for Pauline's floral work.

GARDEN OF JOY
Waharoa

Owners:
Joy and Ken Booker

Address: 106 Wardville Rd, R D,
Waharoa
Directions: Travel north from
Waharoa on SH 27. Turn right into
Wardville Rd, past asparagus growers
to second driveway on right. NZ
Dairy Co. number 7244, or Fire
Number 106
Phone: 0-7-888 8237
Open: September to May, daily,
by appointment
Groups: By appointment, as above
Fee: $3 per adult
Size: Small – 0.26ha (⅔ acre)
Terrain: Flat
Hot water: On request
Nursery: A few plants from garden

Garden of Joy has been a labour of love for Joy Booker since 1976, as she has gradually extended her garden into the surrounding paddocks. Large native and exotic trees provide a framework, with water gardens, cottage plants and over 120 mainly old roses predominating, which she chooses not to spray. She enjoys colour but is aware of form and texture too. Joy doesn't like mono-colour, using whites such as mignonettes and lychnis to separate different colours. She finds silver artemisias provide good contrasting foliage all year, as do variegated plants and conifers. She likes yellow to give the garden a lift, especially on wet days. Joy loves perennials such as soft, fluffy astilbes and thalictrum, with penstemons, Siberian irises and campanulas among her favourites. She is growing more wisterias, and a huge white one climbs over her ponga pergola. A gazebo is adorned with pink miniature roses including "Fairy", with an old plough languishing nearby. A stone bridge crosses a figure-eight-shaped waterlily pond teeming with goldfish. A huge pepper-tree provides dappled shade over another little pond planted with hostas. Clematis grows up through trees in a native corner, where a third pool has a waterfall splashing into it through a hollow log. This immaculate garden, with its attention to detail, won the local rural garden competition in 1993.

CAROLYN GARDENS
Matamata

Owners:
Joan and Ian Reed

Address: 24 Mangawhero Rd,
Matamata
Directions: From Broadway (the
main street of Matamata), continue
south-east towards Tauranga on
Mangawhero Rd. Garden on left
Phone: 0-7-888 8411
Open: All year, daily except Sunday
mornings, by appointment
Groups: By appointment, as above
Fee: $3 per adult
Size: Medium – 0.8ha (2 acres)
Terrain: Flat with slight contour

 pending

Carolyn Gardens were designed by Jane McGuffie in 1994 for the Reeds and has been landscaped and planted on the site of previous stables. Already this has been a winning garden in local competitions with its rose pergolas and brick patios and paths constructed from the old stables bricks. A broken concrete wall was made from the old floor of the stables and antique farm machinery in the garden reminds visitors of its origins. Moss-covered pergolas and post and rail fences separate the garden from the surrounding countryside while sweeping lawns set off the garden beds. Spring features include camellias, prunus and rhododendrons with spring bulbs, clematis and wisteria. Then the roses bloom with the perennials and an English lavender walk of "Seal" leading from the sun-dial in one of the brick patios. In autumn the foliage of the maples, dogwoods and other deciduous trees begins to colour, in contrast to the native evergreens. Joan has colour coordinated the garden with areas of pinks, blues, mauves and whites separated from areas of creams, salmons, golds and blues. A white, pink and blue garden features a "Bantry Bay" rose climbing above the window of a matching guest room.

85

TUI GRANGE
Matamata

Owner:
Anne McGregor

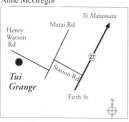

Address: Henry Watson Rd, Peria Hills, R D 2, Matamata
Directions: 8km from Matamata. Take Firth St, then turn right into Station Rd. At end of road, turn left into Matai Rd, then first right into Henry Watson Rd. Tui Grange third property on left
Phone: 0-7-888 5438 evenings
Open: Spring, summer and autumn to groups 10 and over only, by appointment
Groups: By appointment, as above
Fee: $4 per adult
Size: Medium – 0.6ha (1½ acres)
Terrain: Gentle slopes, different levels
Nursery: Perennials

Anne began planting Tui Grange in 1983, gradually transforming a barren, windswept clay hilltop into a lush green garden with tropical foliage and restful atmosphere. Anne loves large-leafed and perfumed species, integrating these in the various garden rooms. She blends colours with textured greens to create light and shade, enclosed areas and open spaces on different levels, with farm boulders, stone steps, ponga walls, pergolas and brick paving. In all her planting, Anne is careful not to obscure the expansive view to the Waikato countryside, using two hahas to merge the garden into the farmscape and bush reserve backdrop. Her favourite area is around the rock-edged pond with its stone fountain and plantings of water-loving species, shaded by an original eucalypt. Anne likes to soften hard lines, growing Virginia creeper over the verandah of her high-gabled cedarwood home. A manuka-thatched summer house and matching dovecote create a South Pacific feeling. A dressage arena features a bank of bright annuals and perennials. In the garden autumn is full of vibrant colour, and summer is kept cool with tropical greens and dichondra in the lawns for lushness. Birds, including white fantail pigeons, peacocks, and tui, frequent Tui Grange, which has won three gardening competitions, including the 1991 Yates/ *Sunday Star* "Great Garden Hunt".

FARNAHARPY
Cambridge

Owners:
Ray and Dorothy Higgins

Farnaharpy

Address: 613 Parallel Rd, R D 3, Cambridge
Directions: Take Cambridge-Te Awamutu Rd. Follow Parallel Rd signs for 4km from turn-off. Garden on left
Phone: 0-7-827 6810
Open: November, Sundays and Wednesdays, 10am–4pm; otherwise September to April, by appointment
Groups: By appointment, as above
Fee: $3 per adult
Size: Medium – 0.4ha (1 acre)
Terrain: Flat

When their house was built on a flat paddock in 1987, the Higgins began developing their garden around it. Trelliswork divides it into rooms and the nearby milking-shed provides an interesting view. Guinea fowl and fantail pigeons add interest. Spring bulbs accompany camellias, prunus blossom, magnolias, viburnums and *Cercis* "Forest Pansy", with new foliage on the robinias, maples and silver birches. A few rhododendrons such as "Trude Webster" and "Unique" can withstand the humid warm Waikato conditions. Then the irises appear, with daylilies and all the perennials in the herbaceous borders. Old roses clamber over Ray's structures, clematis climbs another archway and white wisteria cover the trellis fence that separates off the swimming pool area. Standard white wisteria make a special feature in the white island bed with clematis, mignonettes and a weeping silver pear. Dorothy carefully blends colours, using repeated combinations such as orange with "Blue Bedder" echiums. The pool area is planted to be enjoyed from inside the house or outside, with lilac *Hibiscus huegelii* in a sheltered spot and old roses such as "Albertine" and "Gerbe" surrounding the pool. A tall Norwegian maple, weeping *Sophora japonica* and *Magnolia stellata* provide shade.

SEVEN OAKS GARDENS
Hamilton

Owners:
Alice and Jack Commerer

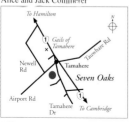

Address: Tamahere Drive, R D 3,
Hamilton
Directions: From Hamilton, take
SH 1 south to Airport off-ramp. Cross
under bridge and turn left at 2nd
roundabout into Tamahere Drive.
Garden on right. Or from Cambridge,
take SH 1 north to Tamahere exit.
Garden on left of Tamahere Drive
Phone: 0-7-856 8003
Open: All year, Monday to Saturday,
by appointment
Groups: As above
Fee: $2 per adult
Size: Medium – 0.4ha (1 acre)
Terrain: Flat
Hot water: Available
Nursery: Cranesbill geraniums,
aquilegias, biennial echiums
Shop: Ceramics for sale
Accommodation: Homestays by
arrangement

Originally seven oaks bordered the roadside of this property, with a sea of daffodils growing underneath, admired by passing motorists. In 1985 Alice incorporated this area into an English cottage garden to overcome a dust-bowl effect in summer. The remaining four huge oaks, over 110 years old, with a big acer, three weeping elms and a white horse chestnut by the gate, provide a canopy for cottage plants underneath. Alice loves self-seeding annuals, including candytuft, nigella and sheets of forget-me-nots that follow the daffodils. Euphorbias pick up the yellows and greens of the daffodils in spring, followed by old-fashioned aquilegias in eight shades from white to deep burgundy. These are complemented by purple honesty and pink clematis, Alice using mainly soft colours with splashes of brighter ones, such as red salvias under the trees and red-hot pokers. Tall blue echiums and named bearded irises feature in November. In summer, standard roses follow mollis azaleas down the driveway, with Livingstone daisies a mass of colour underneath. Climbing roses feature, a red rose and white hybrid clematis covering an archway. Hostas and lilies flourish with colourful impatiens and dahlias. In autumn, bromeliads thrive under beautiful deciduous foliage, with crocuses carpeting the ground. Orchids flower close to the house in winter when camellias bloom.

GAILS OF TAMAHERE
Hamilton

Owner:
Gail Jones

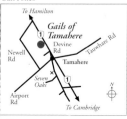

Address: Main Rd, R D 3, Hamilton
Directions: North of Devine Rd,
Tamahere, on SH 1, the main road to
Cambridge
Phone: 0-7-856 6609
Open: All year, daily, 10am–4pm
Groups: By appointment
Fee: No charge
Size: Medium – 1.5ha (3–4 acres)
Terrain: Flat
Nursery: Plants
Shop: Dried flowers, fungi, seed
pods, berries, dried arrangements,
pot-pourri, etc

  by arrangement

Gail is a professional florist, winner of many awards and teacher of design seminars. She uses two old wooden churches as ideal buildings for displaying her dried flower products. The oldest church was the first built in Coromandel in 1867, transported to Tamahere and restored by Gail. The gardens are planned and filled with flowers appropriate for use as fresh cut flowers and for dried flowers. Gail displays dried arrangements, posies, wall hangers, pot-pourri, essential oils, candles set in miniature roses, spice balls, dyed statice, stems of camella berries, pink sponges, budlah nuts, green fungi, red ting tingh, gypsophila, stems of delphiniums, mini roses, and bunches of statice hanging from the arched ceilings. Flower beds outside the churches are laid out attractively, with grass walkways throughout. A sea of English lavender and long beds of roses are broken with lupins, watsonias and agapanthus for height. An ivy-covered fence curves round masses of *Stachys lanata*, white lychnis, pyrethrum daisies and stoechas lavender, with a weeping red standard rose in a rock-edged bed. Yellow conifers contrast with green foliage, and silver birches border the lawn beside a large pool and fountain. Twenty-five metres was cut from Gail's garden for roadway, resulting in an entire revamping of her garden frontage. The changes include an Italian-style garden.

THE POPLARS AT MATANGI
Hamilton

Owners:
Peter and Lesley Ramsay

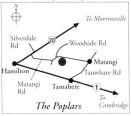

The Poplars

Address: 402 Matangi Rd, R D 4,
Matangi, Hamilton
Directions: From Hamilton, take
SH 26 towards Morrinsville. Turn
right into Matangi Rd. Travel 4.02km
to garden on right. From south, exit
SH 1 at roundabout. Turn right into
Tauwhare Rd, then left into Matangi
Rd. Garden about 2km on left.
Phone: 0-7-829 5551
Mobile: 025 856 793
E-mail: Ramsay@Waikato.ac.nz
Open: 1 September to 15 December,
daily, by appointment
Groups: By appointment, as above
Fee: $5 per adult
Size: Medium – 1.2ha (3 acres)
Terrain: Flat & easy walking in gully
Nursery: Range of plants for sale.
Orders taken for daffodil bulbs

   partial

by arrangement

This country garden has been developed over the past nine years by the Ramsays, although it was landscaped by the original owners 25 years ago, when the stand of huge Japanese poplars or cottonwoods lining the drive was planted. Peter has incorporated a commercial exhibition nursery of named daffodils into the property and thousands of daffodils have naturalised under the trees. Over 80 varieties of camellias emerge in September and blossom trees are joined by over 80 different rhododendrons in October. More than 600 roses of all types are the mainstay in summer, adding to the colour of spring and summer annuals and perennials. A formal sunken garden is symmetrically planted in pinks, purples and white with windows in the trellis looking down to the garden below. Paths through the gully area, a boardwalk and bridge lead across the stream to the large lake where further daffodils cover the banks in spring. Peter is planning a waterfall and developing a bog garden with plants such as primulas, hostas, ligularia, lobelias, gunnera and irises. Weeping blossom trees will form a walkway to the woodland area, where a conifer collection is interplanted with natives and exotics. Many of the daffodil bulbs for sale are exclusive to The Poplars.

TAITUA ARBORETUM
Hamilton

John Mortimer

Owners:
John and Bunny Mortimer

To Ngaruawahia

To SH 1 and Auckland

N

Newcastle Rd

Whatawhata
23

To Raglan

To Hamilton

Taitua Rd

To Otorohanga

Taitua Arboretum

Address: Taitua Rd, R D 9, Hamilton
Directions: Take SH 23 west of
Hamilton. Travel 4km from Dinsdale
to Howden Rd on left. Taitua Rd
veers left. Garden on left
Phone: 0-7-847 5847
Open: By appointment outside the
spring and autumn times advertised in
the *Waikato Times*
Groups: As above
Fee: $5 per adult
Size: Large – 20ha (50 acres)
Terrain: Hilly in places
Nursery: Occasionally
Farm walk: An additional optional
one hour "Tall Trees" farm walk is
available

    limited

Taitua Arboretum focuses on trees and foliage, with over 1,000 different exotic and native species planted since 1970, some with magnificent autumn colour. Paths lead from the informal house garden, through a China-inspired moon gate overhung with Chinese quinces and persimmons, down through the Rainbow Garden to tree collections and specimens, some very rare. Alders, pines, dogwoods, oaks, Australian and North American sections feature, with spring bulbs under magnolias. Over 250 different Chinese species include mulberries and the rare *Glyptostrobus*. A Grecian-style folly in an amphitheatre is accompanied by Mediterranean plantings. New Zealand native coprosma and kowhai line a pathway past a grassed stone circle (no druids!). Three of the five ponds, all bird sanctuaries, contain islands for nesting sites, one edged with "knees" of swamp cypress. Swan Lake is home to mute swans, Canada geese and ducks, with cabbage trees and other hardy natives as shelter. Boardwalks lead over swampy areas and a rustic seat is strategically placed looking down an avenue of elegant "Tasman" poplars. Paths lead through a circle of redwoods, with a slope of maples behind. Arthropodium-edged pathways wind through a woodland garden to a door into a fernery. Through another native area, the one-hour walk ends with a stunning view from the Jacaranda Lawn.

THE BIRCHES
Te Kuiti

Owners:
Don and Marie Lewis

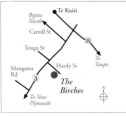

Address: 9 Hardy St, Te Kuiti
Directions: Just south of Te Kuiti off
SH 3, turn into Hardy St. Garden on
right
Phone: 0-7-878 6314
Fax: 0-7-878 6314
Open: All year, daily, early till late
Groups: By appointment;
parking available for coaches
Fee: $3 per adult
Size: Medium – 0.4ha (1 acre)
Terrain: Mostly flat, easy walking
Nursery: Over 200 named fuchsias,
perennials

     by arrangement

The Birches is best known for the fuchsias Don propagates, with around 30 new varieties annually. "Fascination" was his first, his collection now including the popular "Black Prince", "Nancy Lou", "Annabel", "Beacon Rosa", "Seventh Heaven", "Sundial", "White King", "Eusebia" and "Snow Fire". Don built a shade house for his fuchsias, with ponga pergola extension covered in deep red "Dublin Bay" roses. Marie loves the roses, featuring many interesting ones, such as "Hot Chocolate". A sheep paddock in 1983, The Birches was gradually planted, with complementary landscaping creating diverse aspects to provide seasonal colour. Spring bulbs are accompanied by camellias, cherry blossom, azaleas and viburnums. Then the roses and fuchsias bloom, with summer perennials and annuals. In front of the fuchsia shade house is a rocky watercourse trickling into a series of waterlily ponds, with hostas and purple campanula softening the edges. Marigolds and yellow alyssum are bedded round the house, with pots of petunias hanging from the verandah. Autumn colours up the maples, ginkgo and silver birches after which the garden is named. Winter is the time for conifers, and brings early camellias into flower with various bulbs. Natives also feature, with a small bush walk through beeches, rata, rimu, lancewoods, ponga, and kowhai with their beautiful spring blossom.

ARAMATAI
Te Kuiti

Owners:
Trish and Stew Donaldson

Address: Mapara North Rd, Te Kuiti
Postal: P O Box 13, Te Kuiti
Directions: 55km north of
Taumarunui, or 26km south of Te
Kuiti, turn off SH 4 into Mapara
North Rd. Aramatai up private drive
on right, over cattle-stop
Phone: 0-7-878 8071
Mobile: 025 954 289
Fax: 0-7-878 8071
Open: All year, by appointment
Groups: As above
Fee: $3 per adult
Size: Medium – 1ha (2½ acres)
Terrain: Hilly
Nursery: Perennials, shrubs,
seedlings, trees
Shop: Dried flowers

  mostly

  by arrangement

Aramatai (meaning "Matai Path") is the name of the valley, represented by a lovely big matai stump the Donaldsons have in their garden, encircled by a pathway. They began planting in 1992, attracted by the lie of the land, the availability of rhyolite rocks and a magnificent weeping willow over two natural ponds, now connected by a cascading waterfall. Waterlilies add colour to the ponds, edged with irises. Hostas are massed nearby under the willows with yellow and red primulas. A bridge leads to a huge hillside rockery which is the prominent feature of the garden. Rocks gradually moved into place from around the farm are now surrounded with rock plants and groundcovers. Trish loves old-fashioned climbing roses rambling over ponga pergolas and through trees, such as "New Dawn", "Cornelia" and "Cecile Brunner". Summer perennials accompanying the roses include campanulas, evening primroses, rudbeckias, lobelias, arctotis, salvias, penstemons, delphiniums, lavateras and cleomes. Trish is also fond of lilies, especially *Cardiocrinum giganteum* and Easter lilies. Rhododendrons, camellias, spring bulbs and magnolias complement these, with annuals following. Other features include Trish's herb garden, her wildflower area, and a predominantly hazelnut orchard. Stew has planted conifers and young exotics, particularly weeping varieties, among abundant natives.

93

TAPUWAE
Te Kuiti

Owners:
Doff and Howard Tombleson

Address: Tapuwae Rd, R D 7, Te Kuiti
Directions: North of Taumarunui,
travel through Ongarue and Waimiha.
Turn right into Tapuwae Rd & follow
for 5km. Or south from Te Kuiti, take
SH 30 towards Benneydale, travel
through Kopaki and Mangapehi. Take
first right towards Waimiha, then first
left into Tapuwae Rd. Travel 5km to
garden at end of road
Phone: 0-7-878 4837
Open: September to winter, any time
Groups: Groups by appointment
Fee: $5 per adult
Size: Large – 3.2ha (8 acres)
Terrain: Undulating
Hot water: Available

  by arrangement

Tapuwae, meaning "sacred footstep", is sited at more than 500 metres above sea level, as its name suggests. Thirty years ago it was just a small house garden. Trees were planted from 1968 and the garden extended since 1982, to ramble over three hectares now. The high altitude means spring bulbs bloom late, with blossom trees and azaleas providing colour against the new maple foliage. Clematis climbs through trees and rhododendrons display their varied hues. In summer, innumerable perennials flower, with bog plants around large ponds and streams. Sited in pockets created by the undulating landscape, each area has its own special appeal. Everywhere rural views of the surrounding countryside rest the eye, especially in the colourful rhododendron season. The trees are now well established, and natives are interplanted with conifers, magnolias, dogwoods, cercis and camellias. These are underplanted with drifts of forget-me-nots, scillas and ajuga groundcover, and in bog areas with hostas, gunneras, ligularias, rheums and primulas. Old logs and rocks, collected from all over the farm, edge paths and form rustic seats. In the Long Acre, a separate garden to one side of the driveway, cherries and rhododendrons flower on the slope below a huge ancient log, from a tree felled in 1929. Ducks and peacocks are a special feature at Tapuwae.

McKENZIES' GARDEN
Taumarunui

Owners:
Jean and Max McKenzie

Address: SH 4, Taumarunui
Postal: P O Box 88, Taumarunui
Directions: On SH 4, 3km north of Taumarunui. Garden on left
Phone: 0-7-895 7475
Fax: 0-7-895 5166
Open: End September to mid December, and February to March; by appointment
Groups: Turning space for buses, plenty of parking space beyond house
Fee: $4 per adult
Size: Medium – 0.8ha (2 acres)
Terrain: Sloping front section, with plateau above

to top garden only

From the main highway just north of Taumarunui the more recent addition to this garden can be seen – colourful terraces behind a huge retaining wall, with cherries, cannas and *Hemerocallis* (or daylilies) planted right along the fenceline. Up behind is a rhododendron dell, established since 1966 and underplanted with woodland perennials including trilliums, hostas and drifts of purple honesty. This dell looks like fairyland when the rhododendron petals drop and cherry blossoms fall like giant snowflakes carpeting the slopes in colour. Spring also ushers in camellias and magnolias, with standard wisteria and clematis like lace curtains. Peonies thrive on the plateau, as do the delphiniums and bush roses behind the perennial beds. "Fairy" roses cascade from standards of varying heights. Jean's love for roses can be seen in large beds of hybrid teas especially established for her floral work. She similarly grows flowering shrubs such as azaleas for this purpose. Max has built a gazebo for Jean's climbing hybrid clematis. The back garden includes a fun feature of vertical drainage pipes and urns. Rockery plants, their colours interweaving like a tapestry, feature in a sunken rockery, with ericas mirroring the lichen-covered rock shapes. Jean blends her colours as they change with the seasons, always with the King Country hills as a backdrop to the garden.

WICKY'S GARDEN
Matiere

Owner:
Bob Wickham

Address: Mangapapa Rd, Otangiwai,
R D, Matiere, King Country
Postal: P O Box 14 062, Hamilton
Directions: 56km south of Te Kuiti or
30km west of Taumarunui. Turn south
into Mangapapa-Otangiwai Rd and
travel 7km to garden on right
Phone: 0-7-893 7890
Open: August to May; 10am–5pm
Groups: As above
Fee: $5 per adult
Size: Large – nearly 40ha (almost 100
acres) woodland; plus 1ha (2½ acres)
house & rose garden
Terrain: Flat around house, plus hilly
woodland

   partly

  by arrangement

A hillside of white "Everest" rhododendrons welcomes the visitor to Wicky's Garden. Bob began his garden as a colour concept, transforming whole hillsides into single colour masses of rhododendrons. Over a decade later, Wicky's colour theme is developing into a woodland garden, with truckloads of trees introduced, then under-planted to continue the colour throughout the year. Bob is introducing more red which contrasts well against the greenery. An extensive collection of flowering cherries, magnolias and cornuses begin the display from mid August, extending to mid November with the massed rhododendrons and azaleas. The Blue Garden features four levels of blue flowers, from the paulownias above, to the ceanothus, rhododendrons, then bluebells beneath. The roses in the house garden take over in summer, the woodland blooms and water features come into their own. Waterlilies adorn the many stream-fed lakes which are home to Bob's duck families. The deciduous trees, especially the maples, provide a mass of autumn colour, contrasting with the natives. The late Sydney Harpley's sculpture is a special feature in the garden. Gumboots are recommended, as the grass is long in many places while the trees grow up. Although Wicky's Garden is large, pathways are formed for wandering and picnicking. Arrangements can be made to drive elderly people around.

CROWHILL
Manunui

Owners:
Marion and Donald Tidswell

Address: 87 Miro St, Manunui
Directions: 5km south of
Taumarunui, turn left after crossing
Whanganui River into Miro St.
Garden on right
Phone: 0-7-896 8688
Open: October to December, daily,
by appointment
Groups: By appointment, as above
Fee: $3 per adult
Size: Medium – 0.4ha (1 acre)
Terrain: Flat

This semi-formal garden is immaculately kept the year round, a far cry from the land surrounding the 1918 house taken over in 1965. A quarter acre added in 1987 increased the garden area to one acre (0.4 hectares). Some original native trees have been retained, with others planted, as well as interestingly coloured native grasses within the shaped garden beds separated by neat lawns. The grasses are mixed with a wide variety of annuals and over 200 perennials, including a variety of irises. Spring bulbs, tulips and camellias are followed by 250 azalea Mollis and over 180 rhododendrons, both species and hybrids. Then the roses, mainly hybrid teas with a few old-fashioned and climbing, bloom under specimen trees along with summer annuals including nemesia, lobelia, marigold, petunia, alyssum, pansy and viola. Autumn brings colour to deciduous foliage such as ginkgo, liquidambar, beech, prunus and maples. The shapes of these exotics stand out during winter against the conifers in their various green forms, before the spring blossom of magnolias and cherries are complemented by the new growth of soft maples, other trees and shrubs. An old stone wall borders the roadside, enclosing the colourful front garden which is matched by the multitude of summer colours in the back garden beds at Crowhill.

POVERTY BAY AND HAWKE'S BAY

The 22 gardens featured from these two bays extend south from the Bay of Plenty, enjoying the same warm sunshine and temperate climate. The Poverty Bay gardens are situated from Matawai in the gorge south of Opotiki to Whangara on the east cape, north of Gisborne and Muriwai, 32 kilometres south of Gisborne. Being located on the east coast, Gisborne has a low rainfall, and as the sunniest region in the North Island, its beaches are popular. These sunny conditions, along with the fertile alluvial plains, have resulted in Gisborne being well known for its orchards and vineyards.

Burnage, a high-altitude garden at Matawai was planted Buxton-style, now with established English trees and ponds. Just north of Gisborne at Ormond is Braeburn, also an historic garden, with unusual exotic trees. Rosehaven is an urban garden with formal rose beds and water gardens. On the east coast north of Gisborne are three Whangara gardens: Glenroy is a garden of contrasts, from an exposed dry top area to a sheltered moist dell, Wensleydale features roses, and Panikau is one of the best extant examples of an Alfred Buxton garden in New Zealand. South of Gisborne are Karalus Gardens, featuring roses and perennials, while the two most westerly gardens, Eastwoodhill and Hackfalls, are both extensive arboretums.

Gisborne City itself has Botanical Gardens to visit on the banks of the Taruheru River. North of Whangara the road winds up round the picturesque East Cape, lined with pohutukawa, past Te Araroa, the first point of land in the world to greet the touch of dawn each day. To the north-west of Hackfalls Arboretum lies the beautiful Lake Waikaremoana at an altitude of nearly 600 metres, set in the midst of Te Urewera National Park. Walking tracks through lush native forest abound. This lake is 65km north-west of Wairoa, which features an historic cabbage tree, and can also be reached from Hillcrest, a country garden off the Waikaremoana Road, with mature trees, and garden furniture for sale. Another garden south of Gisborne is Wairakaia at Muriwai, originally planted almost a century ago.

Hawke's Bay is adjacent to the Poverty Bay area, sharing a similar climate with warm, mild weather. The Hawke's Bay gardens extend from the northern reaches, just below Poverty Bay, to Waipukurau in the south. The four northerly coastal gardens are: Bremdale at Nuhaka, set amid orchards and featuring roses for much of the year, two Mahia Perennial gardens on the Mahia Peninsula with perennial nurseries, and Opoho Coastal Garden just 22 kilometres north of Wairoa, established on sandhills with mature trees dating back to 1921. Two gardens in the Napier area are both worth a drive inland. Trelinnoe is planted as a park, featuring rhododendrons and trees, while Braehead focuses on roses and alpines. Wahi Pai is a garden situated along the Taihape Road from Hastings with roses and trees. The Ormonds' garden at Havelock North is a dry no-water garden, but features neither cacti nor many succulents. At Waipukurau are the two most southerly Hawke's Bay gardens, both with roses: Rototahi, an artist's garden and Misty Flats, a cottage garden.

Hawke's Bay is well known for its orchards, wineries and sunny, dry climate. Summers are hot and dry, winters are dry and crisp. Napier, the Art Deco city rebuilt after the disastrous 1931 earthquake, is well endowed with public gardens, including the Botanical Gardens up on Hospital Hill, the Sunken Garden on Marine Parade, and, at the northern end, the quarry garden with waterfall. Hastings features a springtime Blossom Festival each September, Frimley Park with rose gardens and Cornwall Park with its gardens. Havelock North's attractions include Keirunga Gardens.

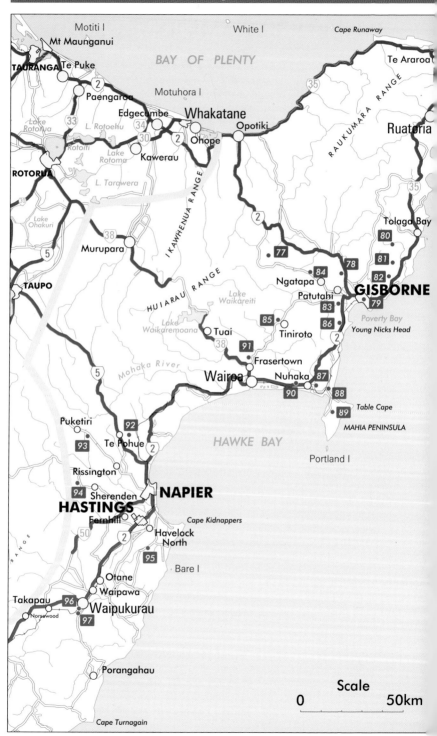

BURNAGE
Matawai

Owners:
Stella and Pete Seymour

Address: Rakauroa Rd, R D, Matawai
Directions: 1 hr from Gisborne. Take
SH 2 towards Opotiki. Travel 68km,
then turn left into Rakauroa Rd.
Continue 12km to garden on left.
From Opotiki, travel 1 hr to Matawai.
Continue 8km, then turn right into
Rakauroa Rd. Garden 12km on left
Phone: 0-6-862 4547
Open: Mid October to end of April,
daily, by appointment
Groups: By appointment, as above
Fee: $3 per adult
Size: Medium – 1ha (2½ acres)
Terrain: Rolling
Nursery: Plants from garden, eg
perennials, cuttings of rhododendrons
& bulbs; seeds for sale

by arrangement

Burnage was first planted in Buxton style by the Tomblesons in 1949. Stella has developed it in the past two years, adding to the bright vivid colourings. Established English trees are a hallmark, with limes, lindens and sycamores as well as huge rhododendrons. The high altitude and acid soil are ideal for azaleas and rhododendrons, a dell of them being Stella's favourite part of the garden, especially in evening. It is the only area where gums will grow and beneath them, around the bird-bath, Stella has planted a circle of the irises she loves. Snowy winters delay the seasons, camellias being joined by early bulbs in spring, followed by magnolia blossom and the rhododendrons. Peonies thrive in the cooler climate and roses predominate. Stella is adding David Austin varieties to the existing hybrid teas. Japanese *Iris kaempferi* are at their best in January and roses continue into April. Perennials lining the driveway are colourful in summer, with Iceland poppies, candytufts and aquilegias. Stella is gradually uncovering the Buxton-style ponds, putting in water features and planting spring bulbs. Near the ponds is a native area where ten pairs of nesting wood pigeons live. The sun-dial is another special feature.

101

BRAEBURN
Ormond

Owners:
Peter and Kay Tomlinson

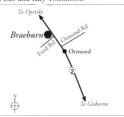

Address: SH 2, Ormond, R D 1, Gisborne
Directions: North of Gisborne, take Back Ormond Rd from city. At SH 2 turn right. Travel about 1km to garden on left
Phone: 0-6-862 5555
Fax: 0-6-867 0483
Open: 1 February to 19 December, 9am–5pm, by appointment
Groups: By appointment, as above – large buses to park on road
Fee: $3 per adult
Size: Medium – 0.6ha (1½ acres)
Terrain: Flat
Nursery: many plants eg begonias, daisies, fuchsias, chrysanthemums, geraniums and tree seedlings

  by arrangement

Planted over 50 years ago by Len Grey, the original avocado grower in New Zealand, Braeburn features a variety of well-established unusual exotic trees. These include the Brazilian grape tree or *Jaboticaba,* grey ears or *Greyia sutherlandii* and the orange flowering *Greyia rodkoferii,* purple flowering *Wigandia caracasana,* weeping conifer *Kashmiriana,* Illawara flame tree and Australian firewheel tree. In addition the weeping maple beside the pond is said to have the widest spread of any in New Zealand. Many other mature exotics in this woodland garden include oaks, claret ashes, crepe myrtles, ginkgoes and chestnuts which provide intense autumn colourings in contrast to the evergreen natives. The driveway is well planted with trees and roses, the trees attracting native pigeons and tui. The first rose to bloom is "Souvenir de Leonie" over an archway in spring, when a great variety of bulbs appear. Roses of all descriptions continue through the summer when a large collection of perennials adds to the colour. Roses climb the trees and cascade everywhere, including the single white "Cherokee", "Alberic Barbier", "Dr Van Fleet", "Pinkie", and "Wedding Day". Winter features an equally impressive array of camellias. Kay's favourites are the roses, delphiniums and hostas.

ROSEHAVEN
Gisborne

Owners:
Sheryl and Roger Turnball

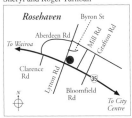

Address: 116 Lytton Rd, Gisborne
Directions: From city centre, take
SH 36 towards Wairoa. Turn right
into Lytton Rd. Garden on right
Phone: 0-6-867 5625 evenings
Open: During the rose season; by
appointment
Groups: By appointment, as above
Fee: $3 per adult
Size: Small – 0.2ha (½ acre)
Terrain: Flat lawns with raised
gardens

 by arrangement

As its name suggests, Rosehaven is predominantly a rose garden, old roses being Sheryl's favourites. She has designed the garden formally with raised beds to add elevation to the flat site. Archways provide structure to rose walkways which divide the garden. A golden banksia tumbles over the arched entrance way with "Bantry Bay" roses. Her favourite standard rose is the weeping "Rosy Cushion". Early roses are accompanied by prunus and malus blossom. Chinese toon trees or *Cedrela sinensis* and rose-pink *Echium wildpretii* also tone in with the pink, purple and white colour scheme. And in summer the hybrid clematises in the waterfall area add to the colour. A pond is the focal point of the waterfall garden which is beautifully lit at night by leadlighting in archways. The pond is over a metre deep and features goldfish, tropical waterlilies and water irises, with a weeping prunus "Falling Snow" beside it. A prunus "Pink Perfection" shades another pond in the front garden and a *Prunus* "Shimidsu sakura" blossoms beside the dovecote. Other trees include a *Robinia frisia*, *Magnolia campbellii*, silver birch grove, Japanese umbrella tree, "Eddie's White Wonder" dogwood, rare maple "Esk Sunset" and silk tree or albizia encircled with begonias.

PANIKAU
Whangara

Owners:
Peter, Norma and Michael Murphy

Address: Panikau Rd, Whangara,
R D 3, Gisborne
Directions: North of Gisborne, take
SH 35 towards Tolaga Bay. After
31km turn left into Panikau Rd.
Continue following signs to garden
Phone: 0-6-862 2683
Open: All year, by appointment
Groups: By appointment, as above
Fee: Donation
Size: Large – 2ha (5 acres), plus
bushwalk
Terrain: Varying levels and steps
Nursery: Plants for sale as available

   by arrangement

Panikau is one of the best extant examples of an Alfred Buxton garden in the country. Buxton's plans were executed in 1919 to 1920 by Edgar Taylor, the first landscape architect to qualify in New Zealand. Many of the original features visible today include the winding tree-lined driveway that hides the view of the house and garden until the last minute, the stone walls and pergola, and the mature tree specimens – both native and exotic. A weeping elm frames the house which replaces the original, burnt down in 1981. Sweeping lawns provide the perfect setting for the trees, shrubs, flowers and stone structures. When he was four years old, Peter laid the foundation stone for the impressive pergola that surrounded three sides of the formal rose garden, now replaced by a swimming pool. A rock garden forms the fourth side, with stone steps leading up to the focal point of the wisteria and wonga-wonga draped pergola, backed by a shelter-belt of mature trees. A hemispherical sun-dial is a typical Buxton feature of the rockery. The Murphys have extended the lawns, planted more roses and bordered the curving pathways with more low box hedging. A native bush walk has also been incorporated into the garden, which provides year-round interest, with panoramic rural views.

WENSLEYDALE
Whangara

Owners:
Nick and Pat Seymour

Address: Waiomoko Rd, R D 3,
Whangara, Gisborne
Directions: 38km from Gisborne, via
SH 35, towards Tolaga Bay. After
28km, at Whangara turn left into
Waiomoko Rd. Travel 10km over 6
cattle stops to garden on left
Phone: 0-6-862 2697
Mobile: 025 725 997
Fax: 0-6-862 2703
Open: October to January, daily,
by appointment
Groups: By appointment, as above;
bus tours a specialty
Fee: $3 per adult, includes tea/coffee
Size: Medium – almost 1ha (2 acres)
Terrain: Flat lawns and sloping
planted banks
Nursery: Plants available seasonally,
g violets, hostas, fuchsias, selected
perennials

  by arrangement

Wensleydale is named after the Yorkshire dales, the original home of the first settlers. The garden has been developed in stages from a bare site since 1966. Early plantings included prunus, silver birch, liquidambar and Japanese umbrella pine (*Sciadopitys verticillata*). The shrubbery and rose gardens are planted in colour waves, a white and pink bed set in paving stones with delphiniums, catmint, statice, and love-in-a-mist complementing pink roses, white daisies and alyssum. Another bed features deep blue lobelia with matching pansies under mixed roses. A row of gold roses edges the lawn and driveway, underplanted with yellow pansies and white daisies. Behind the house is a "Iolanthe" magnolia, with white and pink roses and white daisies. The garden bordering the roadside is pink, white and blue, with a sweeping lawn edged with deep pink lavatera, dark blue delphiniums, white daisies and creamy sisyrinchiums. The lower driveway is lined with hostas, hydrangeas, pink and white watsonias, honesty, and pale blue agapanthus. A waterfall trickles into a lily pond. Spring bulbs accompany camellias, azalea mollis, an extensive hosta collection and prunus and malus blossom. Summer features Pat's orchids, old and modern roses, with large collections of perennials and heat-loving annuals such as petunias and zinnias. The Whangara gardens make a pleasant day trip.

GLENROY
Whangara

Owners:
Jenny and Pip Barker

Address: Glenroy Rd, R D 3, Gisborne
Directions: North of Gisborne, on
road to Tolaga Bay. Turn left before
Whangara to Glenroy. Travel 5km up
Glenroy Rd. Garden on right
Phone: 0-6-862 2636
Fax: 0-6-862 2036
Open: All year, by appointment
Peak times are in spring and autumn
Groups: By appointment – large
buses to enquire re parking
Fee: $3 per adult refundable on
purchase from craft shop
Size: Medium – nearly 1ha (2⅓ acres)
Terrain: Quite steep in parts
Nursery: A few perennials
Shop: Craft shop selling Pip's wood
turning; old English crafts and tools;
gardening things; moon calendars

    to flat areas

    by arrangement

Situated atop a hill, reached by a breathtaking driveway, Glenroy is a garden of contrasts, from the exposed hilltop where proteas and leucadendrons thrive, down to the sheltered dell where bog plants flourish beside a waterlily pond. In 1985 it was just a bare hillside with two poplars growing. South African and Australian plants were all that survived until shelter was established by planting banksias as windbreaks. Then the whole fence was close-battened, which enabled roses to be established. The short slab fences have now disappeared into the undergrowth as a micro-climate has developed, allowing other plants, including rhododendrons, to grow. Jenny loves vireyas, which she grows in a shade house with *Primula obconica*, and hanging baskets galore. Pip has built a chalet-style barn with a well nearby, where Jenny groups her yellows, oranges and apricot colours, nasturtiums contrasting with blue echiums, love-in-a-mist and lavender. Jenny finds that blues are great for lifting yellows. She keeps her flower garden 40 per cent white, with pinks and blues accented by stronger colours. Several *Clematis montana* climb through trees in spring and large hybrid clematis cling to fences. Massed daisies and roses abound, especially old varieties and Austin roses, which grow over Pip's arches and gazebo. Grevilleas feature in the frost-free winter.

KARALUS GARDENS
Manutuke

Owners:
Liz and Mark Karalus

Address: Papatu Rd, Manutuke
Postal: P O Box 94, Manutuke
Directions: South of Gisborne on SH 2
to roundabout, turn left and continue
on SH 2. Take first right into Papatu
Rd, before Te Arai River Bridge.
Garden on left
Phone: 0-6-862 8745
Fax: 0-6-862 8745
Open: Labour Weekend (end of
October) to end of November, Friday
to Sunday, 9am–5pm; other times by
appointment
Groups: By appointment
Fee: $3 per adult
Size: Small – 0.3ha (¼ acre), but
growing
Terrain: Flat to undulating
Nursery: Plants from garden
Shop: Local garden crafts for sale

Karalus Gardens began in the winter of 1988, and are slowly but surely taking over the entire property of 3.5 hectares, as Liz and Mark add new features each year. The central garden is a sunken sun-dial rockery, an ingenious solution to disguise the derelict stone foundations of a previous house. This sun-dial garden sets the theme for all the planting, with a predominance of white, complemented by pinks, mauves, blues and soft yellows with accents of red or deeper blues. Formal elements are incorporated with a clipped dwarf lavender hedge around the sun-dial, standard "Iceberg" roses and *Robinia* "Mop Tops", their shapes repeated by standardised *Lavandula dentata*. Drifts of catmint lead up over the rock walls to the rose pergola, roses being Liz's favourites, especially David Austins and older English roses. She loves the pale pink "Heritage" beside their home, opposite the turning circle in the driveway which features a box-edged rose bed with a lavender-bordered walkway through the centre. A grey garden is a special feature, with a silver birch copse underplanted with masses of soft *Stachys lanata* supplemented by white forget-me-nots, snow-in-summer, erigeron and anthemis daisies. The driveway is lined with perennial borders. Liz and Mark are particularly partial to cottage plants, including herbs, which are established in a separate herb garden.

EASTWOODHILL ARBORETUM
Ngatapa

Owner:
Eastwoodhill Trust Board

Address: Ngatapa, R D 2, Gisborne
Postal: P O Box 865, Gisborne
Directions: 35km from Gisborne.
Travel south to Waipaoa River
roundabout, take Wharekopae Rd to
Ngatapa. Follow signposts
Phone: 0-6-863 9800
Fax: 0-6-863 9081
Open: Daily except Christmas Day
and Good Friday, 9am–4pm
Groups: Guided tours by arrangement
Fee: $5 per adult
Size: Large – 65ha (162½ acres)
Terrain: Varied
Disabled access: Trailer seating 6
disabled persons, by arrangement
Shop: Guide maps and self-guided
tour books for colour-coded walks

  & wheelchair
available

  conferences only

The land for Eastwoodhill was acquired in 1910 by William Douglas Cook, who collected plant material worldwide to create a beautiful park inspired by English gardens. Today, it probably possesses the largest collection of Northern Hemisphere trees in the Southern Hemisphere. Eastwoodhill was gifted to New Zealand in 1975, its Trust Board aiming to develop the Arboretum for educational, scientific and recreational purposes. Ten years later the Friends of Eastwoodhill was formed. The Douglas Cook Centre was opened in 1992 as a venue for seminars. In spring, one hectare of daffodils bloom under the trees, with magnolias and horse chestnuts in flower. Exotic trees are dressed in spring foliage, including the lime needles of swamp cypress. Prunus and malus blossom are complemented with dogwoods, wisteria, then azaleas and rhododendrons. Almost a hectare of a more formal garden around the homestead features bulbs, perennial beds and a spring bog garden. But the most dramatic time to visit Eastwoodhill is in autumn, when over 100 oaks, nearly as many maples, liquidambars, ash, ginkgo, and other deciduous trees are in their full glory, contrasting with conifers and almost 300 camellias. Altogether over 3,000 introduced species are represented, and an indigenous section has been recently established. There are colour-coded walks throughout, with guide-books available.

HACKFALLS ARBORETUM
Tiniroto

Owners:
Bob and Anne Berry

Address: Berry Rd, Tiniroto
Postal: P O Box 3, Tiniroto
Directions: Travel 61km south of
Gisborne or 44km north of Wairoa, to
Tiniroto. Then turn off SH 36 into
Ruakaka Rd. Turn left into Berry Rd
Phone: 0-6-863 7091
Fax: 0-6-863 7083
Open: All year
Groups: By appointment
Fee: $5 per adult
Size: Large – 24ha (60 acres)
arboretum, plus 0.4ha (1 acre)
homestead garden
Terrain: Hilly
Transport: 4-wheel-drive station
wagon to view arboretum – extra cost
Lunches: 4km away at Tiniroto Tavern
Nursery: Trees, shrubs and perennials

   to house garden

by arrangement

Hackfalls Station is named after a Yorkshire property with similar features. Bob has lived at Hackfalls since 1924, and from the early fifties has planted about 50 hectares in a unique arboretum, now a charitable trust, which with four hectares of native bush is covenanted to the QE II National Trust for Open Spaces. He has made several trips to Mexico to gather acorns, and Hackfalls has probably the biggest collection of Mexican oaks in cultivation anywhere. Many other oak specimens also feature; in all 150 different kinds spaced in rolling pastureland, allowing each to develop fully, and limbed up to enable grass to grow underneath. The oaks are complemented by over 2,000 kinds of other trees and shrubs. Two large lakes enhance the area, Kaikiore, a five-hectare wild life sanctuary and Karangata, of 10 hectares. Anne has developed the homestead garden since 1990, including roses, climbers and many unusual alpine and herbaceous plants. She has a good knowledge of plants, evidenced by Rosemoor Garden in England, which she gifted to the Royal Horticultural Society in 1988. Hackfalls garden also features a special area for endangered New Zealand native plants, including *Muehlenbeckia astonii*, hebe species and cultivars.

WAIRAKAIA
Muriwai

Owners:
Sarah and Rodney Faulkner

Address: SH 2, Muriwai, Gisborne
Postal: Wairakaia Station, Private
Bag, Gisborne
Directions: Take SH 2 north of
Wairoa for 68km. Pass under railway
overhead bridge, cross stream &
continue 0.5km to garden on left.
From Gisborne, travel south on SH 2
for 32km to garden on right
Phone: 0-6-862 8607
Open: All year, by appointment
Groups: By appointment, as above
Fee: $3 per adult
Size: Large – 2ha (5 acres)
Terrain: Hilly
Nursery: Perennials from garden
Accommodation: Homestay available
for up to 5 people

  by arrangement

It has been 91 years since the woodland country garden at Wairakaia was begun. Sarah and Rodney, third-generation Faulkners living on the farm, have developed the garden over the past eight years. Many of the exotic trees were planted by Rodney's grandfather, including two prolific avocadoes, a pear and those lining the driveway underplanted with daffodils. Trees form a green tapestry of shape, form and texture, with camellias, magnolias and michelias adding colour in spring, followed by malus and prunus with white wisteria in October. Another spring feature is a valley of arum lilies. Then Sarah's old roses display their beauty in summer and a bed of 50 white "Margaret Merril" and "Iceberg" roses supply many a wedding. The trees and shrubs create a restful oasis over the hot dry summer months, with annuals providing splashes of colour. Autumn colours the deciduous foliage, then the *Camellia sasanqua* begin flowering in May and the first snowdrops and jonquils open at the end of June. Stone walls were begun by Rodney's parents and a summer house built for his grandmother is the focal point of the lower garden. Two goldfish ponds are crossed by rustic bridges.

BREMDALE COASTAL GARDEN
Nuhaka

Owners:
Rose-Marie and Roger Bremner

Address: Wai St, Nuhaka
Postal: P O Box 58, Nuhaka
Directions: Travel 32km north of
Wairoa, to Nuhaka. Turn off SH 2 and
travel 0.5km towards Opoutama. Take
second turn left into Wai St
Phone: 0-6-837 8729
Open: Labour Weekend (end October)
to end November, 9am–5pm daily;
January; other times by appointment
Groups: As above
Fee: $4 per adult; groups of 10 or
more $3.50 per person; $10 per family
Children's play area: Available
Size: Medium – 1ha (2½ acres)
Terrain: Flat, slightly sloping
Nursery: Plants from garden
Shop: Flower barn selling dried
flowers and manuka furniture;
certified organic produce

by arrangement

Bremdale is a rustic cottage garden designed by Rose-Marie to create a romantic atmosphere and landscaped by Roger, featuring his manuka furniture, with stone and ponga walls. The Bremners took over Roger's parents' farm in 1978, extending the garden into a series of rooms separated by creeper-covered archways. Roses predominate, especially climbers, flowering in this mild climate for most of the year, with "Madam President" a favourite. Winter camellias are followed by drifts of daffodils and multi-coloured bearded irises. Rose-Marie bases her colour scheme on floral-art principles, each colour being enhanced by deeper shades with a touch of contrast. Soft pinks, blues, whites and lavenders with greens are the spring theme, highlighted by bolder colours. Foliage, too, is important, from broad-leafed acanthus to ajuga ground cover. Shrubs abound, the favourite being *Hibiscus huegelii*, with self-seeding annuals and perennials throughout. Fragrant plants abound, from lilac trees to the herb garden. Birdsong from native birds is supplemented by birds in dovecotes and aviaries. Certified organic persimmon, kiwifruit and cash-cropping orchards adjacent to the garden provide vistas to the hills beyond. A recently developed pond area with a rustic gazebo is set in spacious lawns, contrasting with the densely planted areas around the house.

MAHIA PERENNIALS
Opoutama

Owners:
Sue and Merv Goodley

Address: 300 Mahanga Rd,
Opoutama, R D 8, Nuhaka
Directions: Travel 32km north of
Wairoa, to Nuhaka. Turn off SH 2 &
travel 11km to Opoutama. Continue
3km on Mahanga Rd to garden on right
Phone: 0-6-837 5828 evenings
Open: September to April, daily,
by appointment
Groups: By appointment, as above
Fee: No charge
Size: Medium – 0.6ha (1½ acres)
Terrain: Flat
Nursery: Perennials, unusual annuals,
rose cuttings, salvias, verbascum,
campanulas, lavenders, digitalis,
abutilons, imported seed
Catalogue: Mail order available;
Agrow agent – fish bark garden spread

 partial

by arrangement

S ue's garden has been established over the past 16 years on the site of the original orchard and 1875 homestead, with winding paths and surprises around the corners. An original jacaranda tree flowers in the summer when Sue's 150 or more roses bloom, mostly old varieties. A history of floods has enriched the soil with river silt. Perennials are in abundance, especially salvias, penstemons, campanulas and verbascum. Unusual annuals are also grown and sold, over 50 varieties including gilia, crepis, phacelia, nemophila and poppies. Autumn features white Japanese anemones beneath the white fantail pigeon cote and Michaelmas daisies, with liquidambars and Taiwan cherry trees providing foliage colour in the mild climate. Over 50 camellias form the backbone of the garden, flowering from winter with magnolias, *Prunus campanulata* and early spring bulbs. Then the crab apples blossom with the viburnums, lavender hedges, aquilegias and cinerarias. The wild-flower garden under the magnolias flowers from October. Sue plants to attract the butterflies, bees and birds. Fruit is grown all year and Sue has a large vegetable garden. She is also establishing a rock garden with water features. Four fox terriers are an added attraction.

MAHIA PERENNIALS
Mahia Beach

Owners:
Leanne and Kevin Symes

Mahia Perennials

Address: Taylor St, Taylors Bay,
Mahia Beach
Postal: R D 8, Nuhaka
Directions: 32km north of Wairoa, to
Nuhaka, turn off SH 2 and travel
11km to Opoutama. Turn right to
Mahia Beach along Moana Drive.
Turn right into New Castle St and
travel 1.5km to Taylors Bay. Garden
signposted on Taylor St
Phone: 0-6-837 5528
Open: September to April, daily,
by appointment
Groups: By appointment, as above
Fee: No charge
Size: Small – 0.2ha (½ acre)
Terrain: Flat
Nursery: Perennials from garden –
see Sue's nursery list
Catalogue: Mail order available

partial
by arrangement

A good sealed road takes you from Sue's to Leanne's garden, along the uninhabited coast with limitless views of the ocean. Leanne's is a coastal cottage garden developed since 1988. It was originally very wet and overrun with blackberry, so the Symes removed all the top soil, built the section up by half a metre, then spread the top soil over again. Young native trees now surround the garden, with brick and gravel pathways meandering between garden beds and native areas. The beds of old roses and perennials encroach on the lawn, the full range of colours spilling over on to the greenery. Spring features daffodils, green ixias, aquilegias, dianthus, stoechas lavenders, daisies and early flowering roses. Old roses follow, with all the summer perennials such as penstemons, verbascums, campanulas, foxgloves, salvias, gladioli, nepetas and English lavenders. In the autumn the asters, dahlias and late-flowering roses bloom, then the winter is coloured with camellias, a buddleia tree and the winter foliage of the natives, such as the pohutukawa, pittosporum, coprosma, pseudopanax, karaka, kowhai, cabbage tree, kauri, totara, puka and hebes. Specimen trees include a melia. Kevin is building more structures for Leanne's climbing roses.

OPOHO COASTAL GARDEN
Wairoa

Owners:
Elizabeth and John Powdrell

Address: SH 2, Wairoa
Postal: Private Bag 2012, Wairoa
Directions: Travel 78km south of Gisborne or 22km north of Wairoa, on SH 2 to garden. Well signposted
Phone: 0-6-837 7848
Fax: 0-6-837 7440
Open: Labour weekend (end October) to end November, 9am–5pm, daily; January & early February, most days; other times by appointment
Groups: By appointment
Fee: $4 per adult; $10 per family; groups $3 per person
Size: Medium – 1.2ha (3 acres) plus 0.6ha (1½ acres) under development
Terrain: Flat & gentle slopes
Nursery: Plants propagated from garden, plus bought in varieties

 by arrangement

Some of the mature trees at Opoho, such as the chestnut and elm, date back to 1921 when the homestead began to be built. The Powdrells have expanded the garden since 1962 when they bought the farm. The entire garden is established on sandhills, so it has taken perseverance to grow all the trees, camellias, roses and perennials that predominate today. Design has been all important to the Powdrells who have used strong colour deliberately, à la Helen Dillon. Sweeping lawns set off the house with trees providing structure. It has been planted as a garden for all seasons, the coastal climate allowing roses and perennials to flower for nine months of the year. Polyanthus and camellias bloom all winter and are joined in the spring by flowering prunus, magnolias, vireya rhododendrons, clivias, daffodils and Dutch irises. Masses of primulas seed down and yellow banksias, climbers and, more recently, old roses feature. Autumn is a short season, with colourful foliage depending on the winds. Special attractions include the ponds and waterfall, the knot garden and secret garden beyond the clematis arch. Limestone rock and the use of wood is prominent and birdlife is abundant.

HILLCREST
Wairoa

Owners:
Lorraine and Peter Clifton

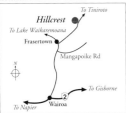

Address: Tiniroto Rd, Wairoa
Postal: Private Bag 2114, Wairoa
Directions: From Wairoa take road
north towards Lake Waikaremoana
for 8km. Before Frasertown, turn
right into Tiniroto Rd. Travel 4km to
garden on left
Phone: 0-6-838 6537
Open: By appointment
Groups: As above
Fee: $3 per adult
Size: Medium – 0.4ha (1 acre)
Terrain: Flat
Nursery: Plants from garden
For sale: Steel plant restrainers;
locally milled macrocarpa for
furniture; home-made jams, sauces
and relishes

  by arrangement

The country garden at Hillcrest farm was begun in 1932 when the new farmhouse was built. Over the past eight years Lorraine has re-designed, developed and refined it, gradually colour-coordinating and grouping plants. Mature trees provide structure for the garden, some of the oaks measuring up to 50 metres across! Camellias also predominate, "Spencers Pink" blossoming from March each year and through the spring. Daffodils cover the front paddock and bloom throughout the garden with hellebores and thousands of violets. Magnolias, azaleas and rhododendrons also feature in spring and paulownias grace the driveway. In summer the roses are the highlight, with climbing roses such as "Dublin Bay" everywhere, underplanted with perennials such as nicotine, aquilegias, watsonias and kniphofias and accompanied by agapanthus and dahlias. The deciduous trees are the mainstay in autumn, with the colours of rhus, maples, viburnums, oaks, plane trees, dogwoods and the golden *Catalpa* or Indian bean tree blending together. These contrast with the group of native rimu trees at the entrance. There are also ponga tree ferns and silver ferns featuring staghorns in the garden. Peter's outdoor wooden furniture and ornamental garden wheelbarrows are an added attraction.

115

TRELINNOE PARK
Napier

Owners:
John and Fiona Wills

Address: Old Coach Rd, R D 2, Napier
Directions: 46km from Napier on
SH 5 to Taupo, turn right down Old
Coach Rd for 5.5km
Phone: 0-6-834 9703
Mobile: 025 465 339
Fax: 0-6-834 9701
Open: Garden:1 August to 31 May, daily
Café: October, November, January, daily;
September, April, May, Thursday to
Sunday; February & March, weekends
Groups: Notify for groups 15 plus
Fee: $5 per adult, $2 children over 12,
$4.50 per head for group of 30,
$12 season ticket
Size: Large – 10ha (25 acres)
Terrain: Fairly hilly
Magnolia Café: Fiona's home cooking
Nursery: Woodland trees and plants
Shop: Art and crafts
Accommodation: Tui Haven simple
retreat at $15 per head

Trelinnoe (pronounced "Tree-linn-o") means "glade in woods". Named after the Cornwall farm where John Wills' grandfather grew up, it is appropriate for John's predominantly woodland garden, carefully landscaped since 1963, with emphasis on shape and design. The undulations of the surrounding slopes have been gradually incorporated, while retaining vistas to the hills beyond, their blues and purples mirrored within the garden. Different areas create different moods, from the expansive lawns patterned by tree shadows to the intimate walks through wooded groves, and from formal walkways edged with clipped hedging to drifts of groundcover under woodland trees. A rockery features some unusual plants, and a native arboretum with kauri grove beside Fiona's café complements the English trees planted for their autumn colour. A large collection of maples is John's favourite, and extensive use of magnolias is the highlight of spring, with dogwoods and rhododendrons followed by jacarandas, pohutukawa and hydrangeas in summer, their blues blending with the distant hills and drifts of arthropodiums like ground mist beneath. John plants in subdued tones using soft creams and whites, some parts deliberately green, with spot-colour emphasis. Plantings of perennials are increasing, especially around the five dams, which attract blue herons and other birds.

BRAEHEAD
Napier

Owners:
Penny and Randall Simcox

Address: 28 Little Bush Rd, R D 4
Puketitiri, Napier
Directions: 1 hour's drive from
Napier along Puketitiri Rd to Little
Bush Rd on left. Garden first on right
Phone: 0-6-839 8870
Open: Nursery: open all year;
Garden: open by appointment
Groups: By appointment
Fee: $3 per adult
Size: Medium – 0.6ha (1½ acres)
Terrain: Terraced slope
Nursery: Perennials, hardy shrubs and
trees
Shop: Restored 100-year-old whare,
"The Matchbox", selling local crafts
and gifts
Attractions: Nearby colonial museum,
other gardens to visit and native bush

  partial

by arrangement

A peaceful hour's rural drive from Napier takes you to Braehead, a cottage garden developed from a bare paddock since 1970. Nearby are magnificent stands of native bush open to visit. Sited at 500 metres above sea level, under the Kaweka Range, Braehead consists of rock gardens and perennial borders, with meandering paths and steps leading to a dam which is home to geese and Pekin ducks. At Puketitiri the gardens blossom late – the rock phlox at Braehead in early spring is spectacular – followed by gentians and *Pulsatilla vulgaris*. Around the dam various irises bloom, then primulas, astilbes, hostas and *Beschornaria yuccoides* with its tall, striking, deep pink flowers. Rhododendrons such as "Lem's Cameo", "Cream Glory" and the creamy "Zelia Plumcocq" grow well here, as do peonies, which Penny loves. There are many rose pergolas flowering mid December, including apricot "Albertine", blowsy pink "Mme Gregoire Stachelin", "Golden Showers" and white "Wedding Day". Mixed borders with roses, filled with perennials of all different varieties, self-seed to give a natural look. Penny has a special alpine garden behind the house, which looks pretty in early spring, her treasures including trilliums, fritillarias, meconopsis and Chatham Island forget-me-nots. *Claytonia nivalis*, with its tiny deep pink flowers, is grown here as a groundcover.

WAHI PAI
Hastings

Owners:
Robin and Doug Nowell-Usticke

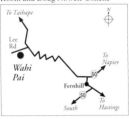

Address: Lee Rd, Otamauri
Postal: P O Box 372, Hastings
Directions: Travel north-west from
Fernhill on Taihape Rd for 29km.
Turn left into Lee Rd. Garden on
corner, on left
Phone: 0-6-874 2863
Fax: 0-6-874 2888
Open: Any time, by appointment
Groups: By appointment, as above
Fee: $3 per adult
Size: Medium – 0.8ha (2 acres)
Terrain: Flat
For sale: Blue Creek gardenwear, eg
waterproof "Snapahapa"
Accommodation: B&B plus dinner,
$75 each, up to 7 people

  by arrangement

Wahi Pai means "pleasant surroundings", the garden so named because of the rolling country view. The house was built in 1918, and the garden extended in 1960 when oaks were planted, contrasting with the blue spruce in autumn. Shape, line and colour are more important to Robin than plants per se. She has developed the garden as a pleasant place for families, with extensive lawns for children. The front garden is formal, with a pool, shaped conifers, clipped box hedging and statuary. Robin is becoming increasingly fond of yellow and white colour combinations, as seen in the bed beside the driveway. Another favourite is the green and white area behind the house where she likes to sit in summer evenings under a tree fern, unusual for Hawke's Bay, by a small fountain, with *Monstera deliciosa* underplanted with hostas. Fragrance from old roses climbing through the tennis court fence is complemented by perfume from a bank of dianthus. English lavender, with more of the old roses that Robin loves, is edged with golden marjoram. Beyond is her special informal rambling woodland, creating a feeling of peacefulness. This newer "wild" area has a packed-earth woodland walk through a rockery planted with spring bulbs, opening out to panoramic views of the hills beyond. Accommodation with meals is available at Wahi Pai.

ORMONDS GARDEN AND NURSERY
Havelock North

Owners:
Peter and Elizabeth Ormond

Address: Kahuranaki Rd, R D 14, Havelock North
Directions: Cross river south of Havelock North. Travel 2km to garden
Phone: 0-6-874 7820
Open: 9am–5pm; 1 September to end February, Wednesday to Sunday except Christmas & Boxing days, every other public holiday; March to September every Friday to Sunday, 9am–5pm; otherwise by appointment
Groups: As above
Fee: Group guided tours, $2 per person
Size: Medium – 1.4ha (3½ acres)
Terrain: Hilly
Nursery: Plants that grow in garden, suited to dry conditions – trees, shrubs, perennials
Shop: Agent for Touchwood Books, quality gifts

   limited

by arrangement

Peter Ormond has been developing the Ormond garden and nursery since 1979. It is a unique garden for hardy plants and trees that grow without watering. Only plants that survive under such conditions are grown and sold at Ormonds. Not a cactus is to be seen, despite popular misconceptions, and only a few succulents. Instead, Mediterranean and South African plants flourish, as they handle frosts as well as hot, dry conditions. Natives such as *Cordyline australis* (cabbage trees) and pittosporums grow well, as do introduced gums, magnolias, oaks and maples. Old roses survive remarkably well, although these are not Peter's favourite plants, except perhaps for the wild, rich yellow rose "Helen Knight". He prefers the buddleias, echiums and hardy perennials that thrive without watering, including North American *Brodiaeas* or hookeras, artemisias, salvias, euphorbias, cistus, campanulas and hellebores. He grows some unusual plants, such as the butterfly or African irises of the moraea and dietes genera, as well as old-fashioned varieties including phlomis, English geraniums and eryngiums. The prevailing westerlies dry the garden, which winds up the hill to superb rural views over the Tukituki River across pasture to the hills beyond. Peter is not expanding the garden further, but plans to develop the detail within the boundaries already laid out.

ROTOTAHI
Waipukurau

Owners:
Brenda and Robert Haldane

Address: 341 Hatuma Rd, R D 1,
Waipukurau
Directions: Travel south of
Waipukurau, on SH 2. Turn left into
Hatuma Rd. Travel 3.4km to garden
on left
Phone: 0-6-858 9471
Open: Garden: 1 November to
December, 10am–5pm;
other times by appointment.
Nursery: 1 March to 1 December;
other times by appointment
Groups: As above
Fee: $3 per adult
Size: Medium – 0.4ha (1 acre)
Terrain: Gently undulating
Nursery: Son Chris Haldane's
Oakwood Nursery, adjacent to
garden, specialising in trees
Art: Brenda's paintings for sale

  by arrangement

Rototahi, meaning "one lake", is adjacent to Lake Hatuma, with views to coastal hills and farmland. Rototahi is essentially an artist's garden; shape and colour are more important to Brenda than particular species. She is mad about trees, especially the backdrop of 80-year-old redwoods planted by Bob's grandfather, complemented by English deciduous trees including ashes, pin oaks, elms, magnolias and cherries. Indigenous species such as pittosporum are dotted around the garden, contrasting with rhododendrons and camellias under the woodland canopy. Brenda is planting more kowhai and native flaxes to attract native birds to an ornamental dam in front of the house. She loves the way the trees change from pale lime to bluey-grey, with greens of all shades predominating, and splashes of seasonal colour provided by self-sown perennials, especially the shasta daisy and poppy families, which enjoy the heat. Daffodils are followed in late spring by pyracantha, with its red berries in winter; then in summer roses bloom in a circular bed. Brenda has converted an attractive garden shed in the grounds into a gallery space for displaying and selling her paintings. These include still-life, landscape and flowers in a variety of media such as water colour, pastel and oil. Son Chris has established his nursery adjacent to the garden where he specialises in propagating and selling a variety of trees.

MISTY FLATS
Waipukurau

Owners:
Betsy and Gordon Mackie

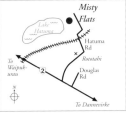

Address: Hatuma Rd, R D 1,
Waipukurau
Directions: South of Waipukurau, off
SH 2. Travel 8km along Hatuma Rd
to garden on left
Phone: 0-6-858 9714
Fax: 0-6-858 9714
Open: All November, 9am–5.30pm;
other times by appointment
Groups: By appointment
Fee: $3 per adult
Size: Medium – 0.4ha (1 acre)
Terrain: Flat
Nursery: Topiary for sale from 1997

  by arrangement

Misty Flats garden has been gradually developed around a modern home over the past 15 years, with an old English rural outlook to Suffolk sheep grazing under century-old exotic trees in the field beyond a rustic gate. Sweeping lawns are bordered with perennial and rose gardens, some edged with buxus and others with lavender. Betsy's favourite plants include lavenders and old-fashioned roses such as "White Wings", "New Dawn", Pemberton's "Cornelia" and "Prosperity" and David Austin's "Mary Rose". She has a great variety of perennials which she colour coordinates by grouping reds, oranges, purples and yellows together in one bright garden bed, while the pastel shades of pink, white and blue are on the other side of the lawn. Beyond the tennis court is a backdrop of *Robinia* "Mop Tops" underplanted with butterscotch achillea and edged with dwarf blue agapanthus, forming a pleasant walk. A new shady area for hostas has been developed under the trees and the swimming pool surrounds have been recently planted with a Portuguese laurel hedge. Nestled into a corner of the garden is a large antique lamp above a fish pond planted with waterlilies. Betsy has begun growing and shaping buxus and other plants into topiary for selling.

THE RANGITIKEI AND THE MANAWATU

We feature 15 gardens from this region. The northernmost garden, Rongoiti, is north of Taihape, but south of Waiouru. Immediately north of Waiouru is the Desert Road, leading through a unique alpine area created by volcanic activity. Lookouts provide opportunities to admire this beautiful barren landscape with its desert flora, petrified wood, and backdrop of mountains in the Tongariro National Park. Severe winters, with snow at times, and fairly cool summers provide ideal conditions for growing alpine specimens. Cold autumn conditions favour good autumn foliage, especially seen among the mature trees at Rongoiti Garden. Rhododendrons also flourish in these conditions.

South of Taihape is the region encompassing the Rangitikei River valley, with a diverse landscape from steep hill country to lush alluvial plains and river valleys. The Rangitikei River carves its course through a plateau, creating extensive terraces and providing rich farming land. The Ruahine Range rises to the east. There are many renowned gardens in this area, as the climatic conditions admirably suit rhododendrons and other plants that enjoy cool nights and summers, a reliable rainfall and above-average altitude. Although it is not as cold as the Central Plateau or as high in altitude, exotics still colour up well in autumn.

The gardens in this region extend from Cairnmuir, just north of Mangaweka, with its views of the Rangitikei River valley, through three Hunterville gardens, to the four gardens in the Marton district. South of Hunterville is Rathmoy, with its two lakes and more formal house garden. On State Highway 1 is The Ridges, with its stunning rhododendron driveway planted 70 years ago. The garden at Maungaraupi also surrounds an historic homestead, this time in the Tudor style of Natusch. Cairnmuir and Maungaraupi provide accommodation for Rangitikei garden visitors. On the road to Feilding is a woodland garden around another historic home, Westoe, this time in Italianate style. In Marton, Royston House provides refreshments at a garden café in the historic homestead, which also offers accommodation. Mungoven features serpentine walls and hedges, and nearby Woodleigh Farm surrounds a Chapman-Taylor home with an inner courtyard garden, also featuring irises in season.

There are three gardens up in the hills north of Kimbolton, the two-hectare Ruapuna Park at Rangiwahia, the well-known rhododendron garden at Cross Hills and the nearby Kimbolton Rhododedron Gardens with a lake for a focal point. Three Manawatu gardens include the classical English terraced garden at Sanson, planted to accompany the historic home of Pukemarama. O'Tara Birch Gardens, located at Rongotea, specialises in dahlias and just north of Palmerston North is Greenhaugh, the most southerly Manawatu garden, with trees from last century in a semi-formal country setting.

The city servicing this area is Palmerston North, centered round The Square, with attractive public gardens at the Esplanade bordering the Manawatu River that skirts the city.

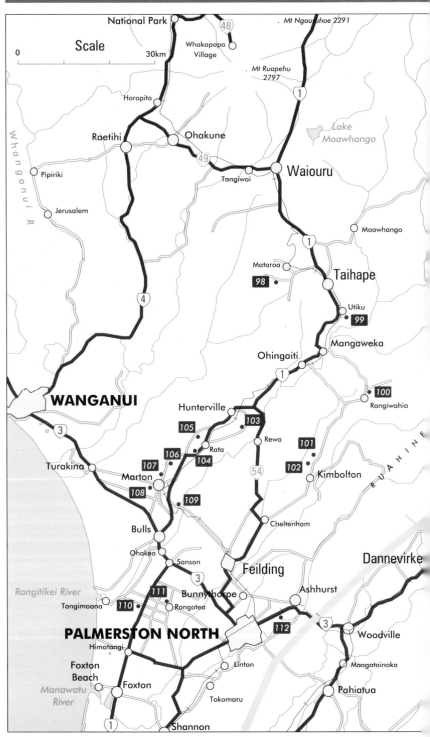

RONGOITI GARDEN
Taihape

Owners:
~~on~~, Helen and Douglas Gordon

Address: Pa-iti, R D 1, Taihape
Directions: Travel north from Taihape
~~~~ SH 1 for 5km. Turn left into
~~~~ataroa Rd, then into Rongoiti Rd.
~~~~ Rongoiti Junction turn right into
~~~~oeke Rd. Garden is 3km on left
~~~~one: 0-6-388 7866
~~~~en: 1 September to 30 April,
~~~~ednesday to Sunday, 9am– 4pm
~~~~oups: By appointment
~~~~e: $5 per adult
~~~~e: Large – 8ha (20 acres)
~~~~rrain: Hilly
~~~~rsery: Primulas, meconopsis,
~~~~rdiocrinum, helleborus, iris,
~~~~ples, daphne, etc

 by arrangement

Pear and plum trees survive from the 1884 surveyors' campsite that gave Rongoiti Garden its name. Ron has developed the garden since 1947, with many thousands of exotic trees planted in the fifties for conservation purposes. These include a redwood grove with *Sequoiadendron giganteum* and a grove of *Thuja plicata*. More recently plantings of 20 golden larch (*Pseudolarix amabilis*) and *Pinus bungeana*, grown from seed imported from China, surround a pond area at the new driveway entrance. The drive winds up through conifers to the established woodland area where rhododendrons feature, including the early tree species, crimson *R. giganteum*, and yellow-trussed *R. maccabeanum*. Spring bulbs also feature with many camellias, cherries and magnolias from September onwards. Various varieties of clematis blossom along with Burmese honeysuckle and dogwoods *Cornus kousa chinensis* and *C. controversa* underplanted with many varied and unusual perennials. The giant lilies, *Cardiocrinum giganteum,* are another feature in mid December. A large western hemlock (*Tsuga heterophylla*) is prominent, with spruces such as *Picea abies* "Aurea" and *P. sitchensis*, as well as native species including kowhai, titoki, tawa and totara which attract native pigeons, bellbirds and tui. The deciduous trees colour up well in autumn.

CAIRNMUIR
Mangaweka

Owners:
Elizabeth and David Buchanan

Address: SH 1, Mangaweka, R D
Directions: Travel 5km north of
Mangaweka, to garden on right,
opposite Manui Rd. Or 16km south of
Taihape, on left opposite Manui Rd
Phone: 0-6-382 5878
Fax: 0-6-382 5747
Open: Labour Weekend (end October)
to end April, daily, by appointment
Groups: By appointment
Fee: $5 per adult; family concessions
Size: Medium – 0.8ha (2 acres)
Terrain: Hilly
Nursery: Variety of plants, eg some
perennials
Accommodation: Dinner, B&B;
attractive accommodation with two
bedrooms, 1 double, 1 twin, with
guest bathrooms

   limited

by arrangement

When the Buchanans arrived at Cairnmuir three decades ago, there were only two macrocarpas and a laurel hedge, with little top soil on the papa rock base. Now the garden is informally textured and flowing, with contours separating different areas, and a large variety of exotic trees providing shade and autumn colour. The driveway is lined with a silver birch grove, beyond which a hillside walk provides spectacular views of the surrounding countryside overlooking the Rangitikei River valley. Spring is announced by hundreds of daffodils and a collection of clematis beginning to flower. Other climbers include roses, wisteria and, in autumn, lapageria. The bog garden features a large variety of primulas, hostas and gunnera under *Betula* (birches), *Metasequoia glytostroboides* (dawn redwoods), and *Taxodium distichum* (swamp cypresses). A pond is surrounded by many other conifers and deciduous trees. Lots of flowering shrubs such as azaleas, rhododendrons, and native olearias are followed by roses of all varieties, delphiniums and many other perennials supplemented by annuals in season, ensuring Elizabeth has flowers for picking all year round. The use of old logs, railway sleepers and stones throughout the garden gives a rustic feel, enhancing the strong design. The Buchanans are developing glass and shade houses.

RUAPUNA PARK
Rangiwahia

Owners:
Ngaire and Alan Hancock

Address: Te Parapara Rd,
Rangiwahia, R D 54, Kimbolton
Directions: 2km north of Rangiwahia,
turn right into Te Parapara Rd
Phone: 0-6-328 2855
Open: Garden: all year, by appointment
Museum: open by appointment
Groups: By appointment
Fee: $3 per adult
Size: Large – 2ha (5 acres)
Terrain: Mainly flat
Nursery: Perennials from garden and
Cardiocrinum giganteum
For sale: Peacocks – bred on property
Museum: Granny's Cottage Museum
with colonial cottage of memorabilia
and vintage farm machinery including
10 working stationary engines

   mostly

  by arrangement

Sited at an altitude of 600 metres, Ruapuna Park features an alpine rockery and other frost-hardy plantings. A registered totara tree, almost one thousand years old, stands amid a woodland area underplanted with large-leafed rhododendron species. Camellias and spring bulbs, including 500 red tulips, are followed by a blazing bed of azaleas, then a bank of David Austin roses. Giant lily-like *Cardiocrinum giganteum* flower around Christmas, followed by a stream bank of fuchsias. Two ponds lead into the "moat" spanned by arched bridges. Gunneras, hostas, irises and cerise primulas flourish around the edges, with heaths and heathers growing on an island of clay. Alan was brought up here, his grandfather having farmed the land since 1886. Revamped and expanded over the past three decades, the resulting parklike garden retains views to the snowcapped Ruahine Range. Alan is keen on conifers, and is also increasing his collection of 14 native olearias, along with acers that survive frost. Stepping stones intersect a garden planted with ornamental grasses, rushes and sedges. Other features include a laburnum archway, a snow gum growing horizontally, two original golden willows underplanted with drifts of blue forget-me-nots and pink primulas, and birdlife, including breeding peacocks and an aviary of zebra finches, quail, and canaries. Granny's Cottage Museum is adjacent.

CROSS HILLS GARDENS
Kimbolton

Owners:
Rodney and Faith Wilson

Address: Rangiwahia Rd, R D 54, Kimbolton
Directions: Take SH 54 to Cheltenham. Turn into Kimbolton Rd. Travel 14km to Kimbolton, then continue 5km to Cross Hills Gardens on left
Phone: 0-6-328 5797
Fax: 0-6-328 5773
Open: September to May, daily, 10.30am–5pm
Groups: Large groups by appointment
Fee: $6 per adult; $1 per child up to 12 years; group concessions
Size: Large – 7.2ha (18 acres)
Terrain: Rolling
Tea kiosk: Open October and November, or by appointment
Nursery: Rhododendron & azalea specialist; mail order nationwide; catalogue $5; flower souvenirs, videos

This park-like rhododendron garden was developed over the past 25 years by the Wilson family. It now boasts over two thousand varieties of rhododendrons and azaleas which peak during October and November. Rodney's favourites are the hardy German hybrids and the unusual standards that his father, Eric, originally developed. These standard *R. yakushimanum* crosses are very popular in smaller gardens. Rhododendrons cover the full range of the colour spectrum, more so than other plants, Rodney coordinating them, such as planting pinks with lavenders and purples with oranges. But Cross Hills is not just rhododendrons. In spring, the cherry blossom, magnolias and camellias accompany the early rhododendrons, then a whole host of perennials begin flowering. In December the cardiocrinum walk is in its full glory and the hostas complement the late-flowering rhododendrons. Perennials and a dahlias continue into autumn when the mature deciduous trees show off their colours against the crisp blue skies. These include beeches, maples, liquidambars, *Nyssa sylvatica*, parrotia and an original oak, which complement the conifers and natives. Two huge macrocarpa feature by the front gate and kauri are unusual at such an altitude. Other features include the clematis bank above the waterfall and the Azalea Bowl with massed deciduous and evergreen azaleas.

129

KIMBOLTON RHODODENDRON GARDENS
Kimbolton

Owner:
The NZ Rhododendron Association

Address: Haggerty St, R D 54, Kimbolton
Directions: Take SH 54 to Cheltenham. Turn into Kimbolton Rd. Travel 14km to Kimbolton, then continue 1km and turn left into Haggerty St. Garden 500m on right. Parking on main lawn
Phone: 0-6-328 5746
Open: First weekend October to mid December, daily, from 9am; other times by appointment
Groups: By appointment
Fee: $5 per adult; members free
Size: Large – 4ha (10 acres)
Terrain: Undulating
Nursery: Plant sales planned for 1997
For sale: Crafts during season

   limited

 large groups please notify

The Kimbolton Rhododendron Gardens were established in 1970 as a home for the New Zealand Rhododendron Association's large collection of rhododendrons that were under the care of Dr Yeates at Massey University. The site at Kimbolton was selected for its excellent free-draining soil, good rainfall, altitude and "sharp" seasons. It has become an educational showplace for rhododendron hybrids and species for the general public, as well as NZRA members, to enjoy. There are now over one thousand mature specimens of rhododendrons and deciduous azaleas in a park-like setting overlooking the countryside. Spacious open lawns are bordered by rhododendrons with a backdrop of mature trees. Rhododendron-lined grassy avenues lead to three linked ponds which are home to white swans. Rhododendrons are reflected in the waters with hostas, gunneras and trees planted round and waterlilies multiplying in the corners. Some of Dr Yeates' lilium and auratum hybrids are grown in the gardens beneath silver birches, chestnut trees, ginkgo, maples, oaks, blue spruce and other conifers as well as native kowhai trees. The rhododendron collection is being expanded to include the best of New Zealand-raised hybrids and species. The peak time for viewing the rhododendrons is during October and November.

RATHMOY
Hunterville

Owners:
Susanna and Christopher Grace

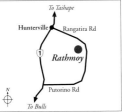

Address: Rangitira Rd, R D 6,
Hunterville
Postal: P O Box 13, Hunterville
Directions: Turn east into Rangatira
Rd from the centre of Hunterville.
Travel 4km to Rathmoy on right
Phone: 0-6-322 8334
Mobile: 025 420 253
Fax: 0-6-322 8380
Open: 1 September to 30 November,
daily, 10am–5pm; other times
by appointment
Groups: All year, by appointment
Fee: $5 per adult
Size: Large – 2.4ha (6 acres)
Terrain: Gently sloping

 by arrangement

Rathmoy, named after an Irish farm in Christopher's family, is an expansive garden sited on a plateau at 500 metres above sea level. A pair of century-old linden trees provide height and structure to the garden, developed over the past two decades around the homestead, with brick walls and archways enclosing a series of intimate garden rooms, intensively planted in roses, lavenders and perennials. These contrast with the newer park-like proportions surrounding the two large lakes in front of the linden trees. A long curving driveway sweeps past the lakes, lined with dwarf rhododendrons and edged with white lychnis and daisies. Susanna loves simple garden plants like daisies, which she masses together in blocks of white or colour much as brush strokes fill a canvas. Pink and red predominate above the pond, a lot of white in the more formal house garden with "Wedding Day" and white wisteria climbing over brick archways, a yellow border under a golden elm, and pink with blue around the dovecote. Susanna enjoys the quiet, broken by birdsong from fantail pigeons and doves and other residents at Rathmoy, including Basil the llama, kunekune pigs, coloured Jacob sheep, donkeys, St Bernard dog and water fowl. Two elegant swans grace the lakes, and baby ducklings feature in spring, with geese as well.

THE RIDGES
Hunterville

Owners:
Marshall family

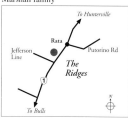

Address: R D 1, Marton
Directions: 13km south of Hunterville
or 21km north of Bulls on SH 1
Phone: 0-6-327 8484
Fax: 0-6-327 8279
Open: 20 September to 30 November,
20 March to 30 April, 10am–4.30pm,
other times when road sign displayed
Closed: Easter
Groups: As above, or by appointment
Fee: $5 per adult
Size: Large – 2ha (5 acres) plus
woodland area
Terrain: Terraced
Nursery: Specialists in unusual and
rare plants, primula, cyclamen, hosta,
meconopsis, aquilegia, arthropodium,
lilium, rodgersia, rheum, fritillaria,
helleborus; mail-order catalogue
Shop: Garden accessories

   mostly

🍽 by arrangement

Sited on a terrace above the Rangitikei River, The Ridges was originally planted by Sally's grandparents from 1924, with design elements by Alfred Buxton in the 1930s. A sunken garden was added in the 1950s. An impressive 70-year-old rhododendron-lined driveway welcomes visitors to this mature garden, where woodland areas are complemented by open lawn with colourful borders. Established trees still allow superb views to the surrounding countryside, Ruahine Range and Tararua foothills beyond. Spring begins with drifts of chionodoxa, dark blue forget-me-nots and dog's-tooth violets under deciduous trees. Flowering cherries, magnolias and dogwoods blossom, underplanted with fritillarias, peonies and early perennials. Masses of rhododendrons and azaleas brighten the green backdrop. Roses and lilies bloom throughout the garden, and summer perennials in the formal sunken gardens frame a central statue of "Spring". Then in autumn pink *Cyclamen hederifolium* carpet the garden beneath the beautiful autumn foliage of notable copper beeches, maples, liquidambars, oaks, and birches. A magnificent *Magnolia campbellii* blossoms in winter, when camellias open. Belladonna lilies stud the entrance, leading past a memorable stand of kahikatea and over three hectares of woodland where Sally is planning a walk past a series of ponds.

MAUNGARAUPI COUNTRY ESTATE
Hunterville

Owners:
Hilary and Ken Cavanagh

Address: Leedstown Rd, R D 1,
Marton
Directions: Turn off SH 1 into
Leedstown loop Rd
Phone: 0-6-327 7820
Fax: 0-6-327 8619
Open: All year, by appointment
Groups: By appointment, as above
Fee: $5 per adult
Size: Large – 2ha (5 acres)
Terrain: Flat
Accommodation: B&B; dinner;
adjoining self-contained flat;
bookings for seminars, weddings, etc
Historic homestead: Open for
viewing by appointment; house tours,
phone John Vickers on 0-6-327 7280

 by arrangement

The garden at Maungaraupi was first planted in 1906, when Tilleard Natusch designed the Tudor-style historic homestead built for William Swainson Marshall, whose descendants lived here until recently. A long, winding driveway through established native trees opens onto the extensive lawns edged with rose beds. Red blooms of "Dublin Bay" brighten the tennis court, and further roses, delphiniums, foxgloves, cosmos, fuchsias, and stocks border the wisteria-festooned verandah where a conservatory once stood. Native arthropodiums and Chatham Island forget-me-nots contribute to the predominantly pink and blue colour scheme. Spring carpets the woodland in bluebells and daffodils, a *Magnolia campbellii* blooms, followed by white clematis, wisteria and rhododendrons, with trilliums featuring in shady areas. Perennials and lavenders complement the roses in summer, providing masses of colour. *Cardiocrinum giganteum* flower around Christmas, then deciduous foliage colours vibrantly in autumn. Enormous Douglas firs add to the backdrop of evergreens in winter. Two hectares of native bush including rimu, kauri and totara attract abundant birdlife, with two glades in the woodland, one featuring a small pond. The garden affords magnificent views to the Rangitikei River valley, rolling farmland and the Ruahine Range beyond.

WOODLEIGH FARM
Marton

Owners:
John and Sarah Vickers

Address: Tutaenui Rd, R D 2, Marton
Directions: 4km north of Marton, on main road (Tutaenui Rd). Garden on right, up driveway
Phone: 0-6-327 7280
Open: October to December, daily, 10am–4pm; other times by appointment
Groups: As above
Fee: $5 per adult
Size: Medium – 0.8ha (2 acres)
Terrain: Flat
Tours: Bookings for historic homes day tour conducted by John Vickers; four beautiful Rangitikei homes with luncheon, $55, 10am–4pm (Finalist in NZ Tourism awards, 1995)

    by arrangement

Woodleigh Farm is centred around a 1911 Chapman-Taylor courtyard house. The remnants of the original 1920s garden provided established trees when the Vickers came here in 1976. Prevailing westerlies dictated their garden layout, with brick walls, trelliswork, rose pergolas and shrubs creating shelter for flowering plants. Green foliage predominates, with pinks and blues grouped together and a separate red garden with purples. John aims to achieve a balance between plantsman and artist, preserving a peaceful restfulness which the flat terrain enhances. An English garden featuring all shades of bearded irises in massed beds is divided by a formal avenue behind a brick wall. Near the summer house is a bed of intense blue delphiniums. Water irises, hostas and ligularias surround a waterlily pond. This contrasts with the formal pool in the inner courtyard, with its clipped box, seasonal colour being added by container plants such as red tulips. Further box hedging formalises the wide turning circle by the solid courtyard gateway, where butterflies are attracted to cherry pie (*Heliotropium arborescens*) next to "Golden Showers", a shrub rose climbing up the house. Roses, old and new, flower with peonies, lilacs, tall echiums, rhododendrons and iris species. Unusual specimen trees feature, such as a *Calliandra* and a weeping Kashmir deodar.

MUNGOVEN
Marton

Owners:
Judy and Bob Christie

Address: 20 Tutaenui Rd, Marton
Directions: Take Tutaenui Rd north of Marton. Travel 1.6km to Mungoven garden on left
Phone: 0-6-327 8343
Open: All year, by appointment
Groups: By appointment, as above
Fee: $3 per adult
Size: Medium – 0.8ha (2 acres)
Terrain: Flat to undulating

Mungoven was established by the Hammonds with landscape designer David Irvine, 25 years before the Christies bought the property in 1989. The attractive lines continue, with a broken concrete serpentine wall and a high, curving golden totara hedge prominent. A shaped ornamental lily pond is planted with Japanese maples, weeping conifers and azaleas, overshadowed by a Judas tree. Judy has introduced roses into a hidden garden beyond a wisteria-covered pergola. Spring also features rhododendrons, dogwoods, and magnolias. Native arthropodiums and primulas bloom in the bog garden by a dam area, which is being revamped. Summer perennials accompany the roses, then lilies and bush cyclamen provide autumn colour, with the deciduous trees, including a large copper beech. Leucadendrons flower in winter, when the heaths and heathers feature and the totara hedge turns a golden yellow. The camellia glen also begins to bloom in June, protected by a tall karo hedge. Nearby is a landscaped bank of conifers. Huge local boulders and rocks add interest. A moon gate leads to a slatted timber shade house sheltering fuchsias, begonias, Chilean bellflowers and hippeastrums. Dramatic *Agave attenuata* succulents, *Silene uniflora* "Druetts Variegated" and black grass-like *Ophiopogon planiscapus* "Nigrescens" flank a stone-filled watercourse round the patio.

135

ROYSTON HOUSE
Marton

Owners:
Glenis and Hamish McMaster

Address: 97 Wanganui Rd, Marton
Directions: East of Marton township,
follow High St into Wanganui Rd.
Garden just past Pukepapa Rd on left
Phone: 0-6-327 6393
Mobile: 025 471 148
Fax: 0-6-327 6393
Open: All year, by appointment
Groups: By appointment, as above
Fee: $3 per adult
Size: Medium – 0.8ha (2 acres)
Terrain: Slightly contoured
Garden café: Open by appointment.
Cater for weddings, etc
Luncheons with views over gardens
in peaceful surroundings
Accommodation: B&B and dinner

    partial

  by arrangement

Situated on the outskirts of Marton is this turn-of-the-century home, typical of the grandeur of its era. Royston House is a solid kauri homestead designed by Cecil Woods in 1896. The grand driveway is formed by an avenue of plane trees for almost its entire 150 metres, underplanted with spring bulbs. Complementing the homestead are the English-style park-like grounds, complete with grass tennis court and unique Gothic tennis house. A secret garden door leads down through a native area to a lagoon, with lawn sweeping down to the water's edge. Glenis has planted gardens around the lawns since 1989, establishing lots of perennials such as penstemons, poppies, phlox, verbenas, synthyris and foxgloves. In springtime, ajuga groundcover grows vigorously with daffodils and azaleas. Over 100 roses bloom through summer, then the foliage of deciduous trees, some as old as the house itself, provides autumn colour, contrasting with green conifers. Hamish loves making furniture in the style of yesteryear, as featured throughout the garden. By the lagoon beyond the bridge he is building a large louvred summer house for luncheon parties. Wildlife enjoy this area, and Hamish has flocks of four species of pigeon as well as doves. Visitors can also explore the "forgotten garden", ivy wall, ponds, aviaries, archways and cottage garden areas.

WESTOE WOODLAND GARDEN
Marton

Owners:
Jim and Diana Howard

Address: Kakariki Rd, R D 1, Marton
Directions: Travel along SH 1 north
of Bulls or south of Marton turn-off.
Turn east into Kakariki Rd. Westoe
Woodland Garden on left
Phone: 0-6-327 6350
Fax: c/o 0-6-327 7015
Open: All year, Tuesday to Saturday,
10am–4pm; other times by
appointment
Groups: Coaches by appointment
Fee: $5 per adult; free to nursery only
Size: Large – 4ha (10 acres)
Terrain: Mainly flat, some gently
sloping
Nursery: Many plants propagated
from garden; unusual trees, shrubs,
perennials, old and new species,
specialising in NZ native plants

Westoe was laid out in the 1870s by Sir William Fox, who named it after his English birthplace in Durham. Owned by the Howard family since 1885, three generations of keen gardeners have left their mark on this woodland garden surrounding the classical homestead. Jim and Diana underplant mature trees with woodland perennials and rhododendrons. Unusual New Zealand natives are a specialty, including an extensive fernery, with an indigenous area established in 1950 on the valley floor below this sheltered park-like garden terraced down to the Rangitikei River. Native bush surrounds Westoe, which also features magnificent specimens of century-old deciduous trees including redwoods, stone pine (*P. Pinea*), Douglas fir, Atlas cedar and Norfolk Island pine. Spring brings prunus, magnolias and dogwoods into blossom, underplanted with drifts of spring bulbs, irises and primulas. Rhododendrons bloom, then *Cardiocrinum giganteum* and other lilies around Christmas. Autumn foliage includes oaks, maples and cornus underplanted with cyclamen, plectranthus and *Lilium formosanum*. The Howards emphasise winter-flowering species such as hellebores, echium, cyclamen and camellias, some now 120 years old. Many other exotics, including a copper beech, were planted from 1920 onwards. Naturalised annuals have intermixed with the woodland perennials.

PUKEMARAMA
Tangimoana

Owners:
Sue and Ian McKelvie

Address: Rosina Rd, Sanson
Postal: R D 3, Palmerston North
Directions: At Sanson, turn west
following SH 1. Turn right into
Rosina Rd, towards Tangimoana.
Pukemarama on left
Phone: 0-6-324 8446
Fax: 0-6-324 8446
Open: 1 October to Christmas
Closed: Saturdays
Groups: Large groups, all year,
by appointment
Fee: $5 per adult
Size: Large – 3.2ha (8 acres)
Terrain: Terraced
Nursery: Small

  limited

  by arrangement

Pukemarama is situated on a hilltop overlooking the west coast. Established at the turn of the century, the gardens are maintained in their original English style by descendants of the McKelvie family. The historic homestead overlooks formal bricked terraces, 51 steps leading down to a sunken garden with adjacent grassed tennis and croquet lawns. Here twin circular parterres, filled with colourful perennials and annuals, are connected by a long rose pergola and edged with English lavender. Surviving trees from the original symmetrical plantings, include a pair of tall Norfolk Island pines, a cedar, a vast horizontal beech, a weeping cherry and an enormous walnut leading into a woodland dell. This features a huge macrocarpa among other mature trees underplanted with camellias, rhododendrons, azaleas, perennials and bulbs. Beyond, a pond area is being developed. Roses predominate at Pukemarama, from "Albertine" climbing the verandah to miniatures encircling the central sun-dial in the forecourt. Cosmos and alyssum soften the concrete steps. "Scarlet O'Hara" bougainvillea climbs the verandah balustrade above box-edged beds of roses, delphiniums and poppies. Other features include statuary, a summer house, a dove aviary, and Sue's scarecrow, with magnificent views over the surrounding countryside. A 1900 woolshed can be seen on the farm tours.

O'TARA BIRCH GARDENS
Rongotea

Owners:
Adrian Ballinger and Eddie Johns

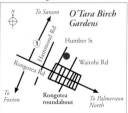

Address: 72 Humber St, Rongotea
Postal: P O Box 81, Rongotea
Directions: Turn off SH 1 south of
Sanson, towards Palmerston North,
left into Rongotea Rd. Travel 4km
towards Rongotea roundabout. Turn
left into Humber St and travel 400m
to O'Tara Birch Gardens on right
Phone: 0-6-324 8490
Fax: 0-6-324 8490
Open: November to mid April, daily,
10am–5pm; evenings by appointment
Groups: By appointment
Fee: $3 per adult
Size: Large – 3.2ha (8 acres)
Terrain: Flat
Nursery & Plant Centre: Dahlias,
grevilleas, irises and roses

  by arrangement

Adrian and Eddie are dahlia enthusiasts, with over 1,000 different dahlias planted in a formal garden in curving beds, radiating out from the centre in concentric circles. Weeping standardised grevilleas encircled by buxus hedging feature in the middle of the garden. Since 1989 hybrids of all shapes and sizes have been grown in this dahlia display garden, now one of the largest in the world. It is a mass of blended colour from mid January to the first frosts of May, with the popular reds, salmons, golds and apricots predominant. But O'Tara Birch is not just dahlias. Established trees, including birches, elders, oaks, maples, *Magnolia campbellii* and *Pinus radiata* "Aurea", surround the garden, separating it into individual rooms, with walks tunnelled through a dense stand of *Thuja plicata*. The adjacent rose garden is being revamped into a formal 16th-century-style open knot garden. A pond area has been developed with surrounding bog garden featuring over 240 varieties of Japanese irises flowering early December. They join the Louisiana and bearded irises which bloom from early November. The Japanese and Siberian irises at O'Tara Birch comprise the largest collection in the Southern Hemisphere. The theme "gardens of the past for the future" encompasses many exciting visions, including a chess garden, a viewing tower and musical events to be held in the gardens.

139

GREENHAUGH
Palmerston North

Owners:
Lynne and Les Atkins

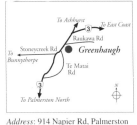

Address: 914 Napier Rd, Palmerston
North, R D 10
Directions: From Palmerston North,
take SH 3 northwards. Continue past
100km sign for 6.5km to garden on
right; signpost at gate
Phone: 0-6-357 3878
Open: All year, Monday to Saturday,
9am–5pm
Groups: By appointment
Fee: $3 per adult
Size: Large – 2ha (5 acres)
Terrain: Gentle terraced slopes
Nursery: Many perennials, foliage
plants including silver foliage, bulbs,
groundcovers, grasses, old roses

Greenhaugh, originally farmed in the 1870s, has been
in the Atkins' family for the past 35 years. This large
semi-formal country garden was developed over the last
decade to extend the colonial homestead's half acre inherited
from Les' parents. Original trees include two mature lindens
or tilia, a copper beech, liquidambar and ginkgo, providing
a wonderful canopy of autumn colour. Lynne loves the old
roses rambling through the orchard and clothing a tennis-
court length pergola along with clematis and wisteria.
Austin roses are also favourites, featured in a salmon,
cream and green area close to the house with *Alchemilla
mollis* and cream Californian poppies. The roses, clematis,
bearded irises and aquilegia steal the scene in spring
together with the *Kolkwitzia* and many euphorbias. Then
the perennial borders come into their own during summer,
with shasta daisies, salvias, penstemons, geraniums,
lavateras and lilies. In autumn, the drier Mediterranean
gardens take over with their hotter colours and lots of
silver and gold foliage. These include *Helianthus*, sedums,
Michaelmas daisies and lavenders, with Japanese anemones
featuring in the herbaceous borders. Winter brings
collections of hellebores to the fore, then 1940s daffodils
lining the driveway bloom. Local limestone is used in the
formal pond areas, steps and paths.

TARANAKI AND WANGANUI

Taranaki is rich dairy land, and some of New Zealand's finest cheese is produced here. Eleven gardens are featured in the fertile Taranaki region surrounding Mt Taranaki and Egmont National Park on all sides, many with spectacular views of the mountain. Four of the gardens are in and around the city of New Plymouth, including Gro-wel Fuchsias and Cedar Lodge Conifers, both catering to specialist markets. Cheney Manor is an urban spring garden with rhododendrons and roses. Pukeiti, the well-known rhododendron garden, is located a little further out, on the foothills of Mt Taranaki. One of the two historic Queen Elizabeth II Trust gardens is also in New Plymouth – Tupare, originally planted by Sir Russell and Lady Matthews in 1932. The other is Hollard Gardens, south of the mountain, first planted by Bernard and Rose Hollard in 1929.

Early each November Taranaki holds its Rhododendron Festival, with 100 gardens taking part. A high rainfall and the alpine climate created by Mt Taranaki particularly favour the growth of rhododendrons and azaleas. New Plymouth also features the renowned Pukekura Park with its fernery, begonia house, lakes, illuminated fountain and waterfall floodlit by night. To the south-west of New Plymouth on the ocean side of the mountain are two gardens: Ngamamaku, with its streamside dell, at Oakura, and the large park-like gardens of Hikurangi surrounding its lake at Okato. Then around on the eastern side of the mountain south of Stratford, just off the highway, is Woodhill, where accommodation is available in its English woodland garden setting. West of Stratford, on the southern flank of Mt Taranaki, are two gardens at Kaponga: one the historic Hollard Gardens, the other the Dudlis' Swiss garden featuring begonias.

South Taranaki stretches down the west coast towards Wanganui. This area has a temperate climate and a fertile strip of land along the coastline down to Wanganui. Westerlies blowing off the Tasman Sea make it essential for these coastal gardens to grow shelter-belts before gardening. Bushy Park, east of Kai Iwi, is in this region, planted around the historic homestead that is open to the public for visiting or accommodation. Walking tracks lead through the adjoining indigenous bush. Other Wanganui attractions include beautiful Virginia Lake, planted with English trees early this century, and featuring an indoor Winter Garden and a fountain illuminated at night. Nearby Bason Botanical Reserve is another horticultural highlight.

Scale

0   50km

CEDAR LODGE CONIFERS
New Plymouth

Owners:
Noeline and David Sampson

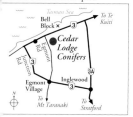

Address: 63 Egmont Rd, Bell Block,
R D 2, New Plymouth
Directions: Take SH 3 north of New
Plymouth. Travel towards Bell Block.
Turn right into Egmont Road, Conifer
Lodge 1 km from SH 3
Phone: 0-6-755 0369
Fax: 0-6-755 0369
Open: All year, Monday to Saturday,
9am–5pm; Sunday 10am–4pm
Groups: As above
Fee: No charge
Size: Large – 2ha (5 acres) plus
nursery
Terrain: Flat and pathed hillside
Nursery: Conifers – largest NZ range
and extensive range worldwide;
catalogue and mail order available

  mostly

This display garden demonstrates the tremendous range of conifers available. The slope behind the nursery was planted in 1978, and has an ideal climate for conifers: wet enough for a wide variety from Siberian to tropical. Conifers vary in growth rates, size, shape, form, and colour. The Sampsons mass-plant in colours which change through the seasons, deepening in the winter from greens to mauves, and from yellows to bronzes. Then the new, soft, pale green spring growth of firs and spruces lightens up and freshens the landscape. Favourites include the pale blue *Picea pungens glauca* and yellow-tipped creamy *Cryptomeria japonica* "Sekkan Sugi". Sizes range from low prostrate forms to bun-shaped, globose, weeping and tall columnar shapes. These show a diversity of textures, from dainty to pendulous. The miniatures are special, such as *Chamaecyparis obtusa* "Densa" or the delicate ground cover *Cedrus deodara* "Prostrata"; the smallest conifer in the world is our dwarf rimu. Many other New Zealand natives fall into the conifer category, including totara, kauri, miro and rimu. Exotics include the largest and tallest trees in the world, the Californian redwoods, as well as spruces, abies and pines. There are 656 different conifers available at Cedar Lodge, with topiary variations. David and Noeline import seed and grow all conifers possible in our climate.

CHENEY MANOR GARDENS
New Plymouth

Owners:
Miro and Frank Willcox

Address: 239c Carrington St,
Vogeltown, New Plymouth
Directions: From New Plymouth city,
turn south into Carrington St. Park on
roadside if possible and walk down
long driveway, to last house on left
Phone: 0-6-753 2334
Open: Labour weekend (end October)
to end November, daily, 9am–5pm;
other times by appointment
Groups: By appointment
Fee: $2 per adult
Size: Small – 0.2ha (½ acre)
Terrain: Flat to sloping with steps
Nursery: Variety of perennials,
groundcovers, rhodohypoxis

 on request

🎋 in nearby Pukekura Park

This urban garden was re-designed and planted by the
previous owners in 1988, with additions and alterations
by the Willcoxes since 1994. It won runner-up to Taranaki
large garden of the year in 1995. The predominant species
are the 140 rhododendrons, with azaleas, and maples
providing shade for many hostas in the bog garden edging
the Pukekura Stream. Primulas and pink and white astilbes
join the hostas and erigeron spreads over the banks. There
are three areas of tropical vireya rhododendrons and
11 different varieties of clematis climbing ponga walls
and pergolas above garden seats. The Willcoxes are
building more archways for roses which are their favourites,
along with hyacinth-like galtonias which also flower in
summer. At present, Cheney Manor is a spring garden, with
flowering cherries, dogwoods and magnolias blossoming
above the rhodohypoxis and irises. White and lilac wisteria
complement the pale pink flowers of the Beauty bush,
Kolkwitzia amabilis. Many kinds of deutzia add to the
spring show, then kalmia display their porcelain-like
flowers later in the season. Exotic trees include a claret
ash and weeping silver pear, interplanted with natives such
as a kowhai, cabbage tree and old kauri.

GRO-WEL FUCHSIA GARDENS
New Plymouth

Owners:
Loraine and Terry Agate

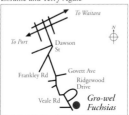

Address: 159 Veale Rd, Frankleigh Park, New Plymouth
Directions: 5km from New Plymouth. Travel south along Frankley Rd. Turn left into Govett Ave, and left again into Veale Rd. Garden on left
Phone: 0-6-753 3437
Mobile: 025 839 255
Fax: 0-6-753 7516
Open: 1 September to 30 April, daily, 9am–4.30pm; 1 May to 30 August, weekdays plus Saturday morning
Groups: By appointment
Fee: No charge
Size: Medium – 0.8ha (2 acres)
Terrain: Flat
Nursery: Fuchsias, junior fuchsias ideal for the traveller, pots, hanging baskets, standards, large bush, etc; *Buxus sempervirens* and a small range of trees and shrubs

Gro-wel Fuchsias, owned by Loraine's parents for the past two decades, was transferred by Loraine and Terry to new premises adjacent to Veale Road Nurseries, which were developed as New Zealand's leading fuchsia specialist. The fuchsia display garden was landscaped in 1990, and now features over 1,000 different fuchsia cultivars and species. Each year the Agates release one or two new varieties, imported from Australia, the United Kingdom and America. Two new releases are large double pink "Acclamation" and almost irridescent "Santa Clara" in royal purple fading to deep rose pink. The fuchsia colours range from bright red to purple-blue, pink, mauve and white. The fuchsia flowering season is longer than for most shrubs, being from early summer to late autumn. This makes fuchsias an ideal garden plant, mostly needing sheltered positions and fertile, moist, but well-drained soil. Gro-wel fuchsias are displayed in beds flanking a winding pathway edged with ponga and complemented with other plantings, including rosemary, pansies, forget-me-nots, alyssum, geums, foxgloves, cinerarias, lavender, roses and red kaka-beak. Established native mahoe trees provide dappled shade over some of the garden. The pathway leads to an extensive shade house where hanging baskets, standards and other fuchsias are displayed. A topiary collection, mainly birds, adds interest.

145

TUPARE
New Plymouth

Manager:
Greg Rine, QE II National Trust

Address: 487 Mangorei Rd, New Plymouth
Postal: P O Box 40, Kaponga
Directions: Travel 7km south of New Plymouth, on Mangorei Rd to Waiwhakaiho River, just before SH 3. Garden on left
Phone: 0-6-758 6480
Fax: 0-6-758 6480
Open: Main season: 1 September to 31 March, 9am–5pm
Winter season: 1 April to 31 August
Groups: As above
Fee: $5 per adult; group discount $4.50 per head
Size: Large – 3.6ha (9 acres)
Terrain: Steep and some flat
Nursery: Choice perennials
Functions: Dinner by arrangement

  partial

during Rhododendron Festival in November

This landscaped English-style garden was named Tupare after the tribe that originally lived in the area, appropriately meaning "a garland of flowers". Tupare is noted for its collection of rhododendrons and azaleas, which thrive in the mild climate. A steep site above Waiwhakaiho River was carefully landscaped and planted with trees, including a kauri in 1932, tulip tree and liquidambar. A waterfall was built over four years, with stone-lined pools and stream creating a cascading water garden planted with primulas, hostas and other bog plants. Maples surround a fountain and provide spectacular autumn colour. A wide variety of hardy subtropical trees and exotics of note include a davidia, dawn redwood and *Magnolia campbellii* flowering in winter. A collection of native ferns is supplemented by rimu, and nothofagus or New Zealand beech. A row of *Thuja pyramidalis* conifers stands in front of the cottage built to match the Tudor-style Chapman-Taylor home, now a small function centre, sold by the original owners, Sir Russell and Lady Matthews, to the QE II Trust in 1984. The Matthews family is remembered by an archway into the Elizabeth Garden, the Richard Walk past ivy-covered buttresses above cineraria beds, the Jill Walk, John Walk and Mary Lane. The Dell is planted with woodland perennials which flower in summer, with the Rose Garden planted more formally.

146

HIKURANGI
Okato

Owner:
Barbara Williams

Address: Newall Rd, R D 37, Okato
Directions: Travel south of New
Plymouth to west of Mt Taranaki, on
SH 45. Turn left at Okato into Oxford
Rd, then right into Saunders Rd. Turn
right again into Wiremu Rd, then left
into Newall Rd. Hikurangi on right
Phone: 0-6-752 4058
Mobile: 025 451 422
Fax: 0-6-752 4058
Open: Mid October to May, daily;
10am–8pm or dark
Groups: By appointment
Fee: $3 per adult
Size: Large – 2.8ha (7 acres)
Terrain: Varied

 x three   partial

  by arrangement

Hikurangi, meaning "tall mountain", is a large parklike garden with a wonderful backdrop of Mt Taranaki. Pioneered in 1904 from virgin bush, this garden is still being developed by Barbara, who has lived here for four decades. This diverse garden comprises a drier area in the older part, with historic points of interest, and newer areas including water gardens. Barbara likes to take her visitors on a tour beginning in the historic 1906 woolshed, which houses a small museum, then walking through the large new native planting including lancewood, pohutukawa and many rare named species. Pathways wind down around the large lake and up past the stream to an old tunnel where a mill supplied electric power in 1906. Paths lead up past a new alpine rockery to the old garden around the house, then down to the newer areas with wide grassed walkways between beds of perennials, with azaleas, rhododendrons and a ponga pergola. Colours change with the seasons, camellias and daffodils announcing spring, then lilies, dahlias and annuals flowering in summer, followed by autumn chrysanthemums. The lake area is being developed, with smaller ponds and a river. A woodland area with tall tree ferns is underplanted with bog plants. Glow-worms feature in the tunnel area in the evenings, and along the banks leading to the tunnel.

PUKEITI
New Plymouth

Owner:
Pukeiti Rhododendron Trust

Address: 2290 Carrington Rd, R D 4,
New Plymouth
Directions: Travel 20km from New
Plymouth, on Carrington Rd. Garden
on right
Phone: 0-6-752 4141 (24 hours)
Fax: 0-6-752 4143
Open: All year, daily, except
Christmas Day, 9am–5pm
Groups: As above or by appointment
Fee: $6 per adult; group discounts
Size: Large – 20ha (50 acres) of
garden in 360ha (900 acres) of land
Terrain: Undulating
Nursery: Rhododendrons, azaleas,
camellias and woodland plants
Restaurant: The Gatehouse on site,
available for weddings & functions
Shop: Souvenirs, crafts and other gifts
at the Gatehouse shop

 mostly

Pukeiti means "little hill", referring to its site on the
foothills of Mt Taranaki. The first 150 of the present
900 acres were purchased by Douglas Cook in 1951, and
a Trust was formed by 23 rhododendron enthusiasts to
develop the rhododendron park. Pukeiti now boasts the
largest collection of species and hybrid rhododendrons
and azaleas in New Zealand. These flower all year, vireya
tropical rhododendrons in late summer, autumn and winter,
with hardy types continuing in spring and early summer.
A new covered walk and Perrott House provide shelter for
the extensive vireya collection, with orchids and other
rare plants. Hybrids are scattered throughout the hills and
valleys of Pukeiti, concentrated in the Hybrid Block, with
New Zealand-raised hybrids in Stead Block, and large-
leafed species in the Valley of the Giants. Founders Garden
features native planting, with countless complementary
shrubs and plants flowering throughout the year, and
rhododendrons underplanted with many damp-loving
specimens. Exotic trees include magnolias, viburnums,
camellias, cornus, prunus, acers and kalmias. The gardens
are surrounded by native rainforest with bush walks
throughout, and a rimu plantation flanks Pukeiti Hill. Two
garden pools, with viewing platforms, are filled by natural
mountain streams that also power a water wheel, which
pumps water to the property.

NGAMAMAKU
Oakura

Owners:
Tony Barnes and John Sole

Address: 781 Main South Rd,
Oakura, R D 4
Directions: Take SH 45 west from
New Plymouth. Travel 4km past
Oakura. Ngamamaku on left, next to
Egmont National Park
Phone: 0-6-752 7873
Open: During October/November
Rhododendron Festival; and 1 August
to 31 March, by appointment
Groups: By appointment
Fee: $3 per adult
Size: Medium – 1.2ha (3 acres)
Terrain: Flat and sloping
Functions: Available for functions by
prior arrangement
Accommodation: Homestay by prior
arrangement

 mostly
by arrangement

Ngamamaku, meaning "the Place of the Tree Ferns", is a richly historic site adjoining Egmont National Park. Battles were fought here during the 1864 Wars, and pre-European stone walling is still a feature. It was later the site of an air force radar base and barracks during World War II. The present garden, with rural views to the Tasman Sea from its elevated position, was begun from nothing in 1986. Ngamamaku is now very sheltered and secluded, being developed on different levels as separate garden rooms, combining to create an harmonious whole. A natural bush stream runs through the centre of the garden, the streamside dell planted with a wide range of damp-loving perennials in delicate, restful colours. Magnolias, acers, azaleas, rhododendrons, camellias and hostas in great variety are feature plants, combining successfully with the bush and mamaku tree ferns. Native birds abound, and pathways wind through the bush, across the stream and up to a tranquil pond area. A formal paved rose garden, a memorial to John's parents, features a central statue and seats within a circular ponga pergola. Nearby is a large circular aviary. A rockery and pool are screened by a curved avenue of *Thuja pyramidalis*. A unique arched summer house opens on to a formal lawn, enclosed by roses and hedges. This leads into a natural native nikau palm bush walk.

DUDLIS' SWISS BEGONIA GARDENS
Kaponga

Owners:
Margrit and Ruedi Dudli

Address: Eltham Rd, R D 29, Kaponga
Directions: Turn west at Eltham, travel along Eltham Rd 16km to Awatuna; Begonia Gardens on left
Phone: 0-6-274 5624
Open: 1 January to 31 May, weather permitting, by appointment
Groups: By appointment
Fee: $2 per adult, $1 per child
Size: Medium – 0.6ha (1½ acres)
Terrain: Flat front garden and steep gully
Nursery: Begonias, ground covers eg Irish moss, succulents

   mostly

The colourful summer garden surrounding the Dudlis' Swiss home has been planted by Margrit over the past 15 years. Once she had established the borders in Swiss colours, predominantly red, with tuberous begonias the main species, Margrit turned her attention to the swamp down the gully behind the house. Over the past decade she has transformed this into a colourful series of paths and terraces, with steps and bridges for navigating the wet areas. Again red begonias feature, with contrasting vivid green edgings of Irish moss. Damp-loving gunneras and flaxes flourish, with red cannas and hostas under ponga tree ferns and other trees. Big clumps of toetoe enjoy the gully. Fibrous begonias join the tuberous varieties, with yellows and whites complementing the reds in the top garden. Passers-by are drawn to this eye-catching garden with its bed of begonias, dahlias and pelargoniums outside the front fence. Window boxes and balcony boxes of the single scarlet multiflora "Flamboyant" begonias brighten the Swiss house. A bed of conifers contrasts with the brick-edged begonia beds, pierced by standard roses at regular intervals. White alyssum borders a red bed, and a novelty garden of Snow White and her seven dwarfs attracts children. Margrit will also dress in Swiss national costume and Ruedi will play his alphona by arrangement.

HOLLARD GARDENS
Kaponga

Manager:
Greg Rine, QE II National Trust

Address: Upper Manaia Rd, Kaponga
Postal: P O Box 40, Kaponga
Directions: From Stratford, travel
14km west along Opunake Rd. Turn
left into Upper Manaia Rd
Phone: 0-6-764 6544
After Hours: 0-6-764 6616
Fax: 0-6-764 6544
Open: Main season: 1 September to
31 March, 9am–5pm
Winter season: 1 April to 31 August
Groups: By appointment preferred
Fee: $5 per adult; 10% group
discount for 10 persons or more
Size: Large – 4ha (10 acres)
Terrain: Easy contour
Nursery: In spring – rhododendrons,
perennials

   & to toilet

The Hollard Gardens were gifted to the Queen Elizabeth II Trust in 1982 by Bernard and Rose Hollard to ensure their future protection and enjoyment. The original garden was reclaimed from bush in 1927, with swampland in 1947. A new garden, developed from pastureland since 1981, incorporates views of Mt Taranaki and plantings amid sweeping lawns edged with cherry trees, in contrast to the older woodland garden with its narrower twisting pathways, providing surprises round each corner. The climate in Kaponga favours azaleas and rhododendrons, and Bernie Hollard bred the bold red rhododendron "Kaponga", flowering in early spring with the clipped azalea hedges. Rhododendrons flourish under the canopy of woodland trees with ferns, camellias, kalmias, pieris and arbutus. Heaths and heathers abound with many groundcovers, including tiny-leafed native gunneras. Large-leafed rhododendron species and magnolias flower in winter. Established trees include many endangered indigenous species, as well as deciduous exotics. A rare New Zealand passion vine (*Passiflora tetrandra*) winds serpentlike up tawa trees on the bush walk. Old-fashioned perennials include aquilegias, agapanthus, anemones and *Aconitum napellus*, and the bog garden features primulas and hostas. A pond and an endangered native plants garden are being developed.

WOODHILL
Stratford

Owners:
Elaine and John Nicholls

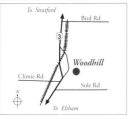

Address: Mountain Rd South, SH 3, Stratford, R D 23
Directions: Travel 2.5km south of Stratford's Pioneer Village. Garden just before Ngaere overbridge on left. Or travel north of Eltham, just past Ngaere overbridge. Garden on right
Phone: 0-6-765 5497
Open: All year, daily, 9am–5pm
Groups: Facilities for retreats and seminars; venue for wedding photography
Fee: $3 per adult
Size: Medium – 0.8ha (2 acres)
Terrain: Mainly flat, with banked area around house
Accommodation: B&B or homestay

  by arrangement

A winding tree-lined driveway reveals tantalising views of the Nicholls' garden along its axis in all seasons. Autumn brings a magnificent golden show, from the ginkgo tree overshadowing the new waterlily pond to the pin oaks reflected red in the swimming pool. Nearby four unusually tall *Picea albertiana* stand sentinel. Even winter has its moment, with giant Himalayan lilies (*Cardiocrinum giganteum*) like huge creamy bells with deep red throats. Early spring is predominantly blue, with ground cover of forget-me-nots and bluebells being joined by the pink/red palette of camellias, azaleas and rhododendrons. Spring also brings magnolias to the fore, with festoons of wisteria and clematis. Hostas and trilliums thrive in this English woodland garden, with aquilegias, white honesty, digitalis and irises abounding. Then summer features old-fashioned roses, creamy dogwood (*Cornus kousa*) and cool shades of greens, especially in the dell. The Nicholls' garden was begun 32 years before they moved in, back in 1956, so is blessed with established trees. Some, such as a huge macrocarpa, are probably as old as the house, which was built in 1886 by Chapman-Taylor's father. A restful peacefulness pervades the garden today, making it a popular venue for retreats, seminars and homestays. Picnickers can enjoy the garden from tables and chairs under sun umbrellas.

BUSHY PARK
Kai Iwi

Owner:
Bushy Park Homestead & Forest Trust

Address: Rangitatau East Rd, Kai Iwi,
R D 8, Wanganui
Directions: Take SH 3 and travel 18km
to Kai Iwi. Turn right into Rangitatau
East Rd. Travel 8km to garden on left
Phone: 0-6-342 9879
Fax: 0-6-342 9879
Open: Daily, 10am–5pm
Groups: As above
Fee: $3 per adult, $1 per child aged
7–16 years, family concessions;
includes access to historic homestead
Size: Medium – 1.2 ha (3 acres)
plus 42.8ha (214 acres) native bush
Terrain: Terraced lawns, sloping
Nursery: Pending eg golden totara
Attraction: Forest Interpretation Centre
in historic stables
Accommodation: Historic homestead
sleeps 15; self-contained bunkhouse
sleeps 10 people
Restaurant: Fully licensed – lunch/dinner

🐕 🚻 🥣 🍽 ♿ & to bush

The gardens at Bushy Park Homestead were
landscaped by I. Cameron in 1906 when Frank
Moore had his classical-style house built on the summit
of the hill there, with expansive views across the countryside
to the Rangitikei plains beyond. A native backdrop of
89 hectares of subtropical rainforest features tall canopy
trees, predominantly rata, tawa, pukatea, and rimu, with
miro, matai, kahikatea, and five species of tree ferns. Tracks
throughout include one leading to New Zealand's largest
northern rata. Epiphytes growing on trees are collospermum,
astelias, native orchids, and puka, with many native climbers.
Further indigenous species growing in the gardens round
the homestead include weeping rimu, puriri, and kowhai.
Frank Moore assisted in planting the original trees, including
two kauri. A golden totara was planted in 1963 after the
Royal Forest and Bird Society took over the management
of Bushy Park. Native birdlife abounds. Terraced lawns in
front of the homestead lead to an arboretum of native
species, which are complemented with exotics. In spring
camellias and rhododendrons flower with kowhai and
kaka-beak. *Kniphofia* and agapanthus brighten the edge of
the lawn in summer and hydrangeas bloom down the
800-metre driveway lined with mature exotics, tall rata
and mamaku tree ferns. An adjacent area features a wetland
pond. Accommodation and a restaurant are available.

THE WAIRARAPA REGION

The Wairarapa lies south of Hawke's Bay, on the east coast. Pastureland, orchards and vineyards flourish in the typical east coast sunshine of the Wairarapa. This wide strip of fertile land to the east of the Tararua Range is very dry and almost Mediterranean in its extremes of climate, from hot summers to cold, frosty winters.

The 11 Wairarapa gardens featured extend from Borderlands at the foot of the Pahiatua Track, east of Palmerston North, with its extensive woodland and beautiful creek, down through the Masterton district, where most of the gardens are situated, on to Awaiti, the Carterton garden sited on almost two and a half hectares of land, with a recently restored colonial cottage tearoom. Then past Featherston down to Lake Wairarapa, where there is Prairie Holm to visit on the western shore, developed around established natives.

The Masterton gardens cover an extensive area, beginning on the outskirts with Fleetwood Gardens and Nursery, specialising in perennials. Tussie Mussie is a small urban garden which developed around an interest in making tussie mussies. Three gardens up the Bideford Valley to the east are diverse, with Te Roto offering accommodation at Acorn Cottage, a restored colonial cottage with food provided, Dursley, a restored Buxton garden, and Rata Hills, a clifftop garden with a steep gully terraced for more sheltered plantings. Two more gardens along the Castlepoint Road provide further interest. Abbotsford Garden and Nursery specialises in hardy perennials, and Beauley, with a dry plateau above a woodland dell, is known for its coloured sheep.

Another garden, not to be missed, down towards Gladstone, south-east of Carterton, is Te Whanga, an English-style garden planted in 1956, with avenues framing vistas to the hills and a woodland gully underplanted with bulbs, lilies and cyclamen. Altogether these 11 Wairarapa gardens feature a great range of plants in different settings, from cottage gardens to sculpturally designed landscapes.

Public Botanical Gardens can also be visited in the Wairarapa, including Queen Elizabeth Park in the centre of Masterton, the gardens at Carrington Park in Carterton, which have the historical significance of having been designed by Alfred Buxton early this century, and Greytown's Memorial Park of eight hectares. The steep Rimutaka Range separates the Wairarapa from Wellington.

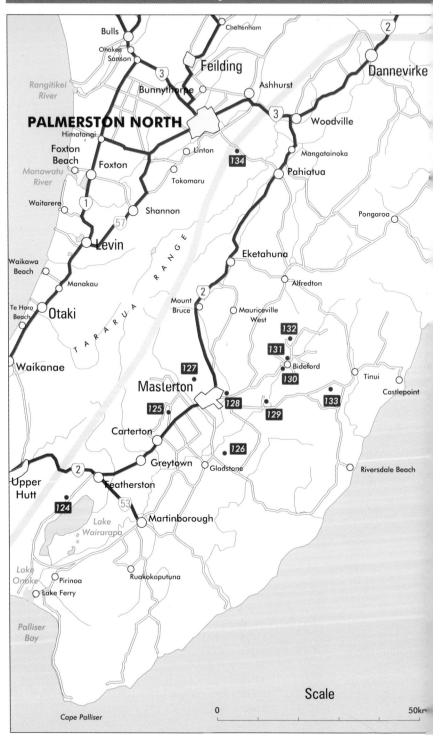

Bulls
Cheltenham
Ohakea
Sanson
Feilding
Dannevirke
3
Bunnythorpe
Ashhurst
PALMERSTON NORTH
3
Woodville
Himatangi
Linton
Mangatainoka
Foxton
Beach
134
Foxton
Pahiatua
Tokomaru
Manawatu
River
Waitarere
Pongaroa
1
Shannon
57
Levin
Eketahuna
Waikawa
Beach
Alfredton
Manakau
2
Te Horo
Beach
Mount
Bruce
Mauriceville
West
132
Otaki
131
Bideford
Tinui
130
Waikanae
127
Castlepoint
Maslerton
128
125
129
133
Carterton
126
Greytown
Gladstone
Riversdale Beach
Upper
Hutt
2
Featherston
124
53
Lake
Wairarapa
Martinborough
Lake
Onoke
Pirinoa
Ruakokoputuna
Lake Ferry
Palliser
Bay

TARARUA RANGE

Rangitikei
River

Scale

0   50km

Cape Palliser

158

PRAIRIE HOLM NURSERY AND GARDENS
Featherston

Owners:
Elaine and Bill Gooding

Address: Western Lake Rd, R D 3,
Featherston
Directions: Travel south from
Featherston, taking Western Lake Rd
for 13km. Garden on right
Phone: 0-6-308 9090 A/H
Mobile: 025 374 932
Fax: 0-6-308 9090
Open: Gardens: all year, daily;
Nursery: 1 July to 30 November
Groups: By appointment
Fee: $3 per adult
Size: Large – 2.4ha (6 acres)
Terrain: Flat
Nursery: Rhododendrons, camellias,
azaleas and a few perennials
Accommodation: Elim Waters chalets
for traumatised people under physical
or emotional stress with special needs

by arrangement

Prairie Holm, named after the children's book *Little House on the Prairie*, has been developed since 1980 around a large grouping of established natives, some planted before World War I. These attract native birds and are underplanted with camellias and rhododendrons. Native tui and wood pigeons feed on tree lucernes planted for shelter from strong northwesterlies and unusual shrubs for windy sites feature. Azaleas begin flowering in winter, with annuals such as polyanthus and violas in the sunken garden. Elaine changes the annual beds each year, colour planting for summer and winter. Above the sunken garden is a bank of perennials with tall purple and rose echiums, a collection of salvias, penstemons and monardas, which thrive in the wind. Further perennials border the nursery. Large plantings of rhododendrons grow in dappled sunlight, including a selection of vireyas. A gazebo is sited in a clearing, and stone-lined paths wind throughout the woodland, with box edging and local stone walls. A rockery by the house is filled with alpines, and another rockery features in the water area, with stonework walls beside two ponds connected by a replica water wheel. A young laburnum arch flowers above, leading to the Elim Waters chalets with dahlias, lilies and perennials. A dovecote stands beside the pines, doves welcoming visitors to Prairie Holm.

AWAITI
Carterton

Owners:
Allan and Jeanette Gates

Address: Chester Rd, R D 1, North
Carterton
Directions: North of Carterton, turn
left into Chester Rd. Travel 2km to
garden on left
Phone: 0-6-379 8478
Open: Garden: open 1 September to
31 May, Tuesday to Sunday,
10am–4pm; plus holiday Mondays
Shop and nursery: open all year
Groups: Welcome, as above
Fee: $3 per adult for garden only
Size: Large – 2.4ha (6 acres)
Terrain: Flat
Nursery: Small nursery – plants from
garden eg perennials and annuals
Shop: Awaiti Gifts selling silk,
porcelain dolls, pot-pourri, china,
dried flowers, etc

Awaiti, meaning "little stream", has evolved around a meandering stream since 1980. Stones from the surrounding farmland are used for lining the waterways and for hand-made walls, with viewing portholes providing glimpses of Japanese irises and lupins beyond. A weir and waterfall are bordered with primulas and lead into pools edged with hostas, astilbes, Japanese irises and azaleas. Jeanette's favourites are the cottage perennials, which grow in abundance in a riot of colourful beds. A lavender walkway borders a rhododendron garden and old totara railings edge the pathways leading out to the lake. Here Allan has crafted a quaint shingle-roofed brick shed and water wheel backed by swamp cypresses and liquidambars. More than 300 rhododendrons are planted among silver birches, ash trees and maples which provide glorious autumn colour. A formal yew-edged rose garden is shaped like a clover leaf around a central wishing well. Clipped *Thuja plicata* "Pyramidalis" separate the garden into lobes and provide a backdrop for the many roses. Archways of climbing roses, pink clematis and mauve wisteria provide viewing frames for vistas of cherry blossom. White fantail pigeons, doves and peacock complement the garden. The original 130-year-old farm cottage is being converted into tearooms surrounded by cottage garden, including two 100-year-old camellia trees.

TE WHANGA
Masterton

Owners:
Robin and Robin Borthwick

Address: Te Kopi Rd, R D 4,
Masterton
Directions: From Masterton, take
Gladstone Rd for 15km, turn left into
Te Kopi Rd. Travel 6km to garden at
end of road, veering right up
driveway
Phone: 0-6-372 7728
Fax: 0-6-372 7798
Open: All year, by appointment
Groups: By appointment, as above
Fee: $5 per adult
Size: Large – 3.2ha (8 acres)
Terrain: Rolling and gullies

 by arrangement

Te Whanga is a garden of vistas in the tradition of the English country garden, planned by Robin's parents in 1956, from bare paddock. Open lawn spaces are balanced with woodland gullies and two long grassy avenues retain vistas to the hills. Broad grass walkways lined with camellias and agapanthus lead to the gully, with established trees merging above. Massed clivias surround a circular courtyard and beyond, rhododendrons including large leafed species grow among maples and oaks, underplanted with fuchsias and ferns. A rare Mexican *Chierostomen pentadactylon* or Devil's Claw, aptly named after its leathery red flowers, blooms in November. Across a bridge are weeping *Acer palmatum* "Dissectum" with cymbidium orchids throughout the woodland. Drifts of bluebells and single snowdrops carpet the woodland in spring, then *Cardiocrinum giganteum* provide summer colour. But autumn is peaktime, with drifts of naturalised *Cyclamen hederifolium* beneath the deciduous foliage. The black leaves of a weeping copper beech, *Fagus sylvatica* "Pendula Purpurea", turn coppery beside the weeping Japanese maples that line the terrace in front of the house. Winter features poinsettias and three large *Magnolia campbellii*, while in summer a huge *Bougainvillea* "Scarlet O'Hara" blooms beside the house, with beds of roses beyond.

FLEETWOOD GARDENS AND NURSERY
Masterton

Owners:
Deborah Tutty and Julia Tutty

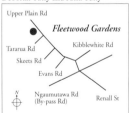

Address: Upper Plain Rd, R D 8, Masterton
Directions: From Masterton, take Renall St north. Continue 5.7km from By-pass Road. Garden on left
Phone: 0-6-378 8340
Open: All year, daily, 9am–5pm
Closed: Christmas Day
Groups: By appointment
Fee: No charge
Size: Medium – 0.8ha (2 acres), plus developing ½ acre
Terrain: Flat
Shop: Craft, self-serve cool drinks, tea and coffee facilities
Nursery: Over 600 varieties perennials, climbers, rhododendrons, azaleas, camellias, natives

A mother and daughter team run this nursery and country garden surrounding the century-old house, although Julia has only designed and planted the garden in the past six years. It was originally a riverbed, so buckets of rocks had to be removed before the peastraw and manure were laid down for planting the perennials. The Tuttys' favourites are perennials, with over 600 varieties for sale. The plants in the nursery can be seen in the garden which flows from one area to another, separated by grassy paths. Husband Andrew's patch includes a wet area under trees and a pagoda he built. A new area in front of the nursery has been designed by Rachel Callaghan to feature a pond surrounded by a bog garden. The Tuttys enjoy a range of colours, not just pastels, with a white area in the shady spot under the trees. Spring features camellias, daffodils, flowering cherries, dogwoods, rhododendrons, azaleas, wisteria and early annuals. Roses accompany all the summer perennials until autumn when the exotic trees, especially prunus and maples, colour up. In winter, the deciduous trees contrast with evergreens, including indigenous species. Fleetwood sell a lot of indigenous species, especially native grasses.

TUSSIE MUSSIE GARDEN
Masterton

Owners:
Beth and Ross Sutherland

Address: 6 Cooper St, Masterton
Directions: North of Masterton, turn
right down the Castlepoint Rd, then
first left into Cooper St. Tussie
Mussie Garden on right
Phone: 0-6-377 3473
Open: Most days
Groups: By appointment
Fee: $3 per adult
Size: Small – 0.05ha (⅛ acre)
Terrain: Flat
Nursery: Herbs, violas, lavenders,
climbers, and unusual plants from
garden
Shop: Beth's paintings & tussie
mussies for sale

by arrangement

This intensively planted garden filled with small
flowers and foliage developed around Beth's interest
in making tussie mussies. After the Sutherlands left their
farm in 1982, Beth established many scented and old-
fashioned varieties in this small retirement cottage garden,
extending it to include herbs. The flowers inspire Beth's
paintings, so she chooses her colours carefully, enjoying
rich but not garish combinations, including greens, pinks,
blues, wine red, lemon and whites. Spring bulbs are
complemented with camellias, apple blossom, *Magnolia
stellata*, dogwood, and a Judas tree. Beth's favourite old
roses climb over pergolas, arbour, gateways and garage.
Bougainvillea brightens the front entrance in summer,
when hanging baskets of begonias and many potted plants
bloom with Beth's unusual old perennials. Autumn features
an ornamental grape and *Prunus subhirtella* "Autumnalis",
which blossoms in winter. A little circular bricked fish
pond in the front garden planted with waterlilies and irises
provides a tranquil spot where the Sutherlands enjoy
watching raindrops on the water on a wet day. Bonsai grow
round a bird-bath nearby. Ross has developed a native
fern area next to a rangiora with banksia climbing through
it. Other natives include rata, tree fuchsia, lancewood,
kowhai, *Brachyglottis compactus* and *B. greyi* (formerly
B. senecio).

ABBOTSFORD GARDEN AND NURSERY
Masterton

Owners:
Tim and Penny Bunny

Address: R D 9, Masterton
Directions: From Masterton, turn off SH 2 into Castlepoint Rd. Travel 10 minutes, then turn left into Abbotsford Rd. Garden on right
Phone: 0-6-378 8763
Fax: 0-6-378 2829
Open: March to May, and September to Christmas; Saturdays only, 10am–5pm; also Labour Weekend (end October) and Easter; other times by appointment
Groups: By appointment
Fee: $3 per adult
Size: Medium – 0.8ha (2 acres)
Terrain: Flat
Nursery: Specialising in hardy plants good for massing, easy care; bulbs, perennials eg lavenders, penstemons, cranesbills

by arrangement

The Bunnys have developed Abbotsford over the past two decades around a 120-year-old house, the original garden overgrown and lost. Nowadays old roses climb over surrounding fences and archways of inner garden rooms, designed with borders in sunny and shady areas. Outer rooms feature formal walks, such as the cherry walk, with a pergola opening into a new lavender-and-box-hedged rondel. An avenue of pin oaks through a paddock provides rural vistas to hills beyond. Predominant colours at Abbotsford are greens, greys and white. Penny loves splashes of yellow among plants grown for form, texture and design, particularly grey and silver foliage. Spring bulbs are accompanied by clematis and flowering shrubs, including viburnum, hydrangea and a philadelphus collection. Aquilegias abound, and many peonies flower mid November. A good selection of lavenders and plants of Mediterranean origin suited to hot, dry conditions flourish in summer. Cool autumn nights result in bright foliage on deciduous trees and shrubs. Penny is particularly keen on bare-wood-flowering shrubs such as winter sweets, witch hazel, japonicas and corylopsis. She specialises in hardy perennials, especially nicotianas, penstemons, cranesbill geraniums, salvias, euphorbias and massing plants suited to difficult areas. A formal Tuscan pool is planned.

TE ROTO
Masterton

Owners:
Di and Tom Bunny

Address: Bideford, R D 11, Masterton
Directions: Turn east off SH 2 into
Castlepoint Rd. Turn left into SH 52,
then up Bideford Valley. 15 minutes
from Masterton. Fire Number 14
Phone: 0-6-372 4800
Fax: 0-6-372 4800
Open: 1 October to end April, daily,
10am–6pm, by appointment
Groups: By appointment, as above
Fee: $3 per adult
Size: Medium – 1ha (2½ acres)
Terrain: Mostly flat with gently
sloped bank
Accommodation: Acorn Cottage
(restored colonial cottage) by
arrangement; everything including
food supplied

  mostly

 by arrangement

Te Roto gardens began early in the century, when Tom's grandparents planted a Wellingtonia (*Sequoiadendron giganteum*), lawsoniana and several acorns which are now large oaks. Di and Tom have extended the garden since 1987, planting a sunken garden round the swimming pool to create a quiet, peaceful spot out of the wind. A walled tennis court has varieties of Virginia creeper around it, with roses and wisterias climbing over the walls. Di is mad on autumn colour, the Virginia creeper turning bright red, an ash tree golden, smoke bushes deep red, maples and cherries brilliant too. After winter, camellias bloom, then the chartreuse *Prunus* "Ukon" and copse of frothy pink *Prunus serrulata* "Shimidsu Sakura" blossom beside Acorn Cottage, with silver birches and dogwoods. Rhododendrons are carpeted with bluebells and snowdrops in spring, then *Cyclamen neapolitanum* in autumn. Old roses bloom in summer, with lots of aquilegias, phlox and daisies, the warmth of pink being lightened by blues which provide depth of colour. In a wetland bog area, Di grows hostas, astilbes and gunneras. Old roses climb over an archway here, with terraced banks of perennials and roses behind, so that the vista can be seen from Acorn Cottage, the restored colonial cottage, available for accommodation. In 1994 a wildfowl pond was developed.

DURSLEY
Masterton

Owner:
Judith Callaghan

Address: Bideford, R D 11, Masterton
Directions: Turn east off SH 2 into Castlepoint Rd. Turn left into SH 52, then up Bideford Valley, past Te Roto garden. Dursley on left. 18 minutes from Masterton
Phone: 0-6-372 4804
Open: September to April (Fathers' Day to Anzac Day), 10.30am–6pm, daily
Groups: As above
Fee: $3 per adult
Size: Medium – 1.2ha (3 acres)
Terrain: Flat with small terrace
Tours: Combined catered tours can be arranged with Te Roto and Historic Church

  mostly

  by arrangement

In 1916 Alfred Buxton designed the garden, then known as Te Rangi Pai. The name was changed to Dursley in the 1930s, but the lines of Buxton's landscaping are still apparent today. A 1917 arbutus and weeping birch give stature, with some original rose bushes featuring among the 300 now growing throughout the garden. Many other established trees, underplanted with naturalised bulbs, form a woodland carpeted with spring bulbs, including daffodils, bluebells, galanthus and grape hyacinths, then drifts of cyclamens in autumn. Long views under the trees are retained in a natural, not contrived way, with pathways through deciduous azaleas, rhododendrons, camellias and tree peonies, their bright colours downplayed by shadows from the canopy overhead. In summer, "Turk's Cap" lilies or *L. martagon* feature throughout the woodland area, and a very large clump of *Romneya coulteri* or California "tree" poppy is striking in full bloom. Three herbaceous borders are sited to provide views from the house. When the Callaghans took over the garden in 1972 they removed seven truckloads of debris before beginning to recover the garden area around the flowing driveway. Care has been taken not to plant out the panoramic views to the hills, with seats abounding for visitors to sit and listen to the birds in the quiet, tranquil atmosphere.

RATA HILLS
Masterton

Owner:
Erroll Warren

Address: The Tanglewood Rd,
Bideford Valley, Masterton
Directions: 28km from SH 2. Take
Castlepoint Rd, turn left into SH 52,
then up Bideford Valley past Te Roto,
and Dursley. Then turn left into
Tanglewood Rd. Garden on right
Phone: 0-6-372 4834
Fax: 0-6-372 4818
Open: September to May, dawn to
dark, daily, by appointment
Groups: By appointment
Fee: $3 per adult
Size: Large – 2ha accessible (5 acres
garden); 5ha including native bush
Terrain: Flat and steep terraced
Nursery: Cuttings given; some plants
for sale

   to flat area

  by arrangement

Few rata remain of those originally covering Rata Hills. Instead, a century-old creamy-cupped *Magnolia grandiflora* is the focal point on the front lawn with giant kanuka and waratahs, an oak, liquidambar and maple. This is a garden of great contrast, from the dry windy clifftop, down a steeply terraced gorge to native bush in the gully below. Erroll has gardened the plateau above the cliff for two decades, and the gorge for one, in order to create a wind-free area. In 1987 pines covering the steep slope were removed, causing a huge slip to occur six years later. This destroyed much of Erroll's plantings, but, undaunted, she is rebuilding terraces, with lavender hedging and handrails forming elegant lines and a sense of scale when viewed from above. Here a claret ash walk leads to where a gazebo will provide shelter from the lookout, over to the opposite side, which Erroll planted in Formosan lilies by abseiling all over the rock face. Native woodland is underplanted with nearly 200 rhododendrons, and hostas feature throughout the gorge. Many olearias flower through to summer, when Erroll's favourite lily-like cardiocrinums bloom. She also loves gentians and mixed perennials, with trilliums and Chatham Island forget-me-nots flourishing. Old roses feature with massed agapanthus, contrasting with the leucadendrons on the clifftop.

BEAULEY
Masterton

Owners:
Phyllis and Bill French

Address: R D 9, Masterton
Directions: Turn off SH 2 at
Masterton into Castlepoint Rd.
Continue for 33km. Beauley on right,
10km past Riversdale turn-off
Phone: 0-6-372 6824
Open: All year, daily, any time
Groups: Buses welcome, as above
Fee: $3 per adult; honesty box if
away
Size: Medium – 0.4ha (1 acre)
Terrain: Flat and sloping
Shop: Natural wool, sheep rugs, and
wool products for sale; spinning open
day second Thursday every month

   mostly

  by arrangement

Beauley garden is sited on a plateau surrounded by century-old English trees with a backdrop of steep, unusual shaped taipo hills and native bush. A driveway loops up in front of the house, then down past a woodland dell where Phyllis grows bearded and Japanese irises and fuchsias. In contrast is the stony dry plateau, where Phyllis mingles formality with cottage beds, her favourite roses growing amid perennials and self-seeding annuals. She alternates rose bushes with camellias, the latter easy-care and flowering in spring, followed by roses in summer that need much care. Beneath spread hundreds of naturalised pansies in soft mauves. Apart from the roses, a perennial border in front of the house is filled with old aquilegias, delphiniums, peonies, Michaelmas daisies, arthropodiums and flaming-bracted euphorbias. Hippeastrum flower in tubs, followed by tuberous begonias in January. Lavateras and dahlias brighten summer beds, and autumn bulbs such as nerines bloom underneath colourful deciduous foliage. Birds are attracted to established trees, including a monkey puzzle (*Araucaria imbricata*), Himalayan cedar, walnut, *Liriodendron tulipifera* and gleditsias. A field of daffodils behind the house flowers in spring, with tulips and camellias. The orchard blossoms and Beauley's famous black and coloured lambs frisk over the hills.

BORDERLANDS
Pahiatua

Owner:
Romayne Abraham

Address: Makomako, R D 3, Pahiatua
Directions: Turn off SH 2 at Pahiatua
and travel west 17km towards
Palmerston North, to Borderlands at
foot of Pahiatua Track on left. Or
travel 18km from Palmerston North
Phone: 0-6-376 7071
Open: Last weekend in August to
end April; weekends, public holidays
and when "open" sign displayed;
10.30am–5pm; mid December to end
April by appointment
Groups: By appointment; bus parking
Fee: $4 per adult
Size: Large – 2.5ha (6–7 acres)
Terrain: Flat and steps to lower levels
Nursery: Many perennials and bulbs,
sometimes trees and shrubs

     mostly

 by arrangement

When the Abrahams moved to Borderlands in 1961, they inherited roadside oaks, large totara, *Acer palmatum*, poplars, lacebarks, pines and the inevitable macrocarpas. A beautiful creek flowed through the garden, now featuring huge *Gunnera tinctoria* contrasting with delicate maple foliage above. An old brick fireplace converted into a pond area by Romayne's late husband, Nigel, now features standard wisteria and weeping maples above waterlilies, irises, pontederia and hostas. Initial plantings of rhododendrons in 1967 are limbed up to accommodate underplanting. Form, texture and colour is carefully considered, with many deciduous trees chosen solely for autumn foliage, others for sculptural trunks, bark, or fragrance. Borderlands is not a pastel garden, Romayne choosing the full spectrum from gentle colours to vibrant combinations, such as the scarlet Chilean firebush (*Embothrium coccineum* "Longifolium"), entwined with creamy *Pandorea pandorana*. A grassy walkway opens into a glade where waratah, *Telopea speciosissima* "Flaming Beacon", echoes a red rhododendron. Romayne prefers the gentleness of rhododendron species, such as creamy *Rhododendron supranubium*, rather than hybrids. In summer, soft light filters through the deciduous trees, adorned with climbing roses, clematis and wisteria. Vistas have been retained to the nearby hills.

KAPITI COAST AND WELLINGTON

Over the exposed Rimutaka Range from the Wairarapa are the final six North Island gardens, in the Wellington region. Wellington is the capital city of New Zealand, situated on the southern tip of the North Island, separated from the South Island by the Cook Strait.

The Kapiti Coast extends down the west coast from Manakau, south of Levin, to Waikanae, north of Wellington. At Otaki, on this coastline, is Totara Grove, with its native totara forest enhanced with shade-loving plants and rose gardens surrounding the house where pot-pourri is made. Blue Heron, at Waikanae, features mature rhododendrons, camellias, magnolias and eucalypts. These West Coast gardens are much wetter than those in the east, although they are sheltered from prevailing westerlies by Kapiti Island. The Tararua Range lies to the east of the Kapiti Coast. Market gardening is popular in the Otaki area, and the soil around Waikanae is rich, but generally full of river stones.

South of Waikanae in Wellington itself four private gardens are featured, the two northern-most being in the Akatarawa Range, halfway between Waikanae and Upper Hutt. Moss Green is a haven for rhododendrons and other plants that enjoy the cool, moist conditions and Efil Doog (or "Good Life" spelt in reverse) is a Sculpture Park again featuring the rhododendrons that flourish here. Contemporary sculpture is displayed in this garden and an added attraction for art lovers is its private gallery specialising in early New Zealand paintings. The clear Akatarawa River flows through both these gardens.

In the Ngauranga Gorge en route to the city is Newlands Alpine Garden, an urban garden planted predominantly in native alpines. The southernmost garden in the North Island is Sudbury, over towards the west coast in Ohariu Valley, featuring rhododendrons and native around a stream-fed lake. The climate in Wellington is notorious for its gale-force winds funnelling through Cook Strait and its steep, hilly terrain. But gardens nevertheless survive tucked away in sheltered spots or with established trees breaking the winds. The climate here is colder than up north, with frosts in winter.

Attractive public gardens include the extensive Botanical Gardens in Kelburn, established in 1869, with their popular tulip displays in early October, and the adjoining Lady Norwood Rose Gardens, a Begonia House, a Herb Garden and a tower building housing the Education and Environment Centre. Nearby, in Wadestown, is the Otari Native Botanic Garden featuring over 1,200 native species.

The South Island is visible from Wellington on clear days and can be reached by the ferry service. Cars are taken on most of the ferries which average about three hours to cross Cook Strait. Advance ferry bookings are advisable. Most of the Interisland ferries land at Picton giving the motorist the option of travelling down the Marlborough east coast towards Christchurch, or across to Nelson where there are also many attractive gardens. The Marlborough Sounds are directly accessible from Picton, featuring further gardens. Fast ferries operate in calm weather across the Strait, with another sailing direct to Nelson from the Kapiti Coast.

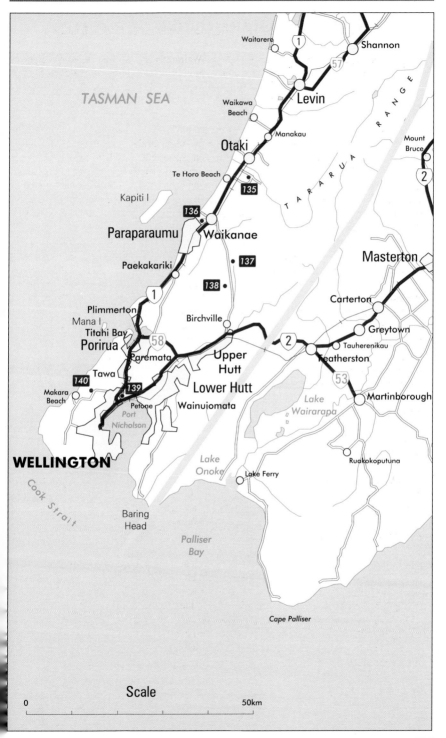

TASMAN SEA

Waitarere

1

57

Shannon

Waikawa
Beach

Levin

Manakau

Otaki

Mount
Bruce

Te Horo Beach

135

2

Kapiti I

136

Paraparaumu

Waikanae

TARARUA RANGE

Masterton

Paekakariki

137

138

1

Carterton

Plimmerton

Birchville

Greytown

Mana I

Titahi Bay

Porirua

58

2

Tauherenikau

Upper
Hutt

Featherston

Paremata

53

Tawa

140

139

Lower Hutt

Martinborough

Makara
Beach

Petone

Wainuiomata

Lake
Wairarapa

Port
Nicholson

WELLINGTON

Lake
Onoke

Lake Ferry

Ruakokoputuna

Cook Strait

Baring
Head

Palliser
Bay

Cape Palliser

Scale

0

50km

175

TOTARA GROVE
Otaki

Owners:
Helen and Hugh Guthrie

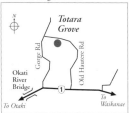

Address: Old Hautere Rd, R D, Otaki
Directions: Travel 1km south of
Otaki. Turn left off SH 1 into Old
Hautere Rd. Garden on left
Phone: 0-6-364 3394
Fax: 0-6-364 3394
Open: Labour Weekend (late
October) and last weekend in
November; other times by
appointment
Groups: By appointment
Fee: $4 per adult; $3 per person for
groups
Size: Medium – 1.3ha (3¼ acres)
Terrain: Flat
Nursery: Roses
Shop: Pot-pourri, fragrant oils, etc

 by arrangement

Totara Grove features coastal totara over a century old, with native beech, matai, kohekohe and titoki, interlaced with native clematis. When the Guthries took over the property in 1986, Helen had room to express her love of roses, after the wandering Jew was removed and the stony soil improved. Spaces were cleared in the woodland, the edges planted with rhododendrons, mollis azaleas, camellias and ornamental trees, underplanted with arthropodiums and groundcover such as campanulas. A weeping "Sanders White" rose features in a glade with tree ferns as a backdrop, near a white and grey garden. Hostas grow along a fern walk, and clivias flourish in the woodland shade, the only orange in the garden blend of pinks, reds, yellows, salmons and apricots. Helen's passion for roses is evident in her collection of over 400 miniatures, new and old roses, as well as David Austin varieties. Roses climb archways, trelliswork, fences, trees and gazebos. They are constrained within different areas, those around a kidney-shaped pond beneath flowering cherries enclosed by box hedging, and roses along the driveway softened with "Pedunculata" lavender edging. An alcove under an archway of "Banksia alba" features a statue of Diana, with box bordering the modern hybrid roses. Helen's rose pot-pourri perfumes the atmosphere around the house.

BLUE HERON
Waikanae

Owners:
Irene and Cliff Chillingworth

Address: 39 Greenaway Rd,
Waikanae
Directions: At Waikanae lights, turn
west down Te Moana Rd. Travel 2km,
then turn left into Greenaway Rd.
Garden on left
Phone: 0-4-293 6099
Open: By appointment
Groups: By apointment
Fee: $4 per adult
Size: Medium – 1ha (2½ acres)
Terrain: Flat and sloping

  mostly

Blue Heron is a mature woodland garden developed by the Chillingworths over the past three decades. Gums include an original white-barked peppermint *Eucalyptus linearis*, orange-blossomed *E. ficifolia*, and a rare snow gum (*E. niphophila*). A dawn redwood "fossil tree" or *Metasequoia glyptostroboides* features in autumn. Mature rhododendrons abound, with a collection of magnolias and over 250 camellias, Cliff's favourite being "Grace Caple". An open lawn is dominated by Wilson's early fruiting plum, shedding its white petals over a paved patio and bog garden, where Irene has planted candelabra primulas around a small pond. Beyond is weeping *Prunus subhirtella* "Pendula", its curtain of pink blossom veiling the azalea-lined grassy walkway to a purple beech *Fagus sylvatica* "Riversii", with Japanese maples and an old deep pink "Duc de Nassau" azalea, underplanted with clivias. A gazebo is sited under a white *Prunus serrulata* "Shirotae" beside a vivid blue ceanothus. Many natives thrive too, including the robust *Pomaderris kumeraho* "Golden Tainui" in a new sunny area, exposed to salty northwesterlies. Here hardy South African and Australian species are interplanted with ornamental-foliaged indigenous plants. Above a new camellia dell, a group of persimmons colours brilliantly in autumn along with crab apples, including a rare *Malus trilobata*.

MOSS GREEN GARDEN
Akatarawa

Owners:
Bob and Jo Munro

Address: R D 2, Akatarawa, Upper Hutt
Directions: 21km from either Upper Hutt or Waikanae
Phone: 0-4-526 7531
Fax: 0-4-526 7507
Open: September to April, Wednesday to Monday, public and school holidays, 10am–5pm; Tuesday by appointment
Groups: Preferably by appointment
Fee: $5 per adult, $1 per child
Size: Medium – 1.2ha (3 acres)
Terrain: Mostly flat, some hilly
Nursery: Extensive, specialising in damp-loving & plants from garden
Talks: Gardening classes run in autumn/winter; talks given at other venues by request

  partial

Moss Green is nestled among bush-clad hills in a valley, with the clear Akatarawa River running through it. In 1970 it was a paddock of blackberry and bracken, but now it sits comfortably in the surrounding native bush, with natives planted throughout. A natural fernery features tall ponga. Moss Green specialises in plants that enjoy a cool, moist climate. The Himalayan-like conditions suit meconopsis and rhododendrons, especially the large-leafed species flowering down by the river among ferns and giant cardiocrinums that bloom magnificently in December. Indigenous and exotic trees attract birdlife, with native pigeons frequenting the garden. Magnolias, including a large *M. campbellii*, and prunus blossom in spring, with maples and scarlet oaks adding to the autumn colour. Two natural ponds enhance the woodland tranquillity. Two bog gardens are planted appropriately, one in a shady position with hostas, *Primula florindae*, ligularias and huge *Gunnera manicata*; the other in sunlight with ajugas, irises, borage, forget-me-nots and *Polygonum bistorta* "Superbum". The nursery is attractively walled with river rocks near Bob's misting sentinels, copper figures which house misting units. A rose garden features mainly old roses in soft shades; Jo keeps the brighter colours concentrated up by the house, in the herbaceous borders.

EFIL DOOG GARDEN OF ART
Akatarawa

Owners:
Ernest and Shirley Cosgrove

Address: 1995 Akatarawa Rd, Upper Hutt, R D 2
Directions: From Upper Hutt, turn left at Brown Owl into Akatarawa Rd. Travel 12km to garden on left. Or travel 27km from Waikanae to garden on right
Phone: 0-4-526 7924
Fax: 0-4-526 7904
Open: 1 September to 30 April, Wednesday to Sunday, 10am–4.30pm
Groups: Prefer by appointment
Fee: $12 per adult, $6 per child under 15; groups over 20 concession rates
Size: Large – over 4ha (11 acres)
Terrain: Mixed, but mostly easy
Art Gallery: Specialising in early NZ original paintings

Efil Doog is "Good Life" spelt backwards! And for Ernest and Shirley, life on their four plus hectare Akatarawa property is good. The cool, moist climate in the hills favours the growth of rhododendrons which predominate, complemented by prunus, magnolias and natives including kowhai, several varieties of ponga and silver ferns. The bush backdrop provides an incomparable rural setting for the contemporary sculptures that are exhibited in this park, allowing an uninterrupted appreciation of each piece in relation to its environment. Such a spacious site enables the sculpture not only to interact with changing light and shadow, but also to reflect the surrounding trees, water and sky. A bridge crosses the beautifully clear Akatarawa River that runs through the park, with a series of ponds featuring Japanese irises and azaleas. Since "Akatarawa" is Maori for "Valley of the Hanging Vines", the Cosgroves have planted a lot of climbers. Clematis grow over the trees on the hillside and six varieties cover an arbour in the garden. Laburnum arches by the entrance, a wisteria walk and the "Enchanted Grove" are other special areas. Some 14,000 daffodils welcome the spring round a natural pond guarded by two sculptures: "Metamorphosis" and "Dragonfly Ballerina". In the summer, cardiocrinums join the drifts of perennials, then the deciduous trees colour the autumn.

NEWLANDS ALPINE GARDEN
Newlands

Owners:
Arnold and Ruth Dench

Address: 37 Lyndfield Lane, Newlands
Directions: From Wellington, take SH 1 to top of Ngauranga Gorge. Turn right at lights into Newlands Rd, Then turn sharp right into Wakely Way. Veer left into Lyndfield Lane. Garden on left. On main bus route – 10 mins from Wellington city
Phone: 0-4-478 5873
Open: October to March, daily, 10am–4pm, by appointment
Groups: By appointment
Fee: $3 per adult
Size: Small – 1000 sq m (⅓ acre)
Terrain: Hilly
Nursery: Range of plants from garden for sale

This predominantly native garden, with particular emphasis on native alpines, began in 1956 as a vegetable garden on a bleak Wellington hillside. There the Denches developed a flat area before landscaping the slopes. Since 1985 they have been replacing exotics with natives, although they have retained a 30-year-old waratah, dwarf berberis and small conifers, with calunas and ericas in a South African section. Newlands Alpine Garden has been planned as a small botanic garden with an entirely native rockery at the front and an exotic rockery on the northern side. A new scree garden for wind-resistant alpines is designed to withstand the blast of northerly winds. A moraine garden catering for difficult plants is adjacent to a fernery beside the creek. An extensive primula collection is a favourite with the owners, who also grow a variety of irises. Of the natives, they specialise in hebes, with about 130 types ranging from miniature varieties to large shrubs. The spring bulb garden features hundreds of daffodils, muscaris, sparaxis and ixias. Lilies, dahlias and perennials add to the native summer display and then the nerines in the bulb garden appear in autumn when the maples are colouring. It is the owners' vision to provide visitors with the opportunity to see and study many rarely seen native and exotic plants.

SUDBURY
Ohariu Valley

Owners:
Suzy and Mark Pennington

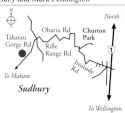

Address: 60 Takarau Gorge Rd,
Ohariu Valley, Wellington
Directions: Turn left at Johnsonville
roundabout. Keep left into Ironside
Rd. Take Takarau Gorge Rd towards
Makara Beach. Garden is No. 60 on
right, 600m from start of Takarau
Gorge Rd
Phone: 0-4-478 4846
Fax: 0-4-478 4846
Open: October to December, and
February to March; by appointment
Groups: By appointment, as above
Fee: $3 per adult
Size: Large – 2ha (5 acres)
Terrain: Flat and hilly
Nursery: Perennials from garden

 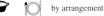 by arrangement

Sudbury is a romantic-style garden planted since 1975,
centred around a wooden homestead and overlooking
a small stream-fed lake. The garden design blends with
surrounding farmland and hills, exotics combining with
natives. Irises, primulas, hostas and other bog plants
among ferns and ponga line a path following the stream,
by two ponds which feed the lake. Rhododendrons, azaleas,
kowhai, willows and perennials cover the banks. An arched
bridge spans the lake to "Gnomes Island", where kowhai
are underplanted with daffodils and gunneras. Behind the
lake, walkways meander through a rhododendron dell and
woodland area, with hostas, peonies, perennials and bulbs
beneath. Kowhai and cherry blossom accompany the spring
bulbs, with naturalised fritillaria and *Cardiocrinum
giganteum*. Surrounding banks are planted in young kauri.
Expansive lawns link the lake with the house garden,
featuring roses, perennials and grey-foliaged plants. Nearby,
a magnolia walk is underplanted with cream and pink tulips
and blue and white forget-me-nots. A wisteria tunnel, formed
by a white Japanese floribunda, leads through a perfumed
area including many roses, old and new, lavender hedge and
philadelphus. An enclosed brick courtyard behind the house
is beautiful in late spring with apricot cedrelas, roses and
abutilon.

183

New Zealand

North Island

Auckland

South Island

Wellington

Christchurch

Dunedin

SOUTH ISLAND

Motueka

Richmond

NELSON

Blenheim

Westport

Reefton

Kaikoura

Greymouth

Kaiapoi

CHRISTCHURCH

Ashburton

Timaru

Waimate

Queenstown

Alexandra

Te Anau

DUNEDIN

Gore

Balclutha

INVERCARGILL

NELSON AND MARLBOROUGH

Nelson and Marlborough cover the northernmost tip of the South Island. We present 23 gardens to visit in this region. Sunny Nelson is renowned for its tramping, fishing and limestone caves. Motueka is famous for its orchards – the most prolific in the country. The region has several national and forest parks, including the well known Heaphy Track in north-west Nelson.

The 13 gardens featured in Nelson are spread throughout the district. Nelson city boasts the formal Queens Gardens, and just north off the main highway is Miyazu Japanese Garden, a contemplative stroll garden featuring paths, bridges and stepping stones through water gardens and a Zen garden. South at Richmond are two more of the City Council's gardens: Isel Park and Broadgreen Rose Gardens, both with trees planted before the turn of the century. Just south, at Hope, is Etheringtons' Garden Park encompassing "Gardens of the World". One kilometre along the coastal highway towards Motueka is Hedgerow, a cottage garden and nursery also selling garden accessories. Further along the highway is Fable Cottage with rhododendrons, camellias and fruit trees surrounding the cottage which is available for accommodation.

In the Orinoco Valley are two gardens: Briar Rose Cottage with a meadow garden adjacent, and Craigholm with its woodland garden and ponds. Further west on State Highway 61 are two more gardens. Just south of Ngatimoti is Margy's Garden beside the Motueka River and featuring a solarium and craft shop selling Margy's hand-made pottery. South is Woodstock Garden with a bog garden in a woodland setting. Motueka features Tasman Bay Roses, with the roses thriving in the mild climate, and Jacaranda Park with many spring trees and plants and a new adobe-built restaurant, as well as the summer jacarandas. Over the hill at Takaka is Beautiful Begonias which is worth a visit in summer to see the range of varieties in the tuberous-begonia houses.

Marlborough is becoming known as the gourmet province, with its vineyards producing award-winning wines. Marlborough extends from Nelson right up beyond Picton, the arrival point in the South Island for the Interisland ferries, through the bays and coves of the picturesque Marlborough Sounds and down through the main city, Blenheim, as far south as Kaikoura, famous for dolphin- and whale-watching.

The 10 gardens featured in Marlborough have to contend with the hot, dry summers typical of this region. The gardens stretch from Havelock on the Nelson highway, up to the Sounds and down the east coast to Kaikoura. At Havelock, one of the water gateways to the Sounds, is Braeside, with its planted creek-banks. Up in the Sounds themselves are two more gardens – The Folly where the native bush is cleared in patches for introduced plantings, and The Nikaus Country Garden and Farmstay with rhododendrons and the nikau palms on the slopes behind. Blenheim features three gardens, Bankhouse at Renwick with its terraced plantings along a stream and a dry riverbed, Rosedale just off the main highway, with its 500 roses, and Rhododendron Lodge where rhododendrons surround a guest pool.

Down the east coast at Seddon are two gardens: Richmond Brook, where plantings soften the old stone homestead surrounded by even older trees, and Barewood with its terraced bank and old roses. Further south along the coast at Kekerengu is Winterhome, a formal classically designed garden with long vistas and focal points. At Kaikoura is Fyffe Gallery with its cottage garden beyond the restaurant courtyard, framing a view to the ranges.

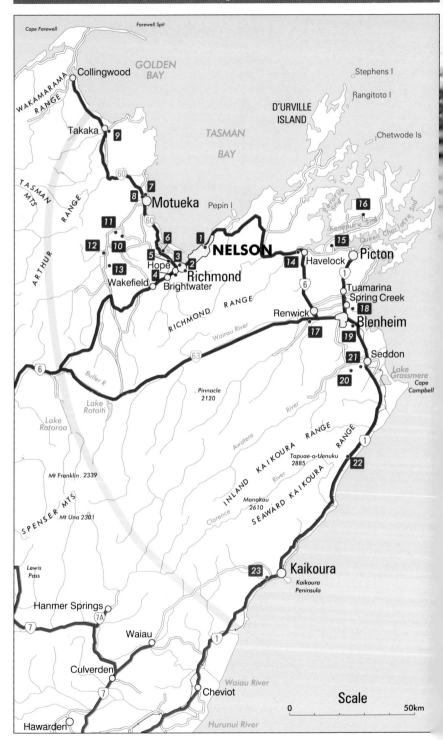

MIYAZU JAPANESE GARDEN
Nelson

Owner:
Nelson City Council

Address: Atawhai Drive, Nelson
Postal: P O Box 645, Nelson
Directions: From north turn left off
SH 6 into Atawhai Drive. Travel past
Miyazu Park for 200m to garden on
right. From south, turn right off
Queen Elizabeth II Drive into
Atawhai Drive. Travel 200m to
garden on right
Phone: 0-3-546 0244
Fax: 0-3-546 0239
Open: All year, daily
Groups: As above
Fee: No charge
Size: Large – 2ha (5 acres)
Terrain: Flat

from carpark

Miyazu Garden is a Japanese stroll garden named after Nelson's sister city. The first planting by the Japanese ambassador in 1990 was followed by the official opening three years later by the Deputy Mayor of Miyazu. The garden features traditional Japanese aesthetic concepts and symbolism using water, rocks, gravel and a combination of New Zealand natives and Japanese plants to create green on green hues of varying texture, with highlights of seasonal colour. Cherry blossoms announce the spring when the camellias, azaleas and the wisteria arbour flower.

A Welcome Gate, with its authentic granite *yukimi-gata* lantern, overlooks the Dragon Pond. Large granite stepping stones traverse the still water towards the 25-year-old bonsai on the far bank, the stone beach contrasting with the water. A stone cleansing basin or *tsukubai* is adjacent to the pondside pavilion which provides contemplative views of a century-old camellia. Many bridges and stepping stones cross the ponds with their water irises and raupo. Waterfalls, streams and bamboo fountains create musical sounds and a sense of tranquillity. Many seats strategically placed throughout the garden allow absorption of the peaceful atmosphere and contemplation of the special features, such as the Zen garden or *Karesansui* where asymmetrically placed rocks are surrounded by a sea of raked gravel.

ISEL PARK
Stoke

Owner:
Nelson City Council

Address: Main Road, Stoke, Nelson
Postal: P O Box 645, Nelson
Directions: Take SH 6 for 8km to
Stoke. Entrances to Isel Park on left
just past Marsden Rd or off Hilliard St
Phone: 0-3-546 0376
Fax: 0-3-546 0239
Open: Garden: daily, 8am till dusk.
Provincial Museum: Tuesday to
Sunday, hours vary. Isel House: 2pm–
4pm, weekends and public holidays
Groups: As above
Fee: No charge for garden; museum
$2 per adult, $1 per child, $5 per
family; Isel House $1 per adult
Size: Large – 6ha (15 acres)
Terrain: Flat
Restrictions: Vehicles & bicycles on
roadway only

 at museum & in park

Isel Park is a woodland garden incorporating trees
planted as early as 1845. Neo-Gothic Isel House was
originally a cottage, built in 1848 by Thomas Marsden
who began planting English oaks, beech, hornbeam,
chestnuts, cedars and poplars on the property. His son
James continued planting trees. The Nelson City Council
bought Isel Park in 1959, creating roads through the old
Marsden trees and converting the woodlot into the woodland
garden, with extensive plantings of rhododendron
collections. Notable trees include colossal specimens of
Sequoiadendron giganteum, a Canary Island pine at
38 metres high to the side of the house, the tallest recorded
tulip tree in the country at 36 metres, and a Corsican pine
of 41 metres. Doves strut across the lawns and the woodland
is carpeted with naturalised bluebells, tulips, daffodils,
and Dutch crocus in spring. Other bulbs such as colchicums
and crocuses provide colour beneath the deciduous trees
in autumn. A wide range of perennials scattered throughout
the park include hostas, polyanthus, agapanthus and lilies,
with *Cardiocrinum giganteum* lilies featuring in summer.
The mature rhododendrons bordered with deciduous
azaleas provide spring colour, and a glasshouse features
vireya rhododendrons and orchids. A cactus house and
fish pond are further attractions.

BROADGREEN ROSE GARDENS
Stoke

Owner:
Nelson City Council

Broadgreen Rose Gardens

Address: 276 Nayland Rd, Stoke
Postal: P O Box 645, Nelson
Directions: Take SH 6 for 8km from
Nelson to Stoke. Turn right into
Songer St, then 3rd right into Nayland
Rd. Broadgreen Gardens 150m on left
Phone: 0-3-546 0376
Fax: 0-3-546 0239
Open: Garden open daily. Broadgreen
House open November to April:
Tuesday to Sunday; May to October:
Wednesdays, weekends and public
holidays. Hours vary, check by
phoning: 0-3-547 7887
Groups: Garden daily; Broadgreen
House by appointment
Fee: No charge for garden; Historic
House $3 per adult, 50c per child
Size: Large – 1.7ha (over 4 acres)
Terrain: Flat

Broadgreen homestead, an early colonial cob house,
was built in 1853 for Edmund Buxton, who planted
the first garden. An impressive Himalayan cedar, *Cedrus
deodara*, planted by Buxton about 1856, is edged with
native arthropodiums. Other conifers are complemented
by smaller trees such as oaks, walnuts and loquats, which
provide autumn colour. Spring brings daffodils into bloom,
followed by the magnolias and rhododendrons. Then
cottage garden perennials accompany the roses in summer.
Spacious lawns are bordered by the Samuels Rose Garden
established by the noted local rose breeder, Mr S J Samuels,
who donated his entire collection of almost three thousand
roses in 1966. The Samuels Rose Garden is designed in
Victorian style, with formal beds laid out according to
colour and variety of rose. Hybrid Tea and Floribunda are
predominant, with a more recent collection of old-
fashioned roses enhancing the historic atmosphere. A rose
pergola with brick columns displays climbers, and "Wedding
Day" adorns an archway. The crimson *Rosa chinensis*
"Semperflorens", a descendant of one of the original China
roses brought to New Zealand, flowers close to Broadgreen
House. Each year, when the roses peak at the end of
November, a Rose Day Fair is held at Broadgreen.

GARDENS OF THE WORLD
Richmond

Owners:
Geoff and Gillian Etherington

Address: Clover Rd East, Hope, Nelson
Postal: P O Box 3046, Richmond, Nelson
Directions: Take SH 6 south of Nelson. Five minutes south of Richmond, turn left down Clover Rd. Etheringtons' is just past Patons Rd on left
Phone: 0-3-542 3036 or 542 3736
Fax: 0-3-542 3036
Open: 1 August to 31 May, 10am till 1 hour before dusk
Groups: By appointment
Fee: $4 per adult over 12 years
Size: Large – 2.4ha (6 acres)
Terrain: Level with landscaped mounds

A grand dream is coming to fruition with the development of the Etheringtons' Garden Park, designed to represent "Gardens of the World". Originally a large flat orchard, this site has been landscaped to provide rolling mounds surrounding the more formal central areas. Different geographical regions are depicted with native plantings from New Zealand, the Orient, the Americas, Europe and Africa. Other areas include the white garden, four formal gardens, the water garden with a fountain, and an amphitheatre where concerts can be held overlooking the pond. Ex-nurseryman Geoff began planting trees in 1990, with African species – some rare – his favourites. The stream and pond are being lined, with the water circulating from the top rockery to flow into the pond beneath. The nearby New Zealand section is growing well and the formal rose garden with its pergola has been completed. A herb garden is under way and a sizeable herbaceous garden with conservatory is being developed. A building is planned for outdoor functions, with the gardens proving a popular venue for weddings. A mountain backdrop frames the different sections of the world garden which swirl around grassed areas – a far cry from the apple orchard of five years ago!

HEDGEROW
Nelson

Owners:
Joanne McIntosh and Sharon Costar

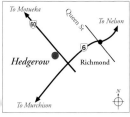

Address: Main Road, Appleby, Nelson
Directions: Take SH 6 south of
Nelson to Richmond. Continue south
to SH 60, turn right towards Motueka.
Travel about 1km to Hedgerow on left
Phone: 0-3-544 1911
Fax: 0-3-544 4057
Open: All year, daily, 9am–5pm
Closed: Christmas, Boxing & Anzac
(25 April) Days, and Good Friday
Groups: As above
Fee: No charge
Size: Medium – 0.4ha (1 acre)
Terrain: Flat
Children: Welcome in the sandpit
Nursery: Cottage plants, lavenders,
fuchsias, pansies, polyanthus, herbs,
bulbs, buxus, daisies, roses – old &
new, garden designer plants

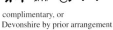

complimentary, or
Devonshire by prior arrangement

Named because of all the lavender, pittosporum and hydrangea hedges surrounding it, Hedgerow is a three-year-old cottage garden with formal elements such as rose archways and gazebos. Special features include a wildflower garden, a sunflower garden and a shade house filled with hanging baskets and potted plants for sale. Garden accessories, such as wire hangers, frames, terracotta pots, picnic tables and seats used in the garden are also for sale, along with garden follies, marble statues, fountains, pillars and other structures. Spring bulbs accompany the cherry blossom and hanging baskets, followed by the lavender hedges flowering and rose arches. Cottage displays of colourful annuals complement the perennials including cornflowers, sages, penstemons, verbena and lavatera, creating a peaceful picnicking spot. Californian poppies brighten the garden entrance beside the carpark. Roses continue flowering into autumn, as do the daisies and hanging baskets of fuchsias, pansies and lobelias. Visitors can sit and enjoy Hedgerow's complimentary tea or coffee in the garden setting. Devonshire teas are also available, by prior arrangement only. A fenced sandpit provides for young children's needs. David and Phillip have designed and garden Hedgerow which is attended by their wives, Joanne and Sharon, all year round.

191

FABLE COTTAGE
Nelson

Owners:
Paul Holdsworth and Trina McKay

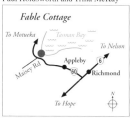

Address: Coastal Highway, R D 1, Richmond, Nelson
Directions: Take SH 6 south of Nelson to Richmond. Continue south to SH 60 (Coastal Highway), turn right towards Motueka. Travel to Maisey Rd on left. Fable Cottage is opposite, on right
Phone: 0-3-544 2657
Mobile: 025 859 748
Open: 1 September to 30 April, Friday to Monday, 10am–4pm; Tuesday to Thursday by appointment
Groups: By appointment
Fee: $2 per adult
Size: Medium – 0.8ha (2 acres)
Terrain: Flat
Nursery: Rhododendrons for sale
Accommodation: Cottage available

Almost a hectare of ornamental garden, lawn, vegetable garden and fruit trees surrounds Fable Cottage, overlooking the estuary. Primarily a spring garden, Trina's favourite plants include her white clematis, magnolias, michelia and maples. The predominant species in the garden would be the rhododendrons, which Trina is specialising in, camellias – a white camellia hedge is replacing a line of pencil willows – and roses. There is a lot of pink in the garden, which Trina has grouped together, with the yellow/orange spectrum out by the estuary, but now she is introducing mainly white flowering plants and evergreens. Daffodils, grape hyacinths and white tulips announce the spring, with the camellias, cherry trees, clematis, irises and azaleas. In summer the roses bloom with perennials such as foxgloves, delphiniums, aquilegias, lavender and hostas. Dahlias add summer colour and Trina is planting more white summer flowers. Trees consist of native pittosporums, conifers such as the recently planted Douglas firs, eucalypts and other exotics including maples, willows, and poplars. Mandarins and other fruit trees grow near the cottage which is available for accommodation. Trina plans to develop a herb garden and Paul will build a bridge over the stream beside the garden.

TASMAN BAY ROSES
Motueka

Owners:
Nigel and Judith Pratt

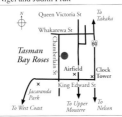

Address: 45 Chamberlain St North, Motueka
Postal: P O Box 159, Motueka
Directions: Take SH 60 north-west of Nelson. At Motueka turn left at clock tower. Travel 3km. Turn right into Chamberlain St, garden 500m on right
Phone: 0-3-528 7449
Fax: 0-3-528 7449
Open: Garden: open from mid November all summer;
Nursery: open daily, noon– 4.30pm
Groups: As above or by appointment
Fee: No charge
Size: Medium – just over 1ha (3 acres)
Terrain: Flat
Nursery: Roses – old and unusual to latest modern; mail-order catalogue $5; potted roses for summer visitors; perennials

At Tasman Bay Roses, a growing collection of old and rare roses is set among mature trees, with the Arthur Range as backdrop. The main garden features a long double border of old roses leading to a summer house covered in "Pax", "Francesca", and "Crépuscule". To one side is a mixed border with further roses, perennials and shrubs, backed by a shelter hedge of conifers. A lavender walk leads between beds of predominantly purple and red roses to another formal garden. Roses climb and ramble through an adjacent orchard, and every available wall and building is covered in roses, forming their own shapes and reaching spectacular heights. Old roses create a colourful spectacle in November and December, with repeat-flowering varieties such as "Bantry Bay" and "Michèle Meilland" providing interest all summer. A tree-lined driveway leads to the barnyard featuring an historic hop kiln, where roses and perennials are available for sale. Native birds abound, with doves nesting in a large macrocarpa and pheasants, quail and fantails also making their homes in the garden. Visitors are welcomed by 100 climbing roses along the boundary and another 50 cover a massive arbour beside the carpark. The roses enjoy the mild Nelson climate and abundant water supply.

193

JACARANDA PARK
Motueka

Owners:
Robert, Barbara and Alan Atkins

Address: College St West, Motueka
Postal: P O Box 162, Motueka
Directions: From Nelson, take SH 60 to Motueka. Turn left into King Edward St and travel to foot of hill. Jacaranda Park driveway on left
Phone: 0-3-528 7777
Fax: 0-3-528 7797
Open: All year, daily, from 9am
Groups: By appointment
Fee: $2.50 per adult
Size: Large – 2ha (5 acres)
Terrain: Hilly to gentle slopes
Nursery: Excellent range of rhododendrons, magnolias, cornus, perennials; rare specimen trees
Shop/café: New adobe craft shop and café. Licensed; suitable for functions; courtyard dining available; open for evening dining

   & to toilet

Jacaranda Park is named after the jacaranda trees that feature in summer with their beautiful lilac/mauve trumpet flowers. Twenty-five years ago this woodland park was hilly pastureland and gorse, with panoramic views overlooking the Motueka River valley and plains below. The planting of shelter trees, such as eucalypts in the seventies, was carefully planned to retain clear river views, and intensive planting has been carried out in the last decade. Now rhododendrons and deciduous trees dominate the two hectares, providing fresh spring colour and brilliant autumn tones. In spring, camellias are complemented with flowering cherries, magnolias, michelias and dogwoods, with azaleas beneath. The white bracts of *Cornus nuttallii* float above rhododendrons such as the fragrant "Princess Alice" along a walkway edged with a stone wall. Hostas and companion planting are being established. In summer, the jacarandas come into their own, with specimen shade trees underplanted with perennials. Autumn colour includes mass plantings of liquidambar. Even winter has its moment, with the structure of the deciduous trees providing architectural beauty along the walking tracks. A formal garden with box hedging and conifers gives year-round appeal. A water garden is being developed and the walkways extended to cover six hectares of woodland garden.

BEAUTIFUL BEGONIAS
Takaka

Beautiful Begonias

Owners:
Robyn and Graham Hardwick

Address: Rocklands Rd, Clifton, Takaka
Directions: Take SH 60 from Nelson. Turn right at Takaka, towards Pohara Beach. Follow signs, turning right into Clifton Rd, then right again into Rocklands Rd
Phone: 0-3-525 9058
Open: December to May, daily, 10am–6pm
Groups: As above
Fee: No charge
Size: Small – 1,000 square metres of covered begonia houses (¼ acre)
Terrain: Hilly
Nursery: Tuberous begonias, fertiliser, supports and books; mail-order catalogue

Beautiful Begonias is situated near Takaka with superb scenic views across Golden Bay. The Hardwicks have been selling tuberous begonias every summer for the past decade, their collection expanding into numerous shade houses. The seedlings appear in spring, with the peak flowering time from February to April, when thousands of begonias provide a massed display of all the sunset colours in full flower. The blooms come as standard uprights and hanging-basket varieties, ruffled, frilled or picotee in singles or doubles. Special named begonias include "Sweetie", a rare scented begonia with soft-yellow, double hanging flowers. Contrary to popular opinion, tuberous begonias are not difficult to grow. As long as they are given appropriate conditions, they can be easily grown in pots or even in the garden outside in sheltered areas with filtered light. The tubers sprout in early spring and are ready to pot up or plant out by late October. The flowering season is late summer, from January through to April, when the plant dies off and the tubers can be dug up, dried and stored ready for the following season. Robyn also raises begonias from imported seed, which requires quite a degree of skill. An aviary of budgies is an added attraction.

BRIAR ROSE COTTAGE
Orinoco

Owners:
Sue and Ron Smart

Briar Rose Cottage

Address: Orinoco, R D 1, Motueka
Directions: From Nelson, take inland
route for 46km to Lower Moutere.
Turn left into Edwards Rd, left into
Waiwhero Rd and left again to Orinoco.
From Motueka, take Motueka Valley
for 19km to Ngatimoti. Turn left into
Waiwhero Rd, then right to Orinoco.
Garden on left
Phone: 0-3-526 8766
Open: November to January, daily,
10am–5pm
Groups: As above
Fee: $2 per adult
Size: Medium – 1ha (2½ acres)
Terrain: Flat
Shop: Country-style crafts, "Hidcote"
lavender, lace, pottery, ceramic
garden tags, etc; closed winter
Tearooms: Self-service herbal teas
and iced fruit drinks

Sue's meadow garden was a cow paddock four years ago. Now it is ablaze with colourful annuals each summer, contrasting with her cottage garden packed with perennials and roses. A century-old hop kiln and cow bale have been transformed into a country-style craft shop, adorned with a cascading wall of "Wedding Day" rose, providing a perfect backdrop for pink peonies, blue larkspurs and delphiniums, edged with lavender. Roses, such as "Sander's White", form the focal point for each cottage bed. A grassy driveway is divided by a herbaceous median strip with a rustic fence through the centre supporting modern roses such as red "Dublin Bay", white "Iceberg" and pink "Blossomtime", complemented by blue cornflowers and larkspurs on either side. More roses clamber over the cottage fence and climb every available tree. The meadow beyond is separated by manuka "windows" framing the Orinoco hills, with more of Sue's beloved roses, such as the cerise old Gallica "Charles de Mills" rambling over the fence. A rustic gate and mown pathways encourage visitors to wander through the meadow, full of yellows and oranges, such as Californian poppies, contrasting dramatically with the blues of larkspurs and foxgloves. Future plans include planting fruit trees on the far side of the meadow.

CRAIGHOLM
Orinoco

Owners:
Vivienne and Tony Whitaker

Address: 270 Thorpe-Orinoco Rd,
Orinoco, R D 1, Motueka
Directions: From Lower Moutere turn
left into Edwards Rd, left into
Waiwhero Rd and left to Orinoco.
From Motueka, travel 19km to
Ngatimoti. Turn left into Waiwhero
Rd, then right to Orinoco. Craigholm
2.7km on right
Phone: 0-3-526 8703
Open: 1 September to 15 May, daily;
by appointment
Groups: By appointment, as above
Fee: $3 per adult over 15
Size: Medium – 1.5ha (3¾ acres)
Terrain: Undulating
Nursery: Planned
Accommodation: B&B with dinner if
desired, by arrangement

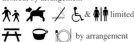

Craigholm, named by the original Scottish settlers in the 1860s, is now a woodland garden with a fern-lined stream running through it. Two ponds are surrounded with bog plants mirrored in the deep reflective water. Ligularia is massed beside bridges crossing the stream, with waterside clumps of hostas, gunneras, primulas and irises. Bamboo shades creamy astilbes and phlomis. Solomon's seal is sheltered by *Nyssa sylvatica* which turn a brilliant red in autumn along with the sassafras, dogwoods, maples and oaks that the Whitakers have planted in the last decade. Unusual trees include a cork oak, Japanese raisin tree and the frost-tender cucumber magnolia with its huge leaves shading astrantia. Original plantings of black walnuts, robinia, sycamores and pines frame the garden overlooking the Orinoco hills. A rock garden beside the house features native shrubs, and spacious lawns slope down to the summer herbaceous border where Vivienne's favourite rhododendrons and massed deciduous azaleas provide spring colour, underplanted with lily-of-the-valley. Paths meander down the gully through a silver birch grove above the ponds, to the gazebo beyond, clad with the old white roses "Sombreuil" Climbing, "Sander's White" and "Mme Alfred Carrière", their beauty matched only by the giant lilies, *Cardiocrinum giganteum*.

197

MARGY'S GARDEN AND NURSERY
Ngatimoti

Owners:
Margy and Paul Brereton

Address: SH 61, Ngatimoti, R D 1, Motueka
Directions: From Moutere Highway turn left into Edwards Rd, left into Waiwhero Rd & travel to Ngatimoti. Turn left into SH 61 (Motueka Valley Rd) & travel 1km to garden on right. From Motueka, travel 20km on SH 61 (Motueka Valley Rd) to garden on right
Phone: 0-3-526 8756
Open: October to mid February, 10am–5pm, weekends; ring weekdays
Groups: By appointment
Fee: $2 per adult
Size: Medium – 0.4ha (1 acre)
Terrain: Flat
Nursery: Perennials and shrubs propagated from garden
Shop: Craft shop selling hand-made dragons by Margy & other pottery

 groups only

mostly   by arrangement

Margy has developed her garden in the past decade from bare paddock beside the Motueka River. First the rock garden was planted, then the native garden, the rose garden and the indoor solarium pool planted with ferns and tropical plants including the banana palm, pawpaw, *Monstera deliciosa,* cymbidium orchids and "Congo Cockatoo" impatiens. In spring Margy's favourite dianthus, daphnes, rock phlox and the rock garden bulbs appear, such as the dog's tooth violets and species tulips. Margy's hostas begin to unfurl their foliage and jasmine perfumes the air. Hebes predominate in the raised native garden, although other indigenous species include tussocks, *Scleranthus* and *Helichrysum.* By mid November the hebes are peaking, then the callas and Asiatic lilies bloom by the boundary overlooking the river. In summer, the roses predominate in their ponga-edged beds, and olearias make a colourful show. Summer perennials include penstemons and taller phlox. Exotics such as maples, paulownias and Chinese wing nuts or *Pterocarya stenoptera* provide shade. Margy plans to plant rhododendrons in the woodland at the far end of her garden where wooden mushrooms have been carved on a tree stump. The craft shop sells a variety of Margy's pottery figures.

WOODSTOCK GARDEN
Woodstock

Owners:
Stephen and Imogen McCarthy

Address: SH 61, Woodstock, R D 2,
Wakefield
Directions: From Motueka, travel
33.3km south on SH 61. Garden just
past Woodstock Junction on left.
From Ngatimoti, travel 14.3km south
on SH 61, as above, to garden on left
Phone: 0-3-543 3852
Open: 1 October to 31 May, daily,
9am–5pm
Groups: By appointment
Fee: $2 per adult, refundable on
purchase
Size: Medium – 0.5ha (1¼ acres)
Terrain: Gentle slope
Nursery: Plants for sale

There are no straight lines and clipped hedges at Woodstock. This informal garden features rhododendrons in a natural-looking woodland setting. The focus is an extensive bog garden with various primulas hostas, irises, gunnera, astilbes and unusual marginal plants. Three ponds featuring waterlilies and goldfish attract water birds and dragonflies. The garden is set in a rural landscape with a river view and a backdrop of mature native beech/podocarp forest. In the springtime, daffodils carpet the banks, complemented with beds of chionodoxa, bluebells and scilla species. Magnolias are followed by prunus and malus in late spring. The rhododendrons predominate from mid October to mid November along with massed Candelabra primulas which thrive in the moist conditions. In early December, the naturalised cardiocrinums flower round the edge of the native bush and in shadier parts of the garden. A collection of old and modern roses bloom in late summer accompanied by perennials and the cyclamens under the trees. Then in autumn the deciduous trees, especially the collection of maples, give wonderful colour against the blue shaded hills.

BRAESIDE
Havelock

Owners:
Dr Vic and Rita Jacobson

Address: Main Rd, Havelock, Marlborough
Directions: From Picton or Blenheim travel to Havelock. Continue 1.5km on SH 6 towards Nelson. Braeside is big white house with grey roof on left
Phone: 0-3-574 2176
Open: October to January, daily, by appointment
Groups: By appointment, as above
Fee: $4 per adult
Size: Medium – 1.2ha (3 acres)
Terrain: Hilly with contoured paths
Nursery: Azaleas, groundcovers, perennials, shrubs and some trees

Over the past decade Rita has developed the garden at Braeside, incorporating trees planted when the homestead was built in 1905. Once she had cleared the hillsides above the creek of noxious weeds, Rita planted groundcovers, providing soft carpets for shrubs and trees. A sloping sea of blue ajuga looks stunning in spring, punctuated by contrasting rhododendrons. Above the drive, a bank of soft white forget-me-nots and billowing daisies contrasts with sharp spikes of yucca. And leading up from a dry creek-bed are slab steps edged with brilliant green Irish moss and overflowing with pink and blue forget-me-nots. Contoured paths climb the slope through natives and exotics to a summer-house lookout facing Pelorus Sounds. The opposite creek-bank features Rita's close-packed nursery and a chamomile walk leading up above a dianthus rockery. A larger alpine rockery backs a crazy-paving rondel, where a stone well is the focal point. A bridge crosses the creek to a yellow and white garden. Other features include dry stone walls and a classical pergola covered with grapes and wisteria. Rita is planting roses to climb into the trees and extending the garden to four times its size further up the hillsides of the creek.

THE FOLLY
Picton

The Folly

Owners:
Val and Graeme Kummer

Address: Kenepuru Rd, Picton, R D 2
Directions: From Picton, take Queen
Charlotte Drive to Linkwater. Turn
right into Kenepuru Rd and travel for
11.5km to The Folly, on left
Phone: 0-3-574 2808
Open: September to May, daily,
10am–5pm
Groups: Large groups by appointment
Fee: $3 per adult
Size: Large – 7ha (18 acres)
Terrain: Flat to hilly, with paths and
steps
Nursery: Fuchsias, natives, perennials
including the unusual
Accommodation: Fully self-contained
apartment, ideal for couples, $70 per
night, by arrangement

  by arrangement

The Kummers have developed the remnants of an early homestead garden and planted the surrounding native bush to create an extensive park concept, with diverse gardens reached by walking-tracks throughout the bush. The original pioneers' graves are adorned with old roses and the Erskine Garden commemorating them is a semi-formal camellia garden set in the bush, encircling a central fountain. An ivy walk leads to Neame's Green – a grassed picnic area surrounded with native trees such as kahikatea. Other major bush clearings are the Rhododendron Dell reached via the Walnut Walk, the pond, and the Perennial Garden. The pond area is found in a glade in the bush planted with lilies, irises, flaxes and other water-loving species. The Perennial Garden edged with lavender and catmint features an extensive range, including some unusual species, with the Fuchsia Shade House nearby. Chamomile steps lead to the garden below the house, with native plantings of red kaka-beak and ponga beyond the verandah. Using predominant colours of blue, white, pink and red, with autumn tonings from introduced English trees, Val has established pockets of garden to enhance rather than detract from the native bush, creating a unique New Zealand style.

THE NIKAUS COUNTRY GARDEN AND FARMSTAY
Marlborough Sounds

Owners:
Alison and Robin Bowron

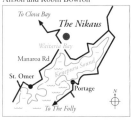

Address: Waitaria Bay, R D 2, Picton
Directions: From Picton or Havelock, travel along Queen Charlotte Drive to Linkwater. Turn north into Kenepuru Rd and drive 1.5 hours to Waitaria Bay. Turn right into Manaroa Rd. The Nikaus Country Garden is on right
Phone: 0-3-573 4432
Fax: 0-3-573 4432
Open: All year, daily, 10am–4pm
Groups: By appointment
Fee: $3 per adult over 15
Size: Medium – 0.6ha (1½ acres)
Terrain: Flat
Nursery: Small – seedlings and perennials from garden; old roses from area
Accommodation: Farmstay available; dinner, B&B; $50 per person per night

Named after the native nikau palms on the slopes behind the house, this 26-year-old garden has been developed over the last three years by Alison, although it was originally designed by another rhododendron lover. Spring begins with sheets of gold daffodils under the orchard and paulownia, while camellias brighten the pathway and vege garden. Then the pinks, creams and blues take over, with flowering cherries, magnolias and michelia joining the rhododendrons. Clematis climbs the fence surrounding the swimming pool, where Alison has planted ferns and begonias under ponga. In November the lilies begin to emerge, continuing till the end of February with massed displays of Asiatic and Oriental lilies including Alison's favourite apricot Asiatic "Hartford". The lilies complement the blue delphiniums and other perennials in the extensive herbaceous border. Old roses are also summer highlights, then chrysanthemums feature in autumn when the oak leaves turn. Maples shelter a kidney-shaped pond backed by a small rock garden to the side of the house. The views out to sea are marvellous in winter through the deciduous trees, and a 25-year-old *Magnolia campbellii* on the lawn blooms in early August. Farm walks lead across a creek up to the nikau grove and a waterfall beyond. Farmstay with dinner is available by arrangement.

BANKHOUSE
Blenheim

Owners:
Geraldine and Tony Sheild

Bankhouse

Address: SH 63, Renwick
Postal: R D 1, Blenheim
Directions: From Blenheim take SH 6
towards Renwick. Turn on to SH 63
and travel about 10 mins to Waihopai
Bridge. Cross Waihopai River and
turn left into either No. 1149 (left
fork) or 1150 driveway to Bankhouse
Phone: 0-3-572 8286
Fax: 0-3-572 9747
Open: By appointment
Groups: By appointment
Fee: $4 per adult
Size: Medium – 0.4ha (1 acre)
Terrain: Terraced
Nursery: Occasional perennials from
garden

   limited

  by arrangement

Named by Tony's great grandfather when the first house was built on the banks of the Waihopai River in 1874, Bankhouse today incorporates a pair of original oaks, two ashes, and several conifers. Geraldine likes the challenge of creating environments to grow what she wants, planting terraces on different levels over the past 18 years. She has established woodland shelter for more delicate plants in the hot, dry Marlborough summers. A waterfall, stream and pond have been constructed beside the river on the lowest level, surrounded with woodland plantings and moisture-loving primulas, hostas, irises, astilbes, meconopsis, foxgloves, rhododendrons and tree peonies. This area is quite a contrast to a newer dry stream on a higher terrace, where daisies and grasses flourish under the Marlborough sun. Geraldine is fond of English David Austin roses that grow well on the top terrace, favourites including the soft pink "Lucetta", creamy "Wild Flower", golden "Windrush", and blush-pink "Claire Rose". Massed lilies are another summer highlight, then in autumn, the foliage of maples and flowering cherries features. In winter the stark forms of the deciduous trees reveal the bark in the winter light, contrasting with summer, when gums and wattles give the garden an Australian feel.

ROSEDALE
Blenheim

Owners:
Jean and Errol Batty

Address: 29 Swamp Rd, Blenheim
Postal: Dillons Point, R D 3,
Blenheim
Directions: 4km from Blenheim
centre. Turn off Grove Rd (SH 1)
across railway line into Dillons Pt Rd.
Turn left into Rowberrys Rd, then
right into Swamp Rd. Rosedale on
corner, on left
Phone: 0-3-578 4535
Open. By appointment
Groups: By appointment
Fee: $3 per adult
Size: Small – 0.3ha (¾ acre)
Terrain: Flat

with outdoor furniture

Established by Jean on farmland 35 years ago,
Rosedale now features 500 roses, mainly modern
bush varieties in blended colours to create different effects.
Visitors are welcomed at the gate by a warm scarlet, gold
and cream rose bed in summer, while another stretches
down to the pergola where white wisteria drips over Jean's
treasures underneath, and purple wisteria complements a
nearby golden ash. Jean plans such colour combinations
throughout the seasons. *Camellia sasanqua* begin to emerge
in autumn, with 36 large camellias, such as the pale pink
"Phyl Doak" shaped like a great Christmas tree, brightening
the winter and early spring. Japonicas join them at the end
of July, then the earliest of 600 tulips appear in September.
Early daffodils, drifts of forget-me-nots and massed
polyanthus border the spacious lawn where the focal point
is a huge flowering peach, "Pink Cloud". An extensive
bank of Mollis azaleas is a spring feature, with evergreens
and mature rhododendrons such as the brilliant red
"Kaponga". Golden Asiatic lilies add their beauty to the
summer perennials, and the roses flower till the end of May,
when the deciduous trees provide good autumn colour.
The many English specimen trees are complemented by
native kowhai.

RHODODENDRON LODGE
Blenheim

Owners:
Audrey and Charlie Chambers

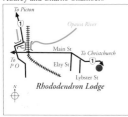

Rhododendron Lodge

Address: 858 SH 1, St Andrews,
R D 4, Blenheim
Directions: Take SH 1 to Blenheim.
Continue south of town on SH 1 to
Rhododendron Lodge on right
Phone: 0-3-578 1145
Open: All year, daily
Groups: By appointment
Fee: $2 per adult
Size: Small – 0.2ha (½ acre)
Terrain: Flat
Swimming pool: Available for use
Accommodation: Quality B&B –
2 twin bedrooms, 1 with ensuite;
$70 double, $50 single

Having retired from full-time farming, the Chambers are enjoying establishing a new garden with an abundant water supply. Audrey's favourite plants are the rhododendrons, roses and delphiniums. In spring the species rhododendrons bloom, beginning with *R. grande*, followed by *R. johnstoneanum* and *R. macabeanum*, then finally *R. yakushimanum*. An extensive collection of hybrid rhododendrons complements these species, accompanied by azaleas, camellias, flowering cherries, crab-apples and maples, underplanted with spring bulbs, lobelias, primulas and forget-me-nots. In summer, the roses take centre stage, with climbers, bush, hybrid teas, floribundas and lots of patio roses predominating. The delphiniums make a lovely contrast with other perennials, blue and white lobelias and white alyssums. The swimming-pool courtyard is bordered by gardens with native ponga tree-ferns a special feature, and a dovecote will soon nestle in the corner. The front garden brims with rhododendrons, azaleas and roses, framed by trees. Audrey is developing a summer hydrangea and agapanthus area here. Native kowhai, matipo and golden totara combine with the exotics which include dogwoods, magnolias, gleditsias, an Indian bean tree and a pepper-tree. Autumn colours the deciduous trees, and chrysanthemums accompany the white fragrant flowering shrub *Bouvardia* "Humboldtii".

BAREWOOD
Seddon

Owners:
Carolyn and Joe Ferraby

Address: Barewood Rd, Seddon,
Marlborough
Directions: From Blenheim take SH 1
south to Seddon. Turn right at Seddon
School into Marama Rd. Travel 17km
to Barewood Rd on left. Continue
1km to Barewood garden
Phone: 0-3-575 7432
Fax: 0-3-575 7432
Open: By appointment
Groups: By appointment
Fee: $3 per adult
Size: Large – 1.6ha (4 acres)
Terrain: Undulating
Nursery: Old roses and perennials
from garden

   mostly

by arrangement

Carolyn has developed the original homestead garden over the past decade, incorporating 80-year-old Douglas firs and oaks. Flowers cascade down the terraced bank in front of the house to the driveway. In spring, clematis and white wisteria adorn the verandahs, with climbing roses taking over in summer. A brick wall is covered with more of the old roses Carolyn loves. Below, a lawn slopes down to a cool woodland spot, where she has established a bog garden of moisture-loving plants under a weeping silver pear. Rhododendrons and viburnums also flourish here, the design influenced by Carolyn's florist background. She likes colours to flow, avoiding any jarring notes. Soft colours, especially pinks and apricots, are used with plenty of green to create a cool atmosphere during the hot, dry Marlborough summers. Whites and silver-greys also lighten the colour scheme, such as soft grey *Stachys lanata* under the pale apricot "Nancy Steen" rose along the driveway. Behind the homestead is Joe's latest project – a summer house – to be draped with roses and approached through a hawthorn avenue. Joe has also built the brick pathways which delineate Carolyn's new potager, featuring espaliered apple and pear arches above billowing lavender borders.

RICHMOND BROOK
Seddon

Owner:
Yvonne Richmond

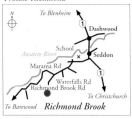

Address: Richmond Brook Rd,
Seddon, Marlborough
Directions: From Blenheim take SH 1
south to Seddon. Turn right at Seddon
School into Marama Rd. Travel 10km
to Richmond Brook Rd on left.
Continue 1.5km to garden
Phone: 0-3-575 7506
Open: By appointment
Groups: By appointment
Fee: $3 per adult
Size: Large – 1.8ha (4½ acres)
Terrain: Flat
Nursery: Perennials from garden

     by arrangement

Richmond Brook has been in the same family since 1848. The first trees were planted in the 1870s, including the huge wellingtonia framing the old stone house built in 1926. The large garden laid out by Yvonne's late husband's grandfather in the 1920s has been revamped by Yvonne over the past decade, to feature shrubs underplanted with perennials in place of the original annual beds. She is gradually replacing the modern roses with old and English varieties, such as her favourites – deep-pink "Constance Spry", blush-pink "Lucetta" and the soft-pink Alba "Félicité Parmentier". Yvonne has festooned the castle-like front facade of the house with cream climbing roses including "Wedding Day", the old "Félicité et Perpétue", banksia-like *Rosa fortuniana*, and Himalayan musk *R. brunonii* that softens the entrance. Other creamy shrubs in front of the house, such as weigela, viburnum, choisya and cistus, are edged with buxus. A further formal box-edged bed of "Iceberg" roses is underplanted with catmint. The curving driveway is edged with a perennial border, more roses, and a row of mature pink rhododendrons providing early spring colour. Soft colours predominate, with lots of green cooling the hot Marlborough summer under the massive established trees.

WINTERHOME GARDEN
Kekerengu

Owners:
Susan and Richard Macfarlane

Address: SH 1, Kekerengu,
Marlborough
Directions: Almost halfway between
Blenheim and Kaikoura, on SH 1.
Travel 70km south of Blenheim or
65km north of Kaikoura to
Kekerengu. Garden on west just north
of Kekerengu
Phone: 0-3-575 8674
Fax: 0-3-575 8620
Open: Labour weekend (end October)
to Easter, daily, 10am–5pm
Groups: As above
Fee: $5 per adult
Size: Large – 2.4ha (6 acres)
Terrain: Flat
For sale: Exclusive imported and NZ-
made garden accessories

   limited

 Devonshire, by arrangement

Winterhome is characterised by boldly straight classical lines, with carefully planned intersecting axes and focal points emphasising perspective. Brick walls clad in espaliered apple trees enclose the white-gravelled carpark, indicating the formal structure of the garden. A brick porthole looks down a formal Dutch-inspired rill or canal at the hub of the central axis, which is being extended to the hills by a cypress avenue. Agapanthus surrounding the carpark brings cool blue and white to the summer, with a pair of Italian cypresses shading bricked steps to a sunken courtyard featuring a raised waterlily pond. Beyond is a formal rose garden of 80 white "Margaret Merril". A jasmine archway frames a view to the swimming pool with a phoenix palm as tropical focal point. A cross-axis leads through wisteria-covered brick pergolas beside the tennis court, or across a swing bridge suspended above the steep driveway, to an avocado grove. Panoramic views stretch over the ocean 30 metres below. A vista across an expansive lawn bordered by a box-edged sea of *Salvia farinacea* "Blue Bedder" leads down a lavender-edged grassy avenue to a white Lutyens-style seat. A woodland path extends to another focal point, where a classical fountain plays in a circular bricked pool.

FYFFE GALLERY AND RESTAURANT
Kaikoura

Owners:
Jan and Graeme Rasmussen

Address: SH 1, Kaikoura, R D 2
Directions: Follow SH 1 south of
Kaikoura for 5.5km (5 minutes).
Fyffe Gallery on right, 2 hours north
of Christchurch
Phone: 0-3-319 6869
Fax: 0-3-319 6869
Open: All year, daily
Groups: By appointment
Fee: No charge
Size: Small – 0.2ha (½ acre)
Terrain: Flat
Restaurant: Seats 60; dinner daily
6pm–8pm in summer; Saturdays only
in winter; book for dinner
Accommodation: 2 doubles and 1
twin, all with en suites, $95 per room
Gallery: Paintings and crafts for sale

  & to toilet

  daily

Behind the adobe restaurant and accommodation house, with cedar shake roof, an English cottage garden has been planted since 1993. Taking care to preserve the magnificent view to Mt Fyffe, the garden has been planted predominantly in blues, whites and yellows. Beyond a manuka railing fence, clad in roses, is a stream crossed by a rustic bridge to a meadow garden of wild flowers. A north-facing brick courtyard behind the restaurant provides a pleasant outdoor eating venue for 30 people, with roses climbing verandah posts and potted standards. Colourful window boxes adorn the two-storeyed building with carpet roses. In spring a weeping prunus blossoms, with white daisies, pink cistus, blue and pink forget-me-nots and potted ranunculus. Then the roses bloom in summer, with the pergola covered in mostly old varieties such as the long-flowering, highly scented white noisette "Mme Alfred Carrière". An urn fountain is the focal point of a brick rondel, and a rustic manuka gazebo is planned as a destination point for the pathways, to provide a resting place for viewing the snow-capped mountains. Trees frame the vista, with tall eucalypts and conifers to the side of this informal garden that was a cow paddock only three years ago.

North, Central and Mid Canterbury, Christchurch and Banks Peninsula

Two-thirds of the population of the South Island lives in Canterbury, which includes the largest city, Christchurch. Thirty-five of the gardens featured are from the northern half of Canterbury. North Canterbury stretches from coastal Kaikoura in the north down to Rangiora, just above Christchurch, then Central Canterbury extends south to the Rakaia River. Mid Canterbury covers the area from Rakaia down through Ashburton. Bordered by the spectacular Southern Alps on the west and the Pacific Ocean on the east, Canterbury enjoys a variety of geographical and climatic changes. The Southern Alps affect the climate, causing rain to fall on the West Coast rainforests. The Canterbury Plains stretch out flat and broad towards the Southern Alps, which appear even more striking in contrast. Many of the gardens incorporate views to the Alps in their garden design.

South of Hanmer Springs is the woodland garden of Lowry Peaks at Culverden, followed by three gardens further south, in the Hawarden area. Flaxmere incorporates vistas to the Alps, with a series of ponds, and Milima features a rockery and climbers over archways, while McDonald Downs is an historic Alfred Buxton garden, retaining many of the original deciduous trees. Closer to the coast at Amberley are two gardens: Brikton, a seasonal garden, and Hunters Garden divided into "rooms", with many planted walkways. At Rangiora is the English country garden Somerset Downs, and nearby is the rose display garden at Littlerose Nursery in Cust. Just north of Christchurch is Ohoka where Wilsons Mill Garden features tree-lined avenues.

Christchurch, of English-style design, is often called the "Garden City". The picturesque Avon River flows through this flat city, crossed by countless bridges. Hagley Park, a sight in spring with its massed daffodils, includes the Botanic Gardens within its boundaries. The Chateau on the Park features a formal rose gardens and moat and nearby are the well known gardens at Mona Vale, surrounding an historic house. Royden is an urban garden planted in 1938 and Fairleigh features a rock garden with miniature alpines and roses. Towards Lincoln is Ballymoney, a woodland garden with pond and birdlife. Overlooking Sumner is Gethsemane, a unique garden with a Christian theme. Banks Peninsula features five gardens: Nydfa, a hillside perennial garden overlooking Governors Bay; Ohinetahi, a formal garden alongside a woodland gully; and Taunton, an old-English-style garden. Towards Akaroa, at Okains Bay is Heaton Rutland Plants and Gardens with its gullies of rhododendrons, and at Pigeon Bay, Annandale is an historic garden featuring mature trees.

South of Christchurch is Weedons, where Willow Tree features herbs laid out in a new garden with adjoining scented shop. In Central Canterbury there are two gardens near Darfield: The Gums with banks of colour, and Bridge Farm with its colonial-style garden. At Dunsandel is Marsal Paeonies where peonies predominate and at Southbridge is the woodland garden of Wendrum. Crossing the Rakaia River, we come to Suzette Gardens with topiary and seasonal flowering walks. In Ashburton itself are two gardens: Coniston, a mature woodland garden surrounding a lake and the more recent Trotts' Garden with a mix of woodland. Just south of Ashburton are three gardens: Willowbank with plantings incorporating a pond, Leafield featuring roses, and Willowpark with established trees. Inland at Ruapuna is Stonehaven with its dry stone walling and meandering woodland paths, and Eden Terrace with a series of ponds. Dunhampton Lily Fields at Mount Somers displays its lilies in summer and 10 kilometres further on is Inverary Station, a mid Canterbury farmstay set in a high-country garden with mature woodland.

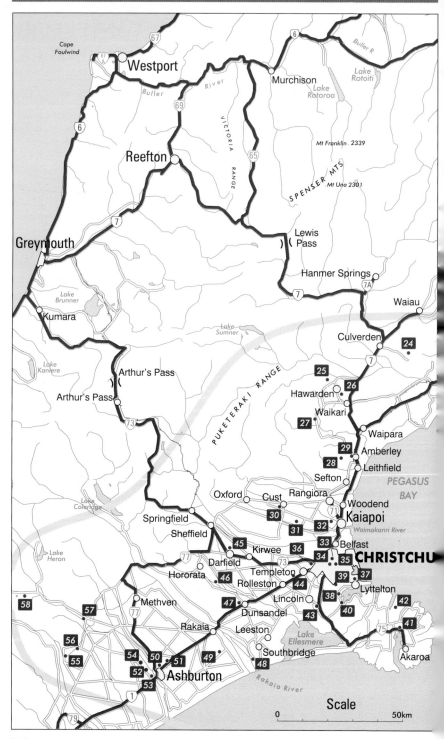

Cape
Foulwind

67
67
A
Westport

Buller R

6

Lake
Rotoiti

Murchison
Lake
Rotoroa

Buller   River

69

VICTORIA   RANGE

65

Mt Franklin . 2339

SPENSER MTS

. Mt Una 2301

6

Reefton

Lewis
Pass

7

Hanmer Springs   7A

Greymouth

Waiau

Lake
Brunner

Kumara

Lake
Kaniere

Lake
Sumner

Culverden   7

24

Arthur's Pass

PUKETERAKI RANGE

25

Hawarden   26

Arthur's Pass

73

Waikari

27

Springfield

Sheffield

Lake
Coleridge

Lake
Heron

Waipara

29

Amberley

28

Leithfield

Sefton

Oxford   Cust   Rangiora   PEGASUS
BAY

30

45   Kirwee

31

71   Woodend

32   Kaiapoi

Darfield   36

33   Belfast

Waimakariri River

77

Hororata   46   Templeton   44   34   35   CHRISTCHU

73   39   37

Rolleston   38   Lyttelton

Methven   47   Lincoln   42

57   43

77   Rakaia   Dunsandel   40   75   41

58   54   50   Leeston   Lake
Ellesmere   Akaroa

56   51   49   Southbridge

55   52   48

53

1   Ashburton

Rakaia River

Scale

0   50km

79

LOWRY PEAKS
Culverden

Owners:
Jossy and David Davison

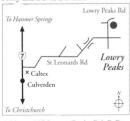

Address: 118 Lowry Peaks Rd, R D,
Culverden
Directions: At Culverden, turn east at
Caltex Mason Motors into
St Leonards Rd. Travel about 10km
to crossroads. Turn left into Lowry
Peaks Rd. Continue about 1.5km to
garden on right
Phone: 0-3-315 8172
Fax: 0-3-315 8014
Open: September to May, daily,
by appointment
Groups: By appointment, as above
Fee: $5 per adult
Size: Medium – 1.4ha (3½ acres)
Terrain: Flat
Functions: Garden weddings by
arrangement

Lowry Peaks is a 16-year-old woodland garden, although its origins reach back to 1913 when the house was built. A vitis vine festoons the verandah and expansive lawns stretch to borders of golden luteum azaleas, underplanted with a sea of blue forget-me-nots, and the new focal point of a Gothic gazebo beyond. Prominent species include davidia trees and David's favourite rhododendrons and magnolias, such as a lovely shaped *Magnolia grandiflora* and *M. loebneri* "Leonard Messel" with its frothy pink stellata-like blooms. Rhododendrons include the fragrant pastel shell-pink "Loderi Pink Diamond", golden-yellow "Crest", and pale-lemon "Unique" under a "Jack Humm" malus. Other spring features to catch are the 25 different old varieties of daffodils under the silver birches along the driveway in September and the prunus blossom – cherries, quinces and crab-apples. David is replacing some original pines with quinces and red oaks, which provide autumn colour along with maples and ashes. Other exotics include four catalpa or Indian bean trees, both golden and green with their large leaves. Summertime features perennials, lilies and roses. A pergola is clad in white, the climbing "Iceberg" rose intertwined with *Clematis armandii*, hybrid "Madame Le Coultre" and a native clematis, while a geometric stone pond is planted in blues and yellows.

FLAXMERE
Hawarden

Owner:
Penny Zino

Address: R D, Hawarden
Directions: From SH 7 turn west to
Waikari. Turn right to Hawarden.
Continue on Lake Sumner Rd for
10km to Westenras Rd on right.
Flaxmere on right
Phone: 0-3-314 4504
Fax: 0-3-314 4493
Open: September to April, by
appointment; also Open Days
Groups: As above
Fee: $5 per adult over 12 years
Size: Large – 2.8ha (7 acres)
Terrain: Terraced riverbed country
Nursery: Mainly roses, shrubs,
climbers, hedging plants

      mostly

   by arrangement

Flaxmere is a garden of vistas and focal points, with framed views to the surrounding hills and Southern Alps. Penny and her late husband John developed Flaxmere for almost three decades, with formal elements and stone walls providing structure, softened by prolific planting. The extreme climate dictates the planting, with severe winters followed by cheerful blossom to welcome the spring. Flowering cherries are underplanted with thousands of daffodils creating a carpet of colour. Grey foliage and a lot of green cool the hot dry summers and show off Penny's roses which she sells each season including her favourite old-fashioned varieties, especially the hybrid musks. Ramblers climb the century-old house and a pergola along the drive. A hexagonal rose garden is planted in graduated colour around a central sun-dial, with pathways radiating in six directions incorporating views to the countryside. From the house, the eastern vista leads down terraced lawns to a reflective pool, with rose pergolas forming a cross-axis. The northern vista extends past one of Penny's ponds, over a curved bridge and down a grassy avenue flanked by bold shrub plantings, to the Alps beyond. Rich autumn colour is provided by the prunus, along with pin oaks, liquidambars, rhus, nyssa and amelanchiers.

MILIMA
Hawarden

Owners:
Shirley and Geoffrey Chart

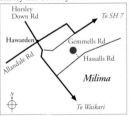

Address: Hassalls Rd, R D, Hawarden
Directions: From south, take SH 7
and turn off to Waikari. Travel
towards Hawarden. Turn right into
Hassalls Rd. Garden is first on left.
Or from north, turn off SH 7 to
Hawarden. Turn left at crossroads,
then take second left into Hassalls
Rd. Garden first on left
Phone: 0-3-314 4522
Open: November to March, by
appointment
Groups: As above
Fee: $2 per adult
Size: Small – 0.25ha (½ acre–¼ acre)
Terrain: Flat and gently sloping

 mostly

 in gazebo

The Charts who emigrated from Kenya 20 years ago
have called their garden by the Swahili name for
a hill – "Milima". The lawn surrounding the house was
turned into a rockery six years ago, when tonnes of earth
were brought in, to create mounds, and boulders were
strategically placed before the planting began. Geoff built
the archways that now support four or five different native
clematis and the gazebo that provides shelter from the
nor'-westers. A Montana clematis climbs its trellis walls,
harmonising with the blue-purple-mauve-pink colour
scheme that Shirley prefers. She likes soft colours in
a garden, avoiding reds and yellows, except where yellows
in her rockery blend in with creams, such as the Dutch
irises. Black wrought iron gates create a "window" in the
pine hedge for viewing the surrounding countryside with
its backdrop of snow-capped mountains. Flanking the
"window" in spring are three malus trees, with three pink
wisteria trees in the paddock beyond. The flowering cherry
"Shimidsu sakura" underplanted with phlox and pansies
blossoms simultaneously with a huge 15-year-old ceanothus.
As the clematis, wisteria and the other spring flowers fade,
annuals and perennials come on, with roses such as "Silver
Moon" over an archway.

McDONALD DOWNS
Hawarden

Owners:
Bill and Phil Paterson

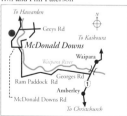

Address: 438 McDonald Downs Rd,
Waipara
Postal: R D, Hawarden
Directions: Travel north from
Amberley on SH 1 for about 10km.
Turn left into Georges Rd. Continue
on this road 10km through Waipara
Gorge to Karetu Bridge. Continue
5km to garden on left. (About 25km
from Amberley)
Phone: 0-3-314 4272
Fax: 0-3-314 4462
Open: September to Easter, daily,
by appointment
Groups: By appointment, as above
Fee: Donations
Size: Medium – 0.7ha (1–2 acres)
Terrain: Flat to hilly

McDonald Downs is one of New Zealand's historic gardens, laid out by the renowned garden landscaper, Alfred Buxton. His influence can still be seen today in typical Buxton elements, such as the sweeping driveway, revealing the house framed by established trees only at the moment of arrival. The spacious box-edged lawns, a water garden, rose garden, and of course the wonderful English trees tightly planted round the perimeter are further Buxton features. The original McDonald was a shepherd at Heathstock Downs when McDonald Downs was divided off in the early 1900s, the homestead built, and Alfred Buxton appointed to design the surrounding grounds. The exotic trees he planted around the large sloping lawn provide a welcome canopy of shade during the hot North Canterbury summer and glorious colour in the frosty autumn. They include golden elms, silver birches, and oaks, complementing the scarlet Virginia creepers draping the verandah. The trees are underplanted with drifts of daffodils which accompany the spring blossom, camellias and rhododendrons. Roses are a feature in summer, and the pond is a mass of colourful waterlilies. Further trees shelter the swimming-pool area, with glimpses to the surrounding hills. McDonald Downs has been in the Paterson family since 1966.

HUNTERS GARDEN
Amberley

Owners:
Freda and Ian Hunter

Hunters Garden

Address: 162 Maskells Rd, R D 1,
Amberley
Directions: Turn off SH 1 at Amberley
Hotel west into Markham St. Turn
right into Douglas Rd, then left into
Lawcocks Rd. Turn left into Balcairn-
Amberley Rd, then right into Maskells
Rd. Hunters Garden fourth on right
Phone: 0-3-314 8391
Open: September to May, daily,
by appointment
Groups: 10 or more preferred
Fee: $3 per adult
Size: Medium – 1ha (2½ acres)
Terrain: Gently sloping
Nursery: Floral art supplies for sale
Floral art demonstrations: "Designing
for Special Occasions" for groups

 by arrangement

The entrance garden features a small waterlily pool set in a rock and alpine garden, with a border of mainly camellias backed by natives. A grape and ivy-clad fence separates off the summer house and "Garden Room" which is planted in trees and shrubs, with white sprays of agonis blossom and standardised choisya in tubs. A woodland path leads to the "View Garden" where rhododendrons and azaleas underplanted with hostas, rodgersias and Japanese irises frame a view to Mt Grey and the surrounding hills. A pathway leads through an archway, covered in the white rose "Albéric Barbier", to the front garden where modern and heritage roses are complemented by fuchsias and dwarf maples. White prunus "Shirotae" is underplanted with pastel roses and dwarf delphiniums. Rock plants complement a sun-dial backed by a weeping pink prunus, while a pottery fountain is surrounded by greys, whites and blues. Curving grassy walkways lead to semi-formal gardens where old roses predominate. A "Pergola Walk" ends at the focal point of a rose-clad Bell House featuring a 130-year-old bell. Beyond is the pond with a pair of black swans. A yellow, blue and white garden leads back to the new potager. Finally, a fernery provides a restful area beneath maples.

BRIKTON
Amberley

Owners:
Ursula and Brian Wright

Address: 45 Douglas Rd, Amberley
Directions: Turn off Carters Rd
(SH 1) west into Douglas St.
Continue across railway line to
Brikton, 45 Douglas Rd, on right
Phone: 0-3-314 8771
Open: September to autumn, daily,
by appointment
Groups: By appointment, as above
Fee: $2 per adult
Size: Small – 0.2ha (½ acre)
Terrain: Flat
Nursery: Occasional plants from
garden

 by arrangement

Since 1990, Ursula has transformed a bare paddock into a flowering garden sectioned into separate rooms. She chooses subtle pastel colours, using a lot of pinks, whites, creams and deep blues to tone in with the recycled-brick house, avoiding overpowering oranges or purples. Ursula's favourite plants include flowering cherries, camellias and rhododendrons in spring, followed by old roses and pickable perennials in summer. She is not keen on bedding plants, preferring container planting and foliage or flowers she can pick, such as the many varieties of leucadendron she is collecting that look so good against the brick. Proteas, too, feature in early spring, then drifts of spring bulbs, wild primroses and forget-me-nots provide a colourful carpet beneath the prunus and malus blossom. Heritage roses ramble over fences and archways, with a summer house and hedges contributing structure and interest to the garden, and dividing it into rooms. Old bricks matching the house have been used to construct patios and edge the pathways that link the different areas. Native lancewoods provide height down the side of the garden and conifers are interplanted with the exotics. Autumn colour is provided by rosehips and the foliage of the cherries, crab-apples, maples and liquidambars.

LITTLEROSE GARDENS AND NURSERY
Cust

Owners:
Jill and John Hughes

Address: 1771 Main Rd (SH 72), Cust
Postal: P O Box 32, Cust
Directions: From Christchurch take
SH 1 north. Take motorway exit left
into Tram Rd towards Oxford. Travel
23km then turn right into Earlys Rd.
At Cust, turn left on to SH 72. Travel
1km to Littlerose on left
Phone: 0-3-312 5704
Open: All year, daily, 9am–5pm,
  or by appointment
Groups: By appointment
Fee: $3 per adult
Size: Medium – almost 1ha (2½ acres)
Terrain: Flat
Nursery: Rose specialist –
old-fashioned, patio and miniatures

The Hughes have developed their rose nursery over the past eight years. They started with miniatures planted alphabetically, now numbering 430 different varieties of bush, standard and weeping roses. Then they added 500 old roses, planted in families, including shrub, climbers, and ramblers. A new section of David Austin roses is an attraction and a copper beech is underplanted with shrub groundcover or "colourscape" roses. The roses are planted in shaped raised beds edged with half-rounds and bordered with pansies, English lavender and silene. A weeping silver pear provides height and contrast. John's favourite rose is the miniature "Rainbow's End" in yellow edged with red, and Jill loves the singles and old roses, such as peachy "Albertine" and salmon-pink "François Juranville" rambling through the silver birches. The vermilion floribunda "Rusticana" (or "Poppy Flash") climbs the wall of the office, while other climbers and ramblers adorn the gums along the roadside, and a new rose walk displays 30 further climbers and ramblers. Potted miniatures edge the nursery. The peak time for viewing the roses is from mid November. The species and Frühlings roses open first in October, while patios and miniatures flower through until the first hard frosts in April.

219

SOMERSET DOWNS
Rangiora

Owners:
Roger and Margaret Southcott

Address: North Eyre Rd, R D 1
Rangiora
Directions: From Christchurch take
SH 1 north. Take motorway exit left
into Tram Rd towards Oxford. Travel
20km, then turn left into Chapmans
Boundary Rd. Turn left again into
North Eyre Rd. Garden on right
Phone: 0-3-312 5864
Fax: 0-3-312 5864
Open: First weekend each month
during spring and summer; other
times by appointment
Groups: As above
Fee: $3 per adult
Size: Medium – 1.2ha (3 acres)
Terrain: Flat
Nursery: Specialist in perennials and
rockery plants; range of trees & shrubs

 by arrangement

Fourteen years ago, Somerset Downs was a bare
paddock. Roger designed an English country garden,
planted eucalypts for quick shelter – now enjoyed by
pheasants, guinea-fowl, bantams, pigeons and peacocks –
and then began planting the English trees he loves. A central
specimen copper beech is complemented by oaks, ashes
and an English beech hedge, which will be trimmed
formally to separate garden rooms. The predominant
species are a mixture of deciduous and evergreen natives
in a park-like setting, with rhododendrons in spring and
roses in summer. Roger likes the pastel shades of
rhododendrons, but enjoys occasional vibrant colour as
well. Daffodils carpet a Chinese poplar copse and bring
spring colour to the recently developed pond area. Roger
loves old roses and David Austin English roses, such
as peachy "Abraham Derby" climbing a silk tree and
"Albertine" rambling over an archway. Foxgloves feature
prominently, with sisyrinchiums and other perennials
beneath silver birches, and rock plants in tufa pots. *Stachys
lanata* encircles a willow and English lavender borders
the beds, separated by sweeping lawns. Clipped box
encloses a weeping silver pear and edges cardoons in
a sheltered corner. The box hedging unifies and provides
formal structure to this flowing garden, while statuary
adds interest.

WILSONS MILL GARDEN
Ohoka

Owners:
Ann and Alan Izard

Address: Christmas Rd, Ohoka,
R D 2, Kaiapoi
Directions: From Christchurch, take
SH 1 north. Take second exit off
motorway, towards Ohoka. Travel
along Mill Rd, then turn left into
Christmas Rd. Garden on right
Phone: 0-3-327 8113
Fax: 0-3-327 8113
Open: All year, daily, by appointment
Groups: By appointment, as above
Fee: $6 per adult
Size: Large – 5.5ha (13–14 acres)
Terrain: Flat and gently undulating
Nursery: Plants from garden
sometimes available

   limited

 by arrangement

The Izards began developing their garden in 1987. Strong lines define the structure, with Alan's favourite trees framing vistas and forming axes. Ann's exuberant plantings soften these lines and provide seasonal colour, using green as the base, with apricots and yellows in profusion and other colours for accent. A colonnade of classical pillars is echoed by rows of columnar trees and clipped hedges such as hornbeam and low buxus. An avenue of cabbage trees leads from the entrance courtyard to the lake featuring waterfowl and lilies. The westerly axis from the house and lake is extended by an avenue of Tasman poplars. Two fastigiate oaks and a golden tree are the focal points of the northerly axis of Leyland cypress. Ginkgoes lining the driveway turn golden in autumn, and the pin-oak grove turns scarlet. Clematis climbs through many of the maturing trees, underplanted with rhododendrons and other shrubs. Spring highlights include a variety of flowering cherries, then hundreds of roses take centre stage in summer. A rose arbour is the central focal point of a formal circular peony garden hedged with box. Other features at Wilsons Mill, named after an original flax mill, include deer and cattle in adjacent paddocks.

221

ROYDEN
Fendalton

Owners:
Dorothy and Norman Gardiner

Address: 8 Royds St, Christchurch
Directions: Take Riccarton or
Fendalton Roads to Straven Rd. Turn
east into Royds St (no exit). Garden
on right
Phone: 0-3-351 7795
Fax: pending
Open: October, November and
March; by appointment
Groups: By appointment, as above
Fee: $3 per adult
Size: Small – 0.25ha (⅝ acre)
Terrain: Flat and terraced

   mostly

 individuals only

Royden is an urban garden established in 1938. Dorothy's father planted maples lining Royds Street and erected the sun-dial on the roadside. Mature trees include a huge copper beech and equally huge chestnut with a woodland created in its shade featuring tree ferns and contrasting reds. A red tulip bed surrounds a weeping cherry tree and pink camellias show beneath the scarlet oak in spring while it is still free of foliage. Dorothy likes pinks and blues such as the "Pinkie" roses along the front stone wall below the magnolias, deep pink peonies and blue irises. Lavenders edge the front path and encircle the maples on the street, along with annuals and daffodils. Behind the house is the Wainairi Stream with its clear waters feeding a waterfall that runs through Haswell stone planted round with native ferns. Other features include a *Grevillea robusta*, unusual as far south as Christchurch, a fernery and an orchid house containing many varieties. An art deco light illuminates the holly against the house. A small pool in the front garden is planted with flaxes and irises. The roses continue into March, along with the perennials in the front borders.

MONA VALE
Fendalton

Owner:
Christchurch City Council

Address: 63 Fendalton Rd,
Christchurch
Postal: P O Box 237, Christchurch
Directions: From the city, take Harper
Avenue along the northern boundary
of Hagley Park. Turn right into
Fendalton Rd. Mona Vale on left
Phone: 0-3-348 9660
Fax: 0-3-348 7011
Open: All year, daily, 7.30am till
1 hour before sunset
Groups: As above; buses to park
outside grounds
Fee: No charge
Size: Large – 5ha (12 acres)
Terrain: Mainly flat, but contoured to
river
Homestead: teas, lunches
also available for private functions

Mona Vale is an historic garden surrounding a turn-of-the-century homestead on the banks of the Avon River. The Edwardian character of the garden has been retained, despite a succession of owners and garden designers. Alice Waymouth originated the garden in 1900; Annie Townend's additions in the next decade included the Fernery purchased from the 1906 Christchurch Exhibition, the Bathhouse and Fendalton Road Gatehouse. Tracy Gough engaged Alfred Buxton to revamp the garden in 1939, resulting in extensive plantings of rhododendrons, azaleas and English trees. The Buxton rose garden was later replaced by Gough with the current lily pond and fountain. Buxton was also responsible for the mound lawn, and the surprise approaches to the homestead seen through weeping trees are a favourite Buxton feature. Mature trees of note include the weeping elms flanking the house, a liriodendron, Lebanese cedar, and weeping willows bordering the river. Native plantings also feature. Mona Vale was saved from demolition in 1967, when the Christchurch City Council and Riccarton Borough Council purchased and restored it for public use. Improvements since then include the new rose gardens, transformation of the Bathhouse into a conservatory, restoration of the Fernery, and extensive additions to the many plant collections.

223

THE CHATEAU ON THE PARK
Riccarton

Manager:
Chris Hill

Address: 189 Deans Ave, Riccarton, Christchurch
Postal: P O Box 8161, Christchurch
Directions: From Christchurch city, take Harper Ave north of Hagley Park. Turn left at end into Deans Ave. Chateau garden on right. From Riccarton Rd, turn left at Hagley Park into Deans Ave. Chateau on left
Phone: 0-3-348 8999
Fax: 0-3-348 8990
Open: All year, daily, any time
Groups: By appointment
Fee: No charge
Size: Medium – 1.2ha (3 acres)
Terrain: Flat
Restaurant: Garden Court Brasserie – dinner available
Accommodation: Available

The garden at the Chateau on the Park has been redeveloped over the last three years on a mature treed site. The predominant species are roses, camellias and rhododendrons, with the formal rose garden a special attraction. Courtyards provide structure, with a moat bordering the reception area, which can be viewed from inside through glassed walls. The water garden around the moat is planted with moisture-loving species such as hostas, native ferns and water fuchsias. Weddings are popular in the inner courtyard at any time of the year, plantings providing seasonal colour mainly in pinks, blues and whites. Spring bulbs and beds of spring flowers accompany the camellias and rhododendrons. Protected trees include a large magnolia which adds to the spring display, and an English oak contributing to the lovely autumn colour. A woodland area attracts many birds to enhance the spring atmosphere. The rose garden is the prime summer feature with the Garden Court Brasserie looking out on to the roses. Summer also features prolific cottage plantings of perennials including candytuft, phlox, lobelia and salvia which complement the annual begonias, alyssum, pansies and polyanthus. This unusually extensive garden in a hotel setting borders Christchurch's famous Hagley Park.

FAIRLEIGH
Harewood

Owner:
Elaine Grundy

Address: 411 Sawyers Arms Rd,
Harewood, Christchurch
Directions: From Christchurch city,
take Harewood Rd. Turn right into
Greers Rd. Turn left at island into
Sawyers Arms Rd. Garden towards
airport on left
Phone: 0-3-359 5734
Open: 1 October to 31 March; daily;
by appointment
Groups: By appointment, as above
Fee: $3 per adult
Size: Small – 0.3ha (¼ acre)
Terrain: Flat
Nursery: Plants from garden –
perennials and rock plants for sale

    shingle

 on lawn  by arrangement

In 1987 Elaine planted her rock garden, put in the trees and tamed the paddocks into lawns. Her favourite plants are the rock plants, miniature alpines and old roses that flourish in the good soil at Fairleigh. The rock garden begins flowering in spring with bulbs accompanied by miniature lilacs, camellias, many clematis including two or three native species and the pink "Freda", magnolias and lots of other blossom trees. Rhododendrons bloom along with other plants in the woodland area. Two ponds featuring goldfish and waterlilies are planted round with trilliums, hostas, miniature bulbs and various irises including bog, Japanese, miniatures and bearded varieties. In summer masses of dianthus feature in the rock garden and the old roses ramble over arches. Four of them – "Dupontii", "Frühlingsmorgen", "Mermaid", and "Sally Holmes" – are painted on cards for sale in Elaine's craft shop. The colour scheme includes lots of white, primrose and the deep blue of gentians. Elaine loves the summer daisies, sweet peas and old-fashioned perennials such as her foxgloves, delphiniums and the lupins that frame the shingle pathways. She has lots of pots and tubs, making the tufa pots herself for her miniature alpines.

225

GETHSEMANE GARDENS
Sumner

Owners:
Bev and Ken Loader

Gethsemane Gardens

Address: 27 Revelation Drive (end Clifton Tce), Sumner, Christchurch
Directions: From Christchurch take Ferry Rd and Main Rd to Clifton. Past Shag Rock turn right up Clifton Tce. Keep left and continue to Revelation Drive (no exit). Gethsemane Gardens on left
Phone: 0-3-326 5848
Open: All year, daily, 9am–5pm,
Closed: Good Friday, Anzac morning (25 April), Easter & Christmas Days
Groups: By appointment
Fee: $2 per adult
Size: Medium – 1.2ha (3 acres)
Terrain: Hilly
Nursery: Alpines, climbers, old roses, groundcovers, large range perennials

🚶 🐕 👫 ♿ partly

🥄 complimentary, tearooms pending

The Christian theme of this garden is spelt out in garden rooms representing each of the letters of the garden's name G-E-T-H-S-E-M-A-N-E. "G" is a curving herbaceous border, "E", "T" and "H" are herb gardens, a knot garden forms the Star of David in the lower half of "H", with the Star of Bethlehem in the top half, "S" is a scented curving pergola, and the second "E" is a rock garden. "M" is another herbaceous border, with a summer house at the apex, and "A" contains a water garden in the lower section, with a white garden in the top triangle. "N" is a larger rock garden and the final "E" is a shade house, each arm filled with shade-loving plants. The dry hill behind is the Mount of Olives featuring recently planted olive trees and lavender. Beyond is a colourful daisy bank with kniphofias massed behind. A lookout provides panoramic views over the coastline and a trellis-built chapel is sited to take advantage of the view. Wedding parties wend their way through the colours of the rainbow in the Bridal Walk towards it. A Rosary Maze features old roses, while a potager is Bev's newest addition. Gethsemane is full of graduated colour all summer, with Marguerite daisies the mainstay in winter.

OHINETAHI
Governors Bay

Owner:
Sir Miles Warren

Address: Governors Bay, R D 1
Lyttelton
Directions: From Christchurch, take
Colombo St over Dyers Pass to
Governors Bay. Continue on Main Rd
1km past shop in Governors Bay.
Garden on left opposite sign
"Ohinetahi Valley" in grassed triangle
at curve in road
Phone: 0-3-329 9852
Fax: 0-3-329 9852
Open: Mid September to mid
December, then mid January to end
February, 9am–4pm, Tuesday,
Wednesday, Thursday
Groups: By appointment
Fee: $10 per adult; groups of 10 or
more $5 per adult
Size: Medium – 1.2ha (3 acres)
Terrain: Flat and steep with steps

 flat area

Ohinetahi is nestled into the hillside overlooking
Governors Bay, within a framework of mature trees
planted in the 1860s by T H Potts, an early botanist.
An original avenue of Burbank plums provides spring
blossom and leads to a double herbaceous border in pinks,
mauves and blues, which ends at the focal point of an ogee
dome-shaped gazebo, reflecting the arches along the
verandah of the historic stone house. This major axis is
one of four which provide strong architectural lines
softened by exuberant plantings. The axes are formed by
clipped hedges, brick pathways and steps, creating vistas
that lead to focal points and views over Lyttelton Harbour.
Within rectangles of topiaried box, a formal parterre rose
garden in white, yellow and terracotta complements the
stone walls of the house. Beyond is a water garden, with
a cross-axis leading up to a walled white garden. A pleached
hornbeam walk extends to a grass oval, with a geometric
"half" garden on the same axis. A swing bridge crosses
a stream running through the woodland garden which
features ancient camellias and rhododendrons. The stream
is interrupted by small pools and edged with bog plants.
This woodland valley contrasts with the formality of the
terraced garden rooms above.

NYDFA
Governors Bay

Owners:
Sharron and Mark Ballantyne

Address: 21 Zephyr Tce, Governors
Bay, Lyttelton, R D 1
Directions: From Christchurch, take
Colombo St over Dyers Pass to
Governors Bay. Turn first right into
Zephyr Tce. Nydfa gardens
signposted on left
Phone: 0-3-329 9621
Fax: 0-3-329 9621
Open: All year, daily, 9am–5pm
Groups: Buses by appointment
Fee: No charge
Size: Small – 0.3ha (¼ acre)
Terrain: Sloping
Nursery: Lavenders, perennials, old
roses and rockery plants
Toilets: At local community centre,
1km away

Welsh for "the nest", Nydfa nestles into the rocky
hillside overlooking Governors Bay. A bare paddock
surrounding an old cottage only eight years ago, Nydfa is
now an exuberant cottage garden carefully planned with
intersecting pathways meandering up the hillside to the
nursery, spilling over with fragrant flowers in spring and
summer. Mark concentrates on the practical aspects at
Nydfa, while Sharron is the designer. The frost-free spring
allows colour to predominate, with drifts of the white and
purple biennial honesty and massed violets overflowing
beneath the flowering cherries. Sharron specialises in
lavenders with over 20 varieties, including the longer-
bracted stoechas lavenders in spring and the traditional
English spiky varieties perfuming the air in summer,
a 7.5-metre lavender hedge flanking the pathway to the
cottage door. Sharron loves her fragrant shrubs such as
the lilacs which feature in spring. A mainly white bed is
a contrast to the favourite bright yellows mixed with purples.
Sharron plants Mediterranean colours, with purple, mustard,
red and cream blended together like a rich tapestry. Old
roses and hybrids welcome the summer, and many varieties
of buddleias attract butterflies to Nydfa. Even winter is
colourful, with proteas, grevilleas and Marguerite daisies
still in flower.

TAUNTON GARDENS
Allandale

Owners:
Barry and Lyn Sligh

Address: Governors Bay, R D 1, Allandale
Directions: From Christchurch, take Colombo St over Dyers Pass to Governors Bay. Turn right, then travel 2km to Taunton Gardens on right
Phone: 0-3-329 9746
Fax: 0-3-329 9746
Open: September to April, 9am–5.30pm; Tuesday to Sunday; nursery also open May to August, Friday to Sunday
Groups: By appointment
Fee: $5 per adult
Size: Medium – over 1 ha (3 acres)
Terrain: Flat and hilly
Nursery: Choice selection of plants eg award-winning azaleas; mail-order catalogue, $5, May to September

by arrangement

After restoring his 1853 stone house, Barry created the garden around two ancient oaks dominating the front lawn. He planted the hillside behind with over 1,000 exotics, retaining vistas to Lyttelton Harbour. Almost two decades later, Taunton's old-English-style garden features award-winning rhododendrons and mollis azaleas that Barry hybridises, and his favourite fragrant plants including an 80-year-old *Viburnum carlesii* and the species *Bullatum edgeworthii* rhododendron. Mauve wisteria clothes the verandah, bordered by the pale-lemon English rose "Windrush" underplanted with "Johnson's Blue" cranesbill geraniums. Vertical accent is provided by Barry's unique dwarf Judas tree, belying its 18 years' growth from a seedling. Forget-me-nots drift round a gazebo, its shake roof mirroring the house. Cornus and magnolias bloom above trilliums and fritillarias. A stream meanders into two ponds which Barry is developing – one large enough for an island with cabbage trees. Daylilies are massed among the rocks, a purple and white wisteria walk along the bank is underplanted with *Agapanthus* "Streamline", and a hosta dell features 120 different varieties. Barry groups pastels together, planting strong colours at a distance, with a deep green background, such as the reds beyond the stream. New double deciduous azaleas cover the full colour range.

231

HEATON RUTLAND PLANTS AND GARDENS
Akaroa

Owners:
Heaton Rutland and Alison
Collingwood

**Heaton Rutland
Plants & Gardens**

Address: Okains Bay Rd, R D 1,
Robinsons Bay, Akaroa
Directions: From Christchurch, take
SH 75 towards Akaroa. Past
Duvauchelle, take second turning on
left, Okains Bay Rd. Follow signposts
and travel 2km to garden on right
Phone: 0-3-304 7096
Open: All year, daily, 9am–5pm
Groups: By appointment
Fee: $3 per adult or purchase from
nursery
Size: Large – 8ha (20 acres)
Terrain: Hilly with gently contoured
paths
Nursery: Rhododendrons, shrubs,
alpines, natives, perennials from
garden

 partly

Begun seven years ago in the crater of an extinct volcano, Heaton Rutland's garden keeps spreading. When he filled up the first gully with his favourite rhododendrons, he began on the adjacent valley. Now he is over the hills, planting trees and letting perennials naturalise to provide great drifts of groundcover. Heaton has designed his garden for seasonal colour, although the spring is hard to beat with his massed rhododendrons blooming, underplanted with bulbs and featuring treasures such as drifts of trilliums. Rock plants and alpines intermingle with the perennials – alstromerias, penstemons and ligularias forming carpets of colour. Roses are being planted as a summer attraction, with autumn a blaze of scarlet oaks, maples and many other deciduous trees. A kauri grove is complemented by other native trees going in everywhere. This is planting on a large scale, with always another basin beyond, each valley providing new panoramic views over Akaroa Harbour. Every season is quite distinctive, with many flowers continuing through the winter. Heaton doesn't consciously plant according to colour; if a plant feels right in a given place, that is where he puts it. Peacocks strutting, displaying, flying and calling add to the colourful spectacle.

ANNANDALE
Pigeon Bay

Owners:
Jane and Frank Davison

Address: Pigeon Bay, Banks
Peninsula; *Postal*: P O Box 19,
Pigeon Bay, Banks Peninsula
Directions: From Christchurch, take
SH 75 towards Akaroa. At the Hilltop
Hotel turn left into Summit Rd. Take
the third roadway on the left. At
Pigeon Bay turn right across bridge
and continue to garden at Annandale
Phone: 0-3-304 6800
Open: October to April, daily,
by appointment
Groups: By appointment, as above
Fee: $3 per adult
Size: Medium – 0.6ha (1½ acres);
original 1.6ha (4 acres) accessible
Terrain: Sculptured
Accommodation: Shearers' cottage
sleeps 14 backpackers, $12 per person

  by arrangement

Seventy years ago, James Gibson designed the Davisons' fifth-generation garden on the water's edge, incorporating two cabbage trees and box hedging planted back in 1884 when the house was built as a hotel. Gibson's training by Alfred Buxton still shows in the layout and lines. Overgrown wattles and blue gums were removed and Gibson's elm trimmed to spread elegantly over the sweeping lawn to a perennial border beside the rose pergola, where Jane grows some of her favourite old roses. The original shaggy, two-metre-high hedge of *Lonicera nitida* has been clipped to neatly edge the sweeping lawn. The Davisons created windows through the trees for sea views, with sizeable eucalypts and wellingtonia providing privacy and a windbreak. An enormous golden banksia rose hedge stretches along the far side of the lawn. Formal box hedging flanked by the ancient cabbage trees still borders a straight path, creating a vista seawards. An old Judas tree rises from the adjacent perennial bed, its cerise spring blossom contrasting with the predominantly green colour scheme. Jane groups her pinks and blues together, with reds and blues elsewhere. She restricts yellows to the far end, where the fernery "wilderness" is now fenced off from the garden.

BALLYMONEY
Taitapu

Owners:
Merrilies and Peter Rebbeck

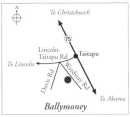
Ballymoney

Address: Wardstay Rd, Taitapu, Christchurch
Postal: R D 2, Christchurch
Directions: From Christchurch city, take SH 75 to Taitapu. Turn right towards Lincoln. Turn left into Wardstay Rd. Garden on right
Phone: 0-3-329 6706
Fax: 0-3-366 6889
Open: All year, daily, by appointment
Groups: By appointment, as above
Fee: $5 per adult including tea/coffee; Groups 10 or more $4 each including tea/coffee
Size: Medium – 0.8ha (2 acres)
Terrain: Flat
Accommodation: 1 self-contained room with ensuite, double & single beds; also 1 double & 1 twin room with shared bathroom

by arrangement

Ballymoney was the name of the property the Rebbecks owned in Ireland. The trees and hedges they planted in 1980, to break the Canterbury winds, now divide the garden into different areas. Once the trees were established, lots of camellias and rhododendrons were planted, then old roses, perennials and groundcover. Silver birches have self-seeded everywhere along with the oaks, creating a woodland. Daffodils, bluebells and other spring bulbs beneath these trees are followed by the camellias and rhododendrons underplanted with white forget-me-nots, foxgloves, violets and trilliums. Summertime is the peak for the David Austin and old roses underplanted with perennials, and the large area of hostas under the trees. A new spring quince avenue leads to the pond where reflections of foliage and berries brighten the autumn. Merrilies keeps colour out of this area, so as not to distract from the surroundings. The pond hosts a large collection of domestic and wild ducks, with guinea fowl and peacocks nearby, and a dovecote housing pigeons. Kunekune and saddleback pigs add interest. The windbreaks such as beech hedges feature in the winter. A small knot garden, summer houses and pergolas provide structure. A potager is being developed and the orchard underplanted with lavender. Quality Bed and Breakfast and farmstay is available by arrangement.

WILLOW TREE
Weedons

Owners:
Priscilla and Jeremy Palmer

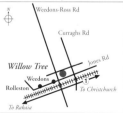

Address: Jones Rd, Weedons, Christchurch
Directions: From Christchurch take SH 1 south to Templeton. Continue, then turn right into Weedons-Ross Rd. Cross railway line, then turn right into Jones Rd. Garden on left
Phone: 0-3-347 9379
Fax: 0-3-347 9379
Open: October to April, daily, by appointment
Groups: As above
Fee: $2 per adult
Size: Small – 0.13ha (⅓ acre)
Terrain: Flat
Nursery: Dried herbs, fresh lavender
Shop: Scented shop selling fragrant and culinary gifts

 herbal, pending

Willow Tree Herbs was uprooted from Rakaia to its present site, the geometric beds barely newly laid out and planted when it was photographed late November 1994. Priscilla is known as the "Lavender Lady" with 30 different lavenders in her garden. Her favourites also include fragrant bergamot, silvery-foliaged artemisias, and old-fashioned roses, which she points out are really herbs too! Jeremy loves the perfume of lemon verbena. Separated, colour-coded and labelled according to herbal usage, the beds border the courtyard in front of the shop. The categories include scented, lavender, biblical medicinal, grey-foliaged medicinal, formal culinary and tea gardens, as well as dye, and bee and butterfly gardens. A small decorative pond will be established in the biblical garden, planted with medicinal irises. Priscilla arranges the beds in colours, with the lavenders colour-coordinated. Honeysuckle emerges in early spring, with blossom trees including almonds, apples, apricots and olives. The long-bracted European lavenders and French *L. dentata* bloom in spring with valerian, catmint and early roses. Willow Tree peaks in summer, with the English spiky lavenders, accompanied in January by bergamot, salvias, catmint, artemisias and elderberry. In February the hops and annual herbs flower, with late roses continuing into autumn.

236

THE GUMS
Darfield

Owners:
Helen and Graeme Loe

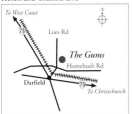

Address: Loes Rd, Darfield, R D,
Central Canterbury
Directions: From Christchurch, take
SH 73 west to Darfield. Continue,
then turn right into Homebush Rd.
Cross railway line, turn first left into
Loes Rd. Garden on right
Phone: 0-3-318 8373
Fax: 0-3-318 8373
Open: October to April, daily,
by appointment
Groups: By appointment, as above
Fee: $2 per adult
Size: Medium – 0.8ha (2 acres)
Terrain: Flat with banks
Nursery: Some plants available

  by arrangement

Set in the vast Canterbury plains, The Gums is encircled by a perimeter of trees and raised banks providing a strong design for the lush plantings within. Paths amble over the banks providing inviting vistas of the garden. Roses, peonies and perennials are massed below the west bank, with the tennis court beyond enclosed with climbing roses. An immaculate lawn bordered by azaleas and rhododendrons leads to a pergola hung with wisteria by the house. Past a waratah, scarlet in the spring, a narrow pathway winds round to a new rose garden and on to a rhododendron dell where the pastel shades of "Naomi", "Lems Cameo", "Pilgrim", "Lady Dorothy Ella" and many others glow in the dappled shade of mature trees. The east bank provides further vistas with walks past climbers including the fragrant peach-coloured old rambling rose "Albertine", the white-flowering bower vine, *Pandorea jasminoides*, and plumbago, to further rhododendrons and roses flowering beneath dogwoods and cherry blossoms, underplanted with annuals and perennials. The reflective waters of the swimming pool mirror the surrounding evergreen shrubs with an occasional splash of colour from rhododendrons, fuchsias, roses and clematis tumbling over a fence or climbing a tree. Seasonal colour has been planted at The Gums over the past 25 years.

BRIDGE FARM
Darfield

Owners:
Dianne and Lindsay Smith

Address: Hororata, Darfield, R D 2,
Christchurch
Directions: From Christchurch, take
SH 73 west towards Hororata.
Continue along Bealey Rd, then turn
left into Derretts Rd. Garden on left
Phone: 0-3-318 0792
Open: September to April, daily,
by appointment
Groups: As above; minimum 6
Fee: $7.50 per adult, including teas
Size: Medium – 0.8ha (2 acres)
Terrain: Flat
Nursery: Plants from garden
For sale: Touchwood books; Dianne's
watercolour paintings of garden themes
Design schools: Spring and autumn
schools; seminars in River Room
Accommodation: Two twin rooms
with private bathroom facilities

by arrangement

Developed from a small cottage garden, the present
colonial-style garden has been influenced by French
design. The recent petanque court is surrounded by
Mediterranean plantings which suit the hot, dry summers,
strong winds and cold winters of the Canterbury plains.
Because of the bright light, Dianne chooses intense
colours for spring and summer, with cooling greens used
extensively. She groups colours to emphasise and repeat
line, texture and form, creating a rhythm and balance.
A brick wall provides long vistas under evergreen archways
to the surrounding countryside, and a catmint walk leads
to the Monet-inspired rose garden where bright pinks and
oranges harmonise. Elsewhere a red, white and blue garden
has been developed around a 50-year-old red polyanthus
rose. Dianne has incorporated 90-year-old trees, such as
the Bon Chrétien pear in the midst of the bluebell rondel.
She has established a woodland setting for naturalised
bulbs, with yellow jonquils in spring and her favourite
coloured purple colchicums in autumn. A potager is filled
with fruit and flowers as well as the culinary herbs and
vegetables. A secret formal garden is designed to be viewed
from the upstairs River Seminar Room, which overlooks
the Hororata River featuring Dianne's river walk. Twilight
suppers by arrangement, with country French-style cookery.

238

MARSAL PAEONIES
Dunsandel

Owners:
Julie and John Allan

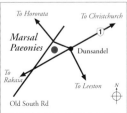

Address: Old South Rd, R D,
Dunsandel, Christchurch
Directions: From Christchurch, take
SH 1 south for 45 mins to Dunsandel.
Turn right into Hororata Rd, then left
into Old South Rd. Travel 1.5km to
garden on left
Phone: 0-3-325 4003
Fax: 0-3-325 4003
Open: Labour weekend (end October)
to mid December, or by appointment
Groups: Open weekends from mid
November to mid December, or by
appointment
Fee: Donation for local charity
Size: Large – 2ha (5 acres)
Terrain: Flat
Nursery: Peonies, perennials from
garden

 open days or by arrangement

The name "Marsal" is a combination of two of the Allan children's names, and "Paeonies" is the botanical spelling of peonies. Julie likes propagating all plants, but tree peonies, "the king of flowers" in ancient China, are her prime love. These flower early, just before Labour weekend, followed by the herbaceous peonies, starting with the corals then white "Miss America" at the beginning of November and reaching a peak towards the end of the month. Julie is also interested in the new intersectional hybrids, which are disease-resistant and feature a tree peony top with herbaceous roots. John's favourites are the trees, particularly maples, along with oaks and a few special birches. Companion plants include daffodils in spring, lilies and roses in summer and many unusual perennials such as the hostas that are predominant throughout the garden, adjacent to the peony field.

A small native area is about nine years old. Panoramic views have been retained to the Southern Alps, but the peonies seem to thrive in windy conditions, enjoying the cold, frosty winters and hot, dry summers. Contrary to popular opinion, certain early peonies can also be grown in warmer climates, providing they are planted close to the surface to maximise the cold in winter.

WENDRUM
Leeston

Owners:
Kathryn and Geoff Millar

Address: Dobbins Rd, Southbridge,
Christchurch. *Postal*: R D 3, Leeston,
Central Canterbury
Directions: From Leeston, turn into
Alexander Rd, then into Cryers Rd.
Turn right into Dobbins Rd. From
Rakaia, cross the Rakaia Bridge, then
turn right into Main Rakaia Rd. Turn
right into Cryers Rd, then as above
Phone: 0-3-324 2511
Fax: 0-3-324 2511
Open: October to late May, daily,
by appointment
Groups: By appointment, as above
Fee: $3 per adult; discount for
horticultural societies
Size: Medium – 1ha (2½ acres)
Terrain: Flat
Nursery: A few perennials and shrubs
propagated from garden

    by arrangement

Starting with only two original trees, Kathryn has developed this woodland garden over the past 25 years, underplanting with her favourite species that love the coolness, especially trilliums. Rhododendrons now predominate, providing spring colour along with deciduous azaleas, unusual woodland plants and blossom trees, including the soft pink *Kolkwitzia*, or beauty bush, by the house. Kathryn is very interested in colour effects, combining blues and yellows and planting lots of whites such as foxgloves and lupins, that glow in the evening. She uses green extensively during the hot, dry Canterbury summer, when her 20-year-old roses bloom among the peonies. Kathryn has recently developed an informal old rose garden with matching borders of colourful perennials, such as the pink lupin-like South African *Diascia* interplanted with creamy sisyrinchiums and phlomis. Kathryn loves the old species *Rosa dupontii* and is increasing plantings of her favourite deep-pink "Bantry Bay" rose. Turkscap martagon lilies add summer interest and flowering continues into autumn when the foliage of mollis azaleas, maples, cercidiphyllum, claret ash and two ginkgoes provides brilliant colour. The form and structure of the garden become apparent when the deciduous leaves fall, a time Kathryn likes best. A small family museum of farm collectables is an additional attraction.

SUZETTE GARDENS
Rakaia

Owners:
Suzanne and Ted Rollinson

Address: Awarua School Rd, Rakaia
Postal: R D 11, Rakaia, Central Canterbury
Directions: From Christchurch, travel 1 hour south on SH 1 to Rakaia. Continue 2.8km, then turn left into Mainwarings Rd. Travel 9km to Awarua School Rd crossroads. Turn left and travel 500m to garden on left. From Ashburton, travel 25 mins north on SH 1 to Mainwarings Rd on right
Phone: 0-3-302 0864
Fax: 0-3-302 0864
Open: All year, daily, by appointment
Groups: By appointment, as above
Fee: $3 per adult
Size: Large – over 2ha (over 5 acres)
Terrain: Slightly undulating

  by arrangement

Twelve years ago Sue landscaped and planted a large paddock, while Ted made the retaining walls and structures, such as the rose pergola featuring "Wedding Day", "New Dawn" and a white banksia rose. He now clips and trims the hedges and trees, including the shaped conifer bed of topiary. A viburnum walk, kowhai trail and lilac walk provide colourful fragrant avenues in spring, while a David Austin walk features the lovely English roses in summer, complemented by old-fashioned and formal rose gardens. Other predominant areas are the camellia bed which includes miniatures, the rhododendron garden, and the woodland area underplanted with spring bulbs. A white camellia garden and separate blue and white, pink, and pastel beds are colour-coordinated. A rockery constructed with rocks from the Rakaia Gorge surrounds a small waterlily pond. Magnolias and over 30 flowering cherries blossom in spring, with clematis climbing the trees. Each summer Sue plants 30 dozen annuals including her favourite Livingstone daisies, asters, petunias, pansies, violas and dwarf phlox. These complement massed perennials such as catmint, daisies, phlox and salvias. Other summer delights include peonies, lilies and dahlias, and the garden is enlivened with peacocks and white and fantail pigeons.

241

CONISTON
Ashburton

Owners:
Robert and Iris Robinson

Address: Coniston, Alford Forest Rd,
Ashburton
Directions: At the south end of
Ashburton, turn west off SH 1 into
Moore St, then continue on Alford
Forest Rd (SH 77) for 3km to
Coniston on right
Phone: 0-3-308 6221
Fax: 0-3-308 6221
Open: October to December, daily,
by appointment
Groups: By appointment, as above
Fee: $5 per adult
Size: Large – 2ha (5 acres)
Terrain: Flat

         mostly

Originally established in 1890, Coniston is now
a woodland garden, developed by the Robinsons
since 1956. Gigantic turn-of-the century wellingtonias,
Lombardy poplars, oaks, elms, ashes, cedars, picea and
thuja form a shelter belt around the perimeter of the garden
and line the curving driveway. A canopy of old pear trees
provides dappled shade for rhododendrons, azaleas and
perennials. Favourites are the tree-like rhododendrons,
especially mauve and blue shades, underplanted with
groundcovers. In early spring, daffodils accompany
camellias, then flowering cherries and dogwoods blossom.
Early magnolias bloom with the rhododendrons and
30-year-old golden and apricot Mollis azaleas, underplanted
with blue ajuga and forget-me-nots. In 1963, a natural
riverbed gully was transformed into a lake bordered with
weeping willows, maples, conifers and swamp cypresses.
Cherry blossom, colourful azaleas and Kingcup calthas
are mirrored in the still waters among waterlilies, while
other moisture-loving plants crowd the banks. Tea roses
and climbers take centre stage in summer, when the
woodland is brightened with *Cardiocrinum giganteum*.
Autumn colours the 30-year-old deciduous trees and a range
of conifers provide contrast, with natives including evergreen
beeches and a 12-metre kauri planted by Bob in 1936.

TROTTS' GARDEN
Ashburton

Owners:
Alan and Catherine Trott

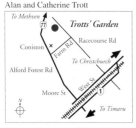

Address: Racecourse Rd, R D 6, Ashburton
Directions: At the north end of Ashburton, turn west off SH 1 into Racecourse Rd. Continue for 3km to Trotts' garden on left
Phone: 0-3-308 9530
Fax: 0-3-308 8568
Open: September to October, daily, 9am–5pm; thereafter 6 days
Closed: Sundays
Groups: As above, but by appointment
Fee: $5 per adult
Size: Large – 3ha (7 acres)
Terrain: Flat
Nursery: Full range including specialist rare trees, shrubs, and perennials; mail order available

Started from a bare paddock in 1984, the Trotts' garden is now a combination of woodland planting and formality. Silver birches, maples, magnolias, prunus, oaks, and many rare trees feature in the woodland, underplanted with tree peonies and Alan's favourite rhododendrons. A stream edged with water-loving plants leads to a bog garden and pond, a focal point of the garden bordered with architectural gunneras and hostas, the white trunks of birches mirrored in the water. Garden structures include two dovecotes, rose arbours, a gazebo and a belvedere, the last providing views over the garden to the mountains beyond and bridging the transition to the formal garden, designed in 1990. This newer area is entered through wrought-iron gates hung between substantial brick columns, opening down a broad grassy walkway between twin herbaceous borders 110 metres long. The formal garden comprises a box-edged rose garden enclosed by neatly trimmed macrocarpa, with symmetrical alcoves and recessed seats. A copse of silvery-leafed *Sorbus aria* "Lutescens" separates this formality from the stream. Alan uses foliage and form effectively, for instance in his hedged square grassy space and in the combination of deep purple and gold, such as copper beeches juxtaposed with *Robinia* "Frisia".

WILLOWBANK
Ashburton

Owners:
Shona and Colin Thomas

Address: Holland Rd, R D 1, Ashburton
Directions: From Ashburton, travel
south on SH 1, crossing Ashburton
River. Take first right under railway
line, then left into Melcombe St. Turn
right into Nixon St. Continue into
Hollands Rd. Garden at end of road
Phone: 0-3-308 4195
Open: September to April, daily,
by appointment
Groups: By appointment, as above
Fee: $3 per adult
Size: Medium – 0.4ha (1 acre)
Terrain: Flat and gently sloping
Nursery: Perennials from garden
Swimming pool: Available
Accommodation: Four singles with
private shared bathroom; meals
optional

 mostly

by arrangement

Twenty-three years ago when they moved into Willowbank, Shona began planting the garden around the century-old homestead. A tall hedge of clipped pine forms a shelter belt on three sides, and weeping willows were planted around a large pond. A pair of white swans now glide on the pond, which features an island with flaxes. Walkways around the pond are sheltered with woodland trees and bordered with lush hostas, architectural gunneras, colourful azaleas and the hanging bells of Solomon's seal. Pathways open off a crazy-paving area edged by low variegated box and lead on over two bridges. Camellias are complemented by prunus blossom underplanted with daffodils in spring, and massed red tulips light up a bed flanking the sloping lawn. Hyacinths flower under the trees, with rhododendrons, azaleas and echiums adding further colour and interest. Shona plants in colours that look right to her, avoiding purples with yellows. Summer features many varieties of roses – miniature, bush, old-fashioned and modern standard roses. Around the waterlily pond white arum lilies predominate, with massed orange lilies under the willows, while belladonna lilies bloom in autumn. The trees are mainly deciduous, accompanied by conifers with native ferns beneath. Peacocks share the limelight with the swans.

LEAFIELD
Ashburton

Owners:
Margaret and Murray Foster

Address: Tinwald-Mayfield Rd,
Ashburton, R D 1
Directions: From Ashburton, travel
south on SH 1, crossing Ashburton
River, to Tinwald. Turn right into
Lagmhor St, then right again into the
Tinwald-Mayfield-Westerfield Rd.
Garden on right
Phone: 0-3-308 8183
Open: October to April, daily,
by appointment
Groups: By appointment, as above
Fee: $3 per adult
Size: Medium – 0.6ha (1½ acres)
Terrain: Flat

    by arrangement

Margaret has revamped the house garden since 1981
and developed the adjacent paddocks. Her favourite
plants are roses – hybrid teas originally, but now old roses
and Graham Thomas English varieties – edged with
a border of purple pansies that seem to flower all year.
She is also increasing the number of perennials, especially
the tall phlox, delphiniums and lupins which provide
vertical accent. The spacious shaped lawn featuring a pale-
pink prunus is edged mainly in blues and pinks, with
patches of brighter colour among the pastels. Margaret
uses yellow for accent, with red tulips in spring. Pockets
of annuals add summer colour, and foliage such as the
yellow, red and green maple leaves is important. Archways
lead to a water-race crossed by rustic bridges and shaded
by a large twisty willow behind the dovecote. White ducks
share the garden with the doves and Margaret is planting
rhododendrons, azaleas and hostas beside the water. White
clematis climbs a manuka pergola, wisteria covers a pergola
over the verandah, and clematis also climbs high into an
old tree near the kowhai beside the house. Two rock gardens
full of Margaret's treasures are interesting features. The
peak times for visiting Leafield are in November and
December.

WILLOWPARK HOMESTEAD
Ashburton

Owners:
Bev and Rex Scarf

Address: Timaru Track Rd, Lagmhor, Ashburton, R D 1
Directions: From Ashburton, travel south on SH 1, crossing Ashburton River, towards Tinwald. Turn right into Lagmhor St, then right again into the Tinwald-Mayfield-Westerfield Rd. Continue past Leafield to crossroads. Turn right into Timaru Track Rd. Willowpark on left
Phone: 0-3-302 5846
Open: Mid September to mid March, daily, by appointment
Groups: By apppointment, as above
Fee: $3 per adult
Size: Medium – 0.4ha (about 1 acre)
Terrain: Flat
Nursery: Perennials from garden

The Scarfs are third generation owners, Willowpark farm being originally owned by Bev's grandfather. Her parents built the house 30 years ago, planted the now mature trees including the big conifers, and established the lawn area. But Bev has doubled the size of the garden in the past decade, including the paddock behind the trees, which provides a hidden area leading to the aviaries. Other fauna attractions include two donkeys, "Marigold" the pig, two goats, rabbits, pet sheep, bantams, fantail pigeons in a dovecote, and a small fish-pond planted with primulas, irises, astilbes and maples. Springtime features camellias, bulbs, cherry blossoms, clematis, over 100 rhododendrons, azaleas and the fresh leaves of the deciduous trees, including all the silver birches. Bev likes planting reds, yellows and blues together and uses blue extensively in the summer when the delphiniums and lupins contrast with the roses. She prefers yellows and bronzes to pinks, and loves the autumn foliage when the oaks, maples, ashes, elms, copper beech, and poplars around the perimeter colour up. These large trees frame the garden with its curving beds of perennials, including aquilegias, irises, geums and sweet William. Bev incorporates a few annuals, such as lobelia and petunias in pots.

EDEN TERRACE
Ruapuna

Owners:
Adrienne and Neil Doyle

Address: R D 5, Ashburton
Directions: Continue from
Stonehaven to Moorhouse Rd. Turn
left into Ealing-Montalto Rd. Garden
on right. Or from Timaru or
Ashburton, take SH 1 then turn west
into Ealing-Montalto Rd. Cross
SH 72 and continue to garden on left
Phone: 0-3-303 6057
Open: October and November, daily,
by appointment
Groups: By appointment, as above
Fee: $3 per adult
Size: Medium – 1ha (2½ acres)
Terrain: Flat

      in groups

The Doyles are the fifth generation on the same farm,
Neil's great-grandfather having built the homestead
in 1876. Adrienne began the garden 17 years ago, starting
with half an acre of old hedges. Now sunken lawns sweep
across to a series of three ponds flowing into each other,
bordered by trees with pastureland beyond. A large blue
gum shades the garden gate and Adrienne's favourite
maples and rhododendrons predominate. These feature
with perennials in shaped beds carved out of the
perimeter of the spacious lawn, like colourful islands in
a sea of green. Clematis climbs a pergola leading through
conifers to an oval swimming-pool area. Beyond are
prunus trees underplanted with aquilegias and peonies.
Colourful borders of moisture-loving plants edge the
ponds, contrasting with foliage of hostas, irises, azaleas,
primulas, Solomon's seal and further rhododendrons.
A weeping willow shades two of the ponds and white
viburnums are underplanted with soft grey *Stachys
lanata*. A bridge to the second water garden is edged with
dry stone walls constructed from the stone that
characterises the area. White ducks enjoy the ponds and
a photinia archway leads back to the lawn again. The
peak time to visit Eden Terrace is in late spring.

STONEHAVEN
Ruapuna

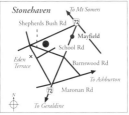

Owners:
Warren and Liz Scott

Address: Ruapuna, R D 5, Ashburton
Directions: From Tinwald turn right into Maronan Rd. Turn right into Barnswood Rd. Cross SH 72 into Shepherds Bush Rd. Pass stone church on right and continue 3km to Stonehaven on right
Phone: 0-3-303 6108
Fax: 0-3-303 6108
Open: Open Days, each Sunday from second Sunday in October to second Sunday in December, 10am–5pm
Groups: Open Days as above, or by appointment October to April
Fee: $4 per adult
Size: Medium – over 1ha (3 acres)
Terrain: Flat
Nursery: Groundcovers, perennials, alpines, bulbs, primulas, gentians

   mostly

 by arrangement

Over the past two decades, Liz has used local stone from the abundant heaps in nearby paddocks, to build the low stone walls that separate Stonehaven into garden rooms. A raised alpine rock garden features lewisias and Liz's favourite blue gentians. A formal malus avenue, underplanted with irises, leads to double perennial borders in blues, whites, yellows and apricots, incorporating a rustic old woolshed. The verandah of the century-old house is draped with purple wisteria, harmonising with the border below. Rose pergolas lead beyond spacious lawns to wandering paths among species rhododendrons, combined with old roses. Groundcover escapees from adjacent beds stud stone-edged pathways meandering through deciduous trees to arrive at a pond hidden in a sea of bluebells beneath rhododendrons. Cherry trees drop white petals around the stony perimeter among primulas, irises and hostas. Elsewhere, a woodland garden is carpeted with honesty, bluebells and forget-me-nots. Woodland paths lead to a bog garden where astilbes and primulas contrast with lush hostas, gunneras and *Cardiocrinum giganteum*. A bank of silver pears tones with soft grey *Stachys lanata* beneath. Rose pergolas and tennis-court netting clad with clematis and roses create windows to paddocks of specimen trees and spring bulbs, with snow-capped mountains beyond.

DUNHAMPTON LILY FIELDS
Mount Somers

Owners:
David and Wendy Millichamp

Address: Hoods Rd, Mt Somers, Ashburton, R D 1
Directions: Take SH 72 towards Mt Somers. Turn west at Stronechrubie Restaurant and Chalets into Hoods Rd. Garden on right
Phone: 0-3-303 9743
Open: October to mid February, daily except Sunday morning
Groups: As above, but by appointment
Fee: No charge
Size: Large – 0.4ha (1 acre) with 3.2ha (8 acres) of lilies
Terrain: Flat
Nursery: Lilies, perennials, maples; free catalogue to visitors

The lily fields are over 13 years old, with the garden nearly half that age. The lily fields peak from late December to mid January, but the garden holds interest throughout spring and summer. The Millichamps specialise in Asiatic lilies which begin flowering in November, then Aurelian trumpets in mid December, followed by Oriental auratum lilies in February. Apart from liliums, there is an extensive maple collection, their leaves unfurling in spring, with daffodils and violas beneath, complementing pink and red camellias, rhododendrons, magnolias, dogwoods and white cherry blossom underplanted with white daisies. A large tree peony grows by the house and wisteria is another spring feature. Deciduous trees include birches and oaks as well as the unusual and rare, many trees raised from seed from the International Dendrology society. Deciduous trees are accompanied by conifers and natives such as New Zealand beeches, brooms, hebes and a grove of toothed ferox lancewoods. A stream runs through the garden, planted with hostas, irises, heuchera and meconopsis, with many other perennials throughout the garden including delphiniums, phlomis, phlox and campanulas that flower with the old roses festooning a pagoda.

INVERARY STATION
Mount Somers

Owners:
Anne and John Chapman

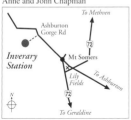

Address: R D 1, Mt Somers, Ashburton
Directions: Take SH 72 towards Mt Somers. Turn west into Ashburton Gorge Rd. Continue past Mt Somers village 9.8km. Inverary Station on left
Phone: 0-3-303 9734
Fax: 0-3-303 9734
Open: All year, by appointment
Groups: By appointment, as above
Fee: $3 per adult
Size: Medium – 1ha (2–3 acres)
Terrain: Contoured
Accommodation: Quality farmstay; 1 double and 1 twin room, with private bathroom

   limited

  by arrangement

For seven years the Chapmans have developed their high-country garden, backed by woodland planted in the fifties by John's father. Tucked into a hillside, the garden provides panoramic views over pastureland, with drifts of white flowers echoing the snow-capped mountains beyond. White wisteria hangs from the verandah and yellow tulips and pink lupins punctuate a froth of white forget-me-nots and arabis, with daffodils lingering into late October! Anne prefers soft colours harmonising with the landscape, rather than the red/orange spectrum. Below the house, blue and white plantings surround the tennis court and barbecue area. The dry stone terracing built by John's family in the sixties is softened with catmint and yellow daisies. Reds used for highlights include the mature rhododendrons in the adjacent woodland gully. A pale-pink prunus walk curves up the lawn behind the house, to the woodland, where a huge flat limestone rock bridges a natural stream, edged with ferns, primulas, astelias and ligularias. Exotics mixed with natives are underplanted with hostas, Chatham Island forget-me-nots and honesty. *Cardiocrinum giganteum* foliage towers among the rhododendrons, flowering in summer when Anne's alpine rockery comes into its own. John's native corner includes hebes, tussocks, flaxes and celmisias gathered from the farm.

SOUTH CANTERBURY,
NORTH AND SOUTH OTAGO AND DUNEDIN

South Canterbury stretches from Geraldine to Waimate in the south. It incorporates Mt Cook National Park, featuring New Zealand's highest mountain, Mt Cook, and a number of beautiful glacial lakes, with ski-fields a major drawcard. The clear waters of typical South Island rivers with their shingled banks are crossed in travelling to many of the 27 gardens featured in these regions.

Towards Geraldine is Orari Estate with its historic woodland garden, and Capricorns Garden nearby features trees and roses with a new pond. Near Temuka is Newlands Rock Gardens specialising in low-growing plants. Towards Fairlie is Kakahu, a natural woodland park-like garden, and at Beautiful Valley is Mulvi-Hill Country Garden with varied walks, rockeries and nursery. At Fairlie is Margaret's Garden Pottery with its tiny garden and her daughter's Trillium Glade, specialising in alpines. Braemar Homestead Garden overlooks the shores of Lake Pukaki, with views of Mt Cook, and near Pleasant Point is Mt Gay Farm with garden vistas to the Pacific Ocean. At Albury is the woodland garden of Woodbank, and south of Cave is Craigmore, an historic Alfred Buxton garden with adjacent peony nursery. Timaru features Ethridge Gardens, a new English-style garden with high brick walls, then south at St Andrews is Birchwood, with beds edging spacious lawns. At Studholme on the coast is Nukuroa, with its park-like woodland, then two gardens at Waimate are Miller's Garden with seasonal garden rooms and The Secret Garden with mature trees incorporated into a formal design.

North Otago includes the main city of Dunedin on the east coast, and begins at Oamaru, famous for its soft pale limestone so easy to carve and build with, making it a useful structural addition to many gardens. In Oamaru is Parkside Stone and Garden with its display garden featuring Oamaru limestone from its quarries. Roxlea Park Fragrant Herb Garden is on the southern border of Oamaru, incorporating a herb nursery and craft gallery, and Joan Elder's Garden a little further south at Maheno provides inspiration for Joan's paintings. Mill Cottage at Waianakarua on the coast is adjacent to the historic Mill House and Bridge and features the creamy Oamaru stone. Inland between Lake Benmore and Lake Ohau is Omarama where The Briars is situated. The formal design of this new garden is based on circles, with panoramic mountain views. Also inland, set in the stark beauty of the Maniototo, not far from Ranfurly, is Clachanburn with a stony creek flowing through the garden.

The main city, Dunedin, settled mainly by Scots, is known as the Rhododendron City because of its annual Rhododendron Week in October. The well known Botanic Gardens and the historic Glenfalloch Woodland Garden on the Otago Peninsula feature many rhododendrons and mature trees. Also on the peninsula is Larnach Castle Garden surrounding the historic castle. Past Portobello is Hereweka Garden and its adjoining nursery in a valley featuring the only extant stand of rimu on the peninsula. The coastal roadway leads to the only mainland Royal Albatross colony in the world. In Abbotsford, south-west of Dunedin itself, is Joy's Bonsai Studio with 450 bonsai for sale. The main road to Central Otago leads south of Dunedin to Milton and continues past Garvan Homestead where an Alfred Buxton garden has been restored round the old home now functioning as a restaurant and providing accommodation.

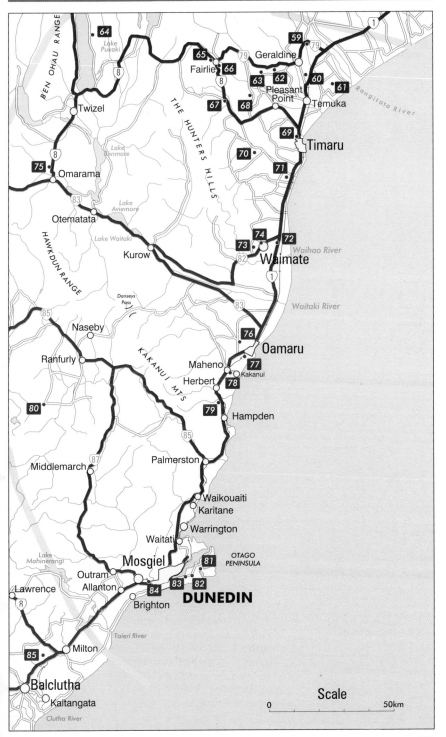

253

CAPRICORNS GARDEN
Geraldine

Owners:
Ros and Philip Burdon
Managers: John and Dorothy Langston

Address: Orari Back Rd, Geraldine
Postal: P O Box 117, Geraldine
Directions: From Ashburton take SH 1
south to Rangitata. Turn right into
SH 79. Then turn left into Orari Back
Rd. Continue 2km to garden on left.
From Timaru, take SH 1 to Orari.
Turn left and travel 2km, then turn
into Orari Back Rd on right. Travel
5km to Capricorns on right
Phone: 0-3-693 9309 (managers)
Open: August to April, daily,
by appointment
Groups: By appointment, as above
Fee: $3 per adult
Size: Large – 3.6ha (9 acres)
Terrain: Flat
Nursery: Perennials, bulbs from
garden

There were two pines, a redwood and wellingtonia, at Capricorns prior to the Burdon family moving there in 1939. Now this mature garden is sheltered by oaks, elms, copper beeches and a rare *Arbutus menziesii* or madrona tree, a favourite of Mrs Burdon senior, with its peeling bark, white spring flowers and orange-red autumn fruits. A natural stream feeds a pond with an island featuring an alder and surrounded by marsh marigolds (*Caltha palustris*), where black swans glide past primulas, dwarf irises, hostas, fritillarias, snowdrops, trilliums, aquilegias, azaleas and cardiocrinum. Ros likes vibrant colours, from the camellias and rhododendrons of spring, to the roses, lilies, perennials and annuals of summer, to autumn crocuses and Michaelmas daisies. Thousands of daffodils in early spring are followed by a sea of bluebells and forget-me-nots lining the driveway. Groundcover in the woodland area includes white wood violets and deep blue *Parochetis* intermingling with yellow celandine. A collection of magnolias is underplanted with forget-me-nots. Drifts of meconopsis, delphiniums, hollyhocks and peonies are interplanted in beds of nearly 300 roses, including Mrs Burdon's favourite, "Peace". The delphiniums are a specialty together with the irises and viburnums. A new native area features rimu, weeping brooms and lacebarks. Tractor tours are available.

ORARI ESTATE
Geraldine

Owners:
Rosie and Ian Morten

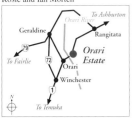

Address: SH 1, Orari
Postal: R D 22, Geraldine
Directions: Take SH 1 south of
Ashburton or north of Temuka.
Garden entrance at Rest Area just
north of Orari River
Phone: 0-3-693 9058
Fax: 0-3-693 9058
Open: All year, daily, by appointment
Groups: By appointment, as above
Fee: $3 per adult
Size: Large – 2ha (5 acres)
Terrain: Undulating

   partial

  by arrangement

Orari Estate has been in Rosie's family since the time of the first settlers, with trees planted back in the 1850s providing a mature woodland. Rosie's grandparents began building the homestead in 1912; a pink kalmia from that era still thrives, with a pear orchard, nut walk, and original main lawn. Rosie's mother began revamping the garden in the 1970s, creating three new garden areas. Sycamores are being progressively culled to open up the woodland, and Rosie is planting old roses. Predominant spring features are the rhododendrons, then in summer cardiocrinum lilies bloom with perennials including irises, delphiniums and groundcovers such as ajuga. A dozen different magnolias announce the arrival of spring, followed by camellias, Mollis azaleas, the rhododendrons, a michelia and a spectacular kowhai. Two creeks flow through the property, one dammed to create a pond where white swans swim. Bridges cross the creeks, edged with pink primulas, ligularias and yellow Kingcup calthas. An old water-race now forms a pathway and drifts of blue forget-me-nots carpet the ground under mature conifers, including an unusual weeping Douglas fir. In autumn the deciduous trees and azaleas feature, while winter highlights the structure of the trees and the garden. Peacocks are an additional attraction.

255

NEWLANDS ROCK GARDENS
Temuka

Owners:
Bev and Peter Davidson

Address: Newland Rd, Clandeboye,
Temuka; *Postal*: "Newlands", Orton,
R D 26, Temuka
Directions: From Christchurch take
SH 1 south through Rangitata. Before
Orari turn left into Farm Rd. Travel
about 11km to Clandeboye. Turn left
into Rolleston Rd, then left again into
Newland Rd. Garden on left
Phone: 0-3-615 9828
Open: Spring to autumn, daily
Groups: By appointment
Fee: No charge
Size: Medium – 0.6ha (1½ acres)
Terrain: Flat
Nursery: Specialises in all low-
growing plants, bulbs & shrubs
(most less than 30cm high). Free
catalogue available. Mail orders taken.

 mostly ⌐ on lawn

individuals   Devonshire
only   by arrangement

Peter's mother planted the large trees round the perimeter of the garden 35 years ago and Peter's sister established the first rock garden. This has been extended to accommodate Bev and Peter's favourite alpines – gentians, dwarf narcissi, dwarf irises and, more recently, peonies. Spacious lawns with seating provide a tranquil setting, the Davidsons' private garden adding to the display garden. Waterlily ponds feature Japanese irises and Peter is developing a rose garden. Early spring is welcomed by the crocuses, dwarf narcissi, cyclamen and aconites. Deep blue gentians and pulsatillas predominate, accompanied by adonis, sanguinaria, scillas, erythroniums, trilliums, wood anemones, muscari, saxifrage, dianthus, and Auricula primulas. Prunus and cornus blossom, weeping maples are clothed with new foliage, rhododendrons bloom and lots of clematis feature too. In summer Peter's roses take over and rhodohypoxis adds to the colour. Bev and Peter specialise in the campanulas which feature from late summer through the autumn months when they are joined by crocuses, colchicums, schizostylis, and the colourful foliage of deciduous trees such as the maples, liquidambars and dogwoods. In winter the cyclamen and narcissi feature with witch hazel and wintersweet trees providing colour for the bare branches.

KAKAHU
Geraldine

Owners:
Sue and Gerald Hargreaves

Address: Winchester-Hanging Rock
Rd, Geraldine
Postal: R D 21, Geraldine
Directions: 15km from Geraldine.
Take SH 79 towards Fairlie. Turn left
into Brenton Rd. At end, turn right
into Winchester-Hanging Rock Rd.
Travel about 5km. Garden on right
Phone: 0-3-697 4858
Fax: 0-3-697 4897
Open: All year, daily, by appointment
Groups: By appointment, as above
Fee: $3 per adult
Size: Large – 3.2ha (8 acres)
Terrain: Flat and sloping to pond
Nursery: Over 1ha (3 acres) of 7 to
9-year-old maturing rhododendrons

  by arrangement

Kakahu is a natural woodland park on a grand scale. Century-old oaks line the driveway and masses of bluebells have naturalised under the Oregon plantation and through the old hazelnut walk, creating a sea of blue in spring. Trees planted since 1890 include some rare species, and some of the largest copper beeches and oaks in the country. Weeping Oregons are among the rare trees and big English limes also feature. Meandering paths lead through the woodland, with a blue and silver walk beneath cherries and dogwoods. A grove of white camellias is another spring attraction. Gerald's mother planted rhododendrons 50 years ago, which now create a mass of colour from mid October to November. Over the past decade, Sue has developed a pond area with bog plants such as gunneras, astilbes, hostas, irises, and marsh marigolds (*Caltha palustris*). Pekin and Muscovy ducks swim under the limestone bridge towards the roses and lilies at the far end. Kakahu is a very green garden, with warm coral colours provided by the roses in summer. The maple area is special and, in autumn, sheets of red and orange foliage splash the garden when the English trees, such as the oaks and ashes, turn.

258

MULVI-HILL COUNTRY GARDEN
Geraldine

Owners:
Valerie and Sandra Mulvihill

Mulvi-Hill Country Garden

Address: Mulvihill Rd, Beautiful
Valley, R D 21, Geraldine
Directions: From Geraldine, take
SH 79 towards Fairlie. Travel 20km,
then turn left into Mulvihill Rd.
Continue 2.3km to garden on right
Phone: 0-3-697 4884 or 0-3-697 4856
Open: October to March, daily,
10am–4pm
Groups: By appointment, as above
Fee: $2 per adult
Size: Medium – 1.2ha (3 acres)
Terrain: Flat and hilly
Nursery: Azaleas, incarvilleas,
trilliums, primulas, auriculas, alpines,
perennials, *Cerinthe major*, *Salvia*
"Blue Patens"
Refreshments: Cold drinks, Moro and
Crunchie bars available for sale

The Mulvihill family has farmed here for four generations, although the garden has been developed only over the last two decades. It is divided into three sections: the level garden and nursery around Sandra's house, the steep driveway full of rhododendrons, azaleas and primulas, and the rockeries around Val's house at the top of the hill. Stone-edged paths are lined with daffodils and splashes of red tulips. A trillium walk displays white and deep-red trilliums in spring, when Sandra's primula collection flowers, and a peony walk features in summer. Behind the shade house, Val has grown a bank of Mollis azaleas from seed. An 80-year-old pear tree stands in the middle of the lower garden, and other trees of interest include *Picea pungens* "Glauca" and an "Eagle claw" maple. Views from the driveway look out over paddocks with deer and willows, to the cattle on the river flats and the forest and hills beyond. The top garden includes roses and alpine treasures, such as the gentians Val loves. A native hibiscus bed self-seeds and a tulip border is followed by annuals, with chrysanthemums and dahlias extending the colour to March. But the peak time to view Mulvi-Hill is from late October to mid November.

259

BRAEMAR HOMESTEAD GARDEN
Lake Pukaki

Owners:
Carol and Duncan Mackenzie

Address: Braemar Station, Lake Pukaki
Postal: P O Box 62, Lake Tekapo
Directions: From Twizel, travel 15km on SH 8 to Lake Pukaki. Turn left into Hayman Rd on east side of lake. Travel 20km to Braemar Station on right. From Tekapo, travel 5km west on SH 8, then turn right into Braemar Rd. Continue 24km to garden on right
Phone: 0-3-680 6844
Fax: 0-3-680 6854
Open: October to April, daily, by appointment
Groups: By appointment, as above
Fee: $3 per adult
Size: Medium – 1ha (2½ acres)
Terrain: Varied – hilly
Nursery: Occasional perennials and roses from garden
Accommodation: Cottage, sleeps 10

🐕 🚻 ♿ to flat areas

🏕 ☕ 🍽 by arrangement

When Lake Pukaki was raised 38 metres in 1976, it flooded the Mackenzies' former home, forcing their move to a hilly paddock overlooking the lake, with spectacular views to Mt Cook. Although advised to grow only hardy natives on such an exposed site, the Mackenzies planted the perimeter in shelter trees, and huge moraine rocks were moved on to the garden. Carol has planted the sheltered courtyard with old rambling roses, clematis, and rhododendrons, where pots of lewisias in sunrise colours love the heat and tolerate the cold. As well as the alpines and natives that are suited to the conditions, Carol finds her favourite old roses – particularly the musks and rugosas – tough enough to survive. She colour-coordinates different areas, with creams, pinks, whites and apricot roses along the driveway, contrasting with lemons, blues and golds on the slope below. Splashes of red provide accent throughout the garden, while yellow irises and blue aquilegias combine elsewhere. A natural stream opens into a pond in a sheltered glade, reached via a grassy avenue. Spring bulbs naturalise under the trees and pulsatillas seed freely. Rose-clad archways lead into a cottage garden where peonies feature among foxgloves, delphiniums, lilies and gentians. An accommodation cottage provides a good base for tramping, boating, fishing, skiing, etc.

TRILLIUM GLADE
Fairlie

Owners:
Francie and Mike Herlund

Address: 3 Ayr St, Fairlie
Directions: From Timaru, take SH 8 to Fairlie. Continue on SH 8 towards Tekapo. After monument, take third road left into Ayr St. Garden on left opposite Medical Centre
Phone: 0-3-685 8352
Fax: 0-3-685 8262
Open: Mid September to end November, daily, by appointment
Groups: By appointment, as above
Fee: $2 per head for bus groups
Size: Small – 0.1ha (¼ acre)
Terrain: Flat
Nursery: Trilliums, unusual woodland and rare alpine plants

Francie has developed her garden over the past 15 years, establishing a micro-climate of dappled shade with an extensive canopy of slatted wood, which creates similar conditions to open deciduous woodland. Elsewhere open areas suit plants that enjoy full sun. Francie specialises in trillium species which she patiently and skilfully propagates from seed. *Trillium nivale* is a tiny pure white miniature trillium appearing first in mid August, with the miniature saxifraga. Later in spring, the rarest trillium, *T. undulatum*, features a "painted" cerise collar around the centre of the flower. *T. luteum*, one of the sessile trilliums, flowers sitting directly on the leaves, is also difficult to grow, but worth the effort when stiff yellow petals appear on the bronze-mottled foliage. Various forms of *T. erectum* flower on longer stems, and the double form of *T. grandiflorum* "Flore Pleno" is eye-catching with up to 30 white petals forming starry blooms. Trillium foliage provides a good background for associated plants such as fritillaria, meconopsis, erythronium, auricula primulas, and peonies, complemented by nearby rhododendrons. Alpine rarities include exquisite forms of *Jankaea*, *Shortia*, Japanese dicentra and alpine verbascum. Francie makes Oamaru limestone and hypertufa pots for difficult plants that require sharp drainage.

261

MARGARET'S GARDEN POTTERY
Fairlie

Owners:
Margaret and Jim Pringle

Address: 8 Railway Place, Fairlie
Directions: From Timaru, take SH 8 to Fairlie. Turn right into Gray St, then left into Railway Place. Garden on right
Phone: 0-3-685 8645
Open: Spring and summer, daily, by appointment
Groups: By appointment, as above
Fee: No charge
Size: Small – 0.05ha (⅛ acre)
Terrain: Flat
For sale: Margaret's garden pottery

Although small and only three years old, Margaret's garden is full of interesting features. Her pottery shed and the adjacent kiln where she fires her pottery are gradually being covered in montana clematis. Margaret's interest in natives is seen in the smaller native clematis varieties that flower later in the spring, and the indigenous alpines down the side of the house accompanying the trilliums from her daughter Francie's nearby alpine garden. Celmisias, the native mountain daisies, are predominant, and native ranunculus also feature. Drifts of white *Galanthus* or snowdrops flower with the early hepaticas in pink, white and blue. Then sheets of deep-blue gentians appear, complementing the small rhododendrons. In summer, a complete hedge of miniature roses accompanies old English roses, rugosas and climbers. A small pond surrounded with native grasses, such as snow grasses and astelias, will become like a pebbled river-bed or mountain stream area. The garden is a wonderful setting for Margaret's hand-crafted pottery – every piece is different. Examples of her outdoor novelty pottery for gardens and patios can be seen throughout her garden and courtyard area softened with potted plants. The peak times for visiting this high-country garden are during spring and summer.

WOODBANK
Albury

Owners:
Mem and Tom Sutherland

Address: Coalpit Rd, Albury, R D 16
Directions: From Timaru, take SH 8
through Pleasant Point to Albury.
Take second road on left into
Chamberlain Rd. Then take Coalpit
Rd on right. Cross bridge and
continue 1.25km into Ardmore Rd.
Woodbank garden on right
Phone: 0-3-685 5714
Open: Mid October to mid February,
daily, by appointment
Groups: By appointment, as above
Fee: $3 per adult
Size: Medium – 0.5ha (over 1 acre)
Terrain: Gentle slope

 limited

 in small groups

  by arrangement

Thirty-four years ago, Woodbank farm was sited on an open-cast coal-mine. Mem had to contend with coal-dust and still finds the occasional piece of coal in the garden. She has added masses of pea-straw, donkey manure and compost over the 17 years she has been developing the garden. Woodbank is now a woodland garden featuring rhododendrons in spring, then roses and perennials in summer. Exotic trees include pin oaks, maples, cherries, small magnolias, and two copper beeches, within a shelter of poplars and Douglas firs. The prunus are mainly "Kanzan" and the chartreuse "Ukon" which blossom in spring and add to the autumn display. Blue carpets of spring groundcover of bluebells, forget-me-nots, grape hyacinths and ajuga contrast with the pink blossom above. Elsewhere Mem has blue and yellow or apricot and blue areas. Old roses and David Austins adorning the tennis court include "Dr W Van Fleet", "New Dawn", "Albertine", "Alchemist" and "Frühlingsgold". A secret garden is hidden behind the tennis court, while a sunken herb garden features a huge rose frame above a rustic seat. Rhododendrons include the "yaks", creamy "Diane" that Mem loves and Tom's favourite "Sir Charles Lemon" which blooms early with its white trusses and speckled throat.

MT GAY FARM
Pleasant Point

Owners:
Flo and Roger Carter

Address: Mt Gay Rd, R D 12,
Pleasant Pt
Directions: From SH 79 turn left into
Gudex Rd. At end turn left into
Middle Valley Rd. Turn right into
Hazelburn Rd, then right again into
Mt Gay Rd. From Pleasant Point
Hotel, follow signs to Raincliff,
turning right at Blacksmith corner into
Raincliff Rd. Turn second left into
Hazelburn Rd, then as above
Phone: 0-3-614 7153
Fax: 0-3-614 7991
Open: All year, daily, by appointment
Groups: By appointment, as above
Fee: $3 per adult
Size: Small – 0.3ha (¾ acre)
Terrain: Terraced and flat
For sale: Sheepskins, hand-made
woollen garments

👫 👶 🐕   🚻 x2   ♿ on flat &
         to toilet
⛱ 🍲 🍽   by arrangement

Tucked into a hillside on Mt Gay, this rural garden provides panoramic views to the mountains and the Pacific Ocean. A walled bank was planted when the house was built 17 years ago. An enthusiastic Iris Society member, Flo planted various iris species from dwarfs to tall beardeds throughout the garden. Peonies bloom in November, then roses and lilies provide summer colour, underplanted with pansies. Daisies are also predominant from summer through autumn, while thousands of hellebores are a winter treat, planted on a bank to be appreciated from a terraced pathway below. Seventy-year-old daffodils feature with bluebells and other spring bulbs, followed by aquilegias and delphiniums for vertical accent. Flo combines yellows with blues, avoiding too many oranges. The third week in October is good for colour with drifts of arabis and phlox against the snowy mountain backdrop. A Norway maple *Acer platanoides* "Crimson King" features in spring with its large deep-crimson-purple leaves turning orange in autumn. Three huge bushes of deep red *Rosa moyesii* bloom in December, with old polyanthus roses beneath a cherry tree and fuchsia. Natives scattered throughout the garden include kowhai, fragrant pittosporums, coprosma, griselinia backing a pond, and a lovely wineberry. Horse riding, shearing and spinning demonstrations are available.

ETHRIDGE GARDENS
Timaru

Ethridge

Owners:
Nan and Wynne Raymond

Ethridge Gardens

Address: 10 Sealy St, Timaru
Directions: Take SH 1 to Timaru.
Turn west north of the town into
Wai-iti Rd. Travel 2km to Sealy St.
Garden on left
Phone: 0-3-684 4910
Fax: 0-3-684 4910
Open: September to May, daily,
by appointment
Groups: By appointment, as above
Fee: $5 per adult
Size: Small – 0.3ha (¾ acre)
Terrain: Flat
Nursery: Many perennials including
Cerinthe major, Alchemilla mollis,
cynoglossum
Functions: Weddings, cocktails,
receptions, by arrangement
Accommodation: By arrangement

by arrangement

This English-style garden, named after Nan's English
great-grandmother, was inspired by Sissinghurst and
Hidcote. Eleven years ago it was virtually a blank canvas.
Nan designed high brick walls to divide it into a series of
rooms and vistas, with grassy axes leading from one colour
scheme to the next, each carefully coordinated throughout
the changing seasons. A century-old oak dominates the front
lawn, fringed with rhododendrons, camellias and roses.
The driveway border in yellows, blues and whites features
"Maigold" roses climbing the high trellis fence. In summer
the herbaceous red, blue and lime-green border is full of
red roses and lilies, with blue irises, delphiniums and lime-
green euphorbias and alchemilla. Further long borders
overflow in pinks, mauves, purples, whites and silver, with
a "Mary Rose" walk edged in box, contrasting with a semi-
circle of silvery, blue- and plum-coloured foliage,
surrounding a silver pear as focal point. A cross-axis takes
the eye to a statue of Atlanta. The first of many archways
leads into the formal courtyard centred around a pond and
fountain framed with "Iceberg" roses. A landscaped
swimming-pool area in bright yellows and blues ends
at the rose gazebo where red "Dublin Bay" climbs to the
Marseilles-tiled roof, matching the 1911 house, and over
the wall into the potager.

CRAIGMORE HOMESTEAD
Timaru

Owners:
Sir Peter, Lady Elworthy and family

Address: R D 2, Timaru
Directions: From Timaru, take
Beaconsfield Rd for 17km. Turn right
into Pareora Gorge Rd. Travel 4km,
then turn left into Craigmore Valley
Rd. Travel 5km, then turn right into
Craigmore Hill Rd. Peonies on right,
homestead across river on left
Phone: 0-3-612 9840 (Kathryn Hill,
Peony Manager)
Fax: 0-3-612 9825
Open: Peony Open Day: first Sunday
in November, 1pm–5pm
Homestead Garden: open September
to Christmas, by appointment
Groups: As above
Fee: $3 per adult
Size: Large – 1ha (2½ acres) plus
1.2ha (3 acres) peony field
Terrain: Flat
Nursery: Peonies, tree peonies

Limestone cliffs and hillsides covered in cabbage trees back the historic Craigmore property, where Herbert Elworthy built a homestead designed by Hurst Seagar in 1907. Deciduous trees planted to Alfred Buxton's landscape plan still dominate the garden. A formal rose garden with paths in the shape of a Celtic Cross was planted after World War II. The Buxton-designed tear-shaped driveway and cherry walk were restored in 1992. In 1981 the Elworthy family began the adjacent peony nursery, with nearly 4,000 herbaceous peonies thriving in the limy soil and hard frosts that characterise this valley. Now, thousands of peonies are exported each November and December and many of them feature in the homestead garden, with single, double and Japanese herbaceous peonies in yellows, coral, scarlet and white complementing the earlier tree peonies. Accompanying plants include spring bulbs, old-fashioned roses, delphiniums and irises. Behind the lawn used for theatrical performances, the steep river bank is being bordered by local native species for protection and landscape effect. Daffodil Day is held on the fourth Sunday in September, annually, in the spacious grounds, with music, Morris dancers and stalls; and the multi-cultural Aoraki Festival of the Arts features biennially in the first weekend of February (next in 1998).

BIRCHWOOD
St Andrews

Owners:
Colleen and Alex Hardacre

Address: Blue Cliffs Rd, R D 24,
St Andrews
Directions: 15 mins from Timaru.
Take SH 1 south to St Andrews, turn
right into Blue Cliffs Rd. Travel 2km
to garden on left
Phone: 0-3-612 6705
Open: All year, daily, by appointment
Groups: By appointment, as above
Fee: $2 per adult
Size. Medium   0.8ha (2 acres)
Terrain: Flat
Nursery: Perennials and alpines from
garden seed

   by arrangement

Birchwood is named after the silver birches planted
15 years ago, with new plantings lining the roadside.
The house was built in a paddock and the angles of the
garden planned to suit the sun, with a flowing driveway
planted in gums and *Cedrus deodara* for shelter. A group
of 14-year-old native trees shelters the garden from
easterlies, with another native corner in the new garden
area where beds flank a spacious lawn. Colleen's favourites
are the alpines in the two rock gardens, including fritillarias,
species tulips and other bulbs, dwarf irises and conifers
for vertical accent. Primulas and Chatham Island forget-
me-nots surround a small fish-pond, and a bog garden
features Japanese and Siberian irises and candelabra
primulas. A new rose arbour will be covered in old-
fashioned roses beside a new rhododendron bed. Both old
and modern roses are planted throughout the garden, with
blues and whites used to soften the colours, apart from the
cottage garden where the colours are mixed. Spring features
include colourful phlox, tree peonies, rhododendrons, and
a fragrant pieris. Spring bulbs are followed by dahlias and
lilies in summer, and autumn colours the foliage of prunus,
maples, cornus, and a new planting of English beeches.
A budgie aviary is an added attraction.

NUKUROA
Studholme

Owners:
Anne and Peter Foley

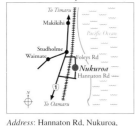

Address: Hannaton Rd, Nukuroa,
R D 10, Waimate
Directions: Exactly halfway between
Timaru and Oamaru off SH 1. Turn
east at Studholme into Foleys Rd.
Turn right into Hannaton Rd.
Nukuroa on right
Phone: 0-3-689 9813
Open: October to November, daily,
by appointment
Groups: By appointment, as above
Fee: $3 per adult
Size: Large – 2.6ha (6 ½ acres)
Terrain: Sloping
Nursery: Sales table of perennials
from garden @ $2.50 each

  by arrangement

Natives and exotics, combined with sweeping lawns, create a park-like atmosphere at Nukuroa, making it a garden of vistas and spaces. Two decades of planting the sloping paddocks with trees and shrubs has created separate areas, with vistas to the Hunter hills beyond. Wide railway-sleeper steps lead down the hillside to flower beds and trees surrounding the spacious lawns, ideal for functions. Daffodils bloom in spring, complemented by drifts of blue scillas, bluebells, forget-me-nots, pansies and aquilegias under michelias, rhododendrons and flowering cherries. A popular October corner is the seat under a pink cascade of montana clematis climbing more than five metres up acer "Kelly Gold". Nearby is Rhododendron "Naomi Exbury" and Peter's favourite 15-year-old pieris. Anne loves the rhododendrons, especially the blush-white "Loderi" group, underplanted with lamiums, forget-me-nots, wood violets, foamflowers and acanthus. Colour is maintained by over 20 deutzias until the English and old roses flower, with dahlias providing additional summer colour. A woodland arboretum incorporates a stream, opening into a pond planted with moisture-loving species Peter is particularly keen on the trees, including the English beeches, planes, limes and his unusual cork oak grove. Donkeys, deer, Cairn terriers and peacocks enliven the landscape.

MILLER'S GARDEN
Waimate

Owner:
Madeleine Miller

Address: Park Rd, R D 9, Waimate
Directions: From Timaru or Oamaru
take SH 1 towards Waimate. Turn
west at SH 82 and continue to Waihao
Back Rd. Turn left and continue to
Park Rd. Turn left and garden on right
Phone: 0-3-689 8498
Open: Late October to March, daily,
by appointment
Groups: By appointment, as above
Fee: $3 per adult
Size: Medium – 0.4ha (1 acre)
Terrain: Flat

Century-old wellingtonias and oaks in the adjacent park provide a wonderful backdrop for Madeleine's garden. Visitors are intrigued to see sows, rather than sheep, grazing the grassy paddocks beyond the garden, screened by Madeleine's prunus grove and mature Leyland cypress hedge. The garden entrance is via a brick courtyard where a central urn features a bay tree encircled with white saxifrage. An archway smothered in pink montana clematis frames a vista to the trellised gazebo. Shingle pathways and grassy avenues finger into different garden rooms with focal points including the Japanese pagoda tree within a grassy circle, and the sun-dial in a sunken garden. Formality continues in the horseshoe-shaped rose garden, with further roses climbing the gazebo and clambering over a serpentine brick wall. Blue wisteria climbs an adjacent pergola and the hybrid clematis "Nelly Moser" adorns the wall in spring. Madeleine plans her colour combinations carefully, using blues extensively with pale pinks, reds or yellows, underplanting rhododendrons and cornus. A kidney-shaped pond in the trees is crossed by a bridge and surrounded with water-loving plants. A further pond with a waterfall was established five years ago when Madeleine extended her native walk into the paddock beyond.

269

THE SECRET GARDEN
Waimate

Owners:
Colin and Jan Wilkinson

Address: Manchesters Rd, Waimate
Directions: From Timaru or Oamaru
take SH 1 towards Waimate. South of
SH 82, turn west into McNamaras
Highway. Then turn right into
Manchesters Rd. Garden on right
Phone: 0-3-689 8461
Open: All year, daily, 9am–6pm
Groups: By appointment for buses
Fee: No charge
Size: Medium – 0.4ha (1 acre)
Terrain: Flat
Nursery: Perennials, lavenders,
species hydrangea, buxus, herbs,
roses, rhododendrons, camellias,
magnolias, cupressus, junipers
Shop: Exclusive gifts
Tearoom: Devonshire tea, light
lunches by arrangement

👫 ♿ wheelchair available

🏕 ☕ 🍽 by arrangement

Incorporating turn-of-the-century English oaks and walnuts, the Wilkinsons' garden has been developed over the past 18 years. Conifers stand guard at the gateway, softened by Montana clematis. Magnolias, viburnums and prunus line the driveway, sprinkled with the petals of the flowering cherries. An archway of roses leads to a stone-edged pond planted with lilies, irises and azaleas. Nearby a dovecote houses white fantail doves. A formal garden within an avenue of pencil cypresses features a twin box-edged border of pink "Alice" rhododendrons underplanted with white forget-me-nots and azaleas, with a bird-bath as focal point. A pair of classical urns flank this avenue leading to a wrought-iron gazebo. Tall hedges enclose a white garden behind a lych-gate, and a blue garden features elsewhere. Hundreds of spring bulbs accompany the blossom trees which form arches overhead. A formal tear-shaped rose bed is divided by a brick path leading to an urn as focal point and a seat in the rose arbour is a welcome summer retreat. Old roses are complemented by bedding plants, with foxgloves, delphiniums and lupins for vertical accent. The deciduous trees provide autumn colour and the formal hedges delineate the structure of the garden in winter. A potager is a recent development. A tearoom offers meals including icecream and strawberries in season, by arrangement.

THE BRIARS
Omarama

Owners:
Marylou and Don Blue

Address: Ahuriri Heights, Omarama
Postal: P O Box 98, Omarama
Directions: On SH 8, travel south
25km from Twizel, or north 2km
from Omarama to Ahuriri Heights.
Turn west and continue 300m to
garden on left
Phone: 0-3-438 9615
Open: All year, daily, 10am–4pm
Groups: As above
Fee: $3 per adult
Size: Medium – 0.8ha (2 acres)
Terrain: Flat, terraced and steep
Accommodation: B&B available,
by arrangement

 partial

In only six years the Blues have transformed a hillside of rabbit burrows and briar roses into a formal garden designed around circles, with even a circular carpark. The garden is named after the wild sweet-briars that now surround the garden, contrasting with the old roses that Marylou has planted throughout. A long pergola walk features 18 pink climbing roses edged with lavender, and a white garden on the top terrace mixes old-fashioned and modern rose varieties. The roses continue into the autumn when the purple and white borders bloom. Spring bulbs and trilliums announce the end of winter. Because of the panoramic mountain views below, Marylou has designed the lower gardens in bold lines, planted with hardy perennials that will survive the harsh climate. Silver birches, gums, oaks and red-leafed malus provide shelter, with dry stone walling adding to the structure of the garden, and pergolas shading the seats placed strategically throughout the garden. A square herb garden contrasts with a traditional circular herb garden featuring a large sunken trough. This opens into Don's potager with its high pergola, which in turn leads to a box-edged square garden, in greens and whites, where an historic font from the Omarama church is focal point.

PARKSIDE STONE AND GARDEN
Oamaru

Owners:
Linda and Bob Wilson

Address: 37 Airedale Rd, Weston, Oamaru
Directions: From Oamaru, take SH 1 south to Weston Rd. Turn right and continue 4km to Weston. Turn right into Main St, then continue into Airedale Rd. Garden 500m on left. From Palmerston, take SH 1 north towards Oamaru. Turn left into Whiterocks Rd at AA sign to Parkside Quarries. Travel 2–3km into Weston
Phone: 0-3-434 7220
Fax: 0-3-434 7220
Open: All year, daily, 9am–5pm
Groups: As above
Fee: $2 per person for quarry and garden bus tour groups
Size: Medium – 0.4ha (1 acre)
Terrain: Flat
Nursery: Full range of trees, shrubs, old-fashioned cottage plants

Parkside is the name of the adjacent farm and stone quarries, the garden created to display Oamaru limestone. Four years ago the Wilsons decided to turn the pony field in front of their home into the garden centre which Linda runs. The central focal point is a large stone rotunda draped in clematis. Extensive use has been made of the soft Oamaru stone which is easy to cut and carve forming pillars, blocks, slabs or even statuary. A stone folly is the focal point at the end of a long herbaceous vista and a walk-through fernery includes a small waterfall and a trellised wall for climbers. A large rockery features plants for all seasons and seasonal beds are changed to demonstrate planting combinations, such as cerise lily-flowered tulips rising from a sea of pink forget-me-nots, white primulas and silvery foliage, edged with box. Grassy pathways curve between beds displaying plants suitable for shade, sun, and cottage gardens, with flowering cherries as centre points. Three formal lily ponds and bridges feature water-loving plants. There are also corners for natives, herbs, and a bed of low maintenance plants such as ericas. Rhododendrons, azaleas and camellias are displayed in a shade house. Parkside is the sole New Zealand supplier of Oamaru limestone. Quarry tours are available and the nursery shop sells Oamaru stone pots, urns, sun-dials and other garden accessories.

ROXLEA PARK FRAGRANT HERB GARDEN
Oamaru

Owners:
Gillian and Murray Cayford

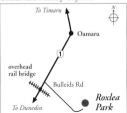

Address: Bulleids Rd, Deborah
Postal: P O Box 255, Oamaru
Directions: Take SH 1 south of
Oamaru for 2.5km. Turn left before
overhead rail bridge into Bulleids Rd.
Travel 300m and turn left to garden
Phone: 0-3-434 6055
Fax: 0-3-434 9880 (work)
Open: Late September to end April,
daily, 10am–6pm
Groups: By appointment
Fee: No charge
Size: Medium – 0.4ha (1 acre)
Terrain: Gently sloping
Nursery: Herbs from garden,
specialising in lavenders and culinary
herbs, some medicinal herbs & salvias
Craft gallery: Sells Gillian's herbs &
pottery, mainly domestic stoneware

♿ mostly   ⚲ by arrangement

This herbal cottage garden, sited in front of an 1860 home constructed from hand-hewn Oamaru limestone, is in its ninth season. Lemon verbena, lavenders, thymes and scented geraniums are Gillian's favourite plants, but a full range of herbs can be seen in raised beds laid out formally. A culinary garden includes marjoram, sage, thyme and balms, which Gillian doesn't allow to flower while in use. A medicinal garden contains well known herbs such as valerian, along with more unusual species including *Echinacea* and *Elecampane*. Labels on French sorrel, comfrey, sweet cicely and other herbs explain their culinary and medicinal uses. A fragrant garden flowers with rosemary, lavender and other perfumed species.
A tranquillity garden planted in blue, white and lemon features a chamomile lawn and a weeping silver pear tree. Low-growing St John's wort, Spanish daisies and salvias surround a small pond and a bird aviary houses budgies, finches, canaries and quail. Spring features climbing creepers such as the wisteria over the house, hardenbergia, pandorea and clematis. A Canadian maple shelters the garden which is surrounded by established poplars, silver birches, gums and macrocarpa hedges. An adjacent craft gallery sells herbal crafts and pottery made and fired by Gillian on the property.

JOAN ELDER'S GARDEN
Maheno

Owner:
Joan Elder

Address: 1 Monkton St, Maheno, Oamaru
Directions: From Oamaru take SH 1 south 9km to Maheno. Turn left into Lambton St, then third left into Monkton St. Garden first on left
Phone: 0-3-439 5859
Open: Spring and summer, daily, by appointment
Groups: By appointment, as above
Fee: No charge
Size: Small – 0.3ha (¼ acre)
Terrain: Flat
Paintings: Joan's watercolours, oils and miniatures of the garden and floral still-life for sale

Joan has established her garden over the past four decades, with favourite roses and rhododendrons, including "White Pearl" which is trimmed like a tree after 30 years' growth. Other predominant species include hostas, meconopsis, trilliums and Auricula primulas. With an artist's eye, Joan has designed her garden for all-year colour, providing inspiration for her paintings. In spring, early rock rhododendrons flower, along with dog-tooth violets and bulbs including a winding narcissi path. Joan plants for colour blends as well as line, using complementary colours such as lavenders under yellow rhododendrons. Red rhododendrons provide strong accents, with different hybrids emerging at various times to maintain the impact of red. Further spring features include dogwoods, kalmias, magnolias, and hybrid clematis such as *C.* "Jackmanii" flowing over an archway with the old rose, salmon rambler "Phyllis Bide". A 150-year-old macrocarpa hedge died, but provides further framework for climbers. A rose bed adjacent to the house continues the red highlights with climbing "Birthday Present" and other sunset colourings, joined in summer by dahlias. Then in autumn the maples, prunus and oaks are really colourful, a pin oak shading the sunken water garden, lush with hostas, Kingcups or marsh marigolds and other bog plants in spring.

MILL COTTAGE
Waianakarua

Owners:
Joan and Jim Wilson

Address: Waianakarua, R D 10.O, Oamaru
Directions: From Oamaru, take SH 1 south for 32km to Waianakarua. Mill Cottage is before an overhead bridge on right, next to historic Mill House
Phone: 0-3-439 5044
Open: September to May, daily, by appointment
Groups: By appointment, as above
Fee: $3 per adult; discounts for groups
Size: Medium – 0.6ha (1½ acres)
Terrain: Flat

  by arrangement

Mill Cottage is adjacent to the historic Mill House and Bridge. A cherry blossom driveway leads to the cottage garden, where a rock-studded bed features tulips, irises, grape hyacinths and polyanthus blending between dwarf conifers and maples. A rose pergola leads into a woodland walk where a row of Spanish cedars provides dappled shade for rhododendrons underplanted with hostas. Pathways are edged with local Oamaru stone which mosses up under the gold, blue and green conifers. Joan's is a seasonal garden, planted in all shades of pink, complemented with pale lemon and blues, rather than purples and reds. A gleditsia shades the rhododendrons in spring, when the creamy Oamaru stone reflects a yellow and cream bed reached through a clematis archway, with meconopsis and delphiniums providing blue highlights. In summer, a blue pansy border contrasts with a rosebed in varying pinks. Formal elements include a paved horse-shoe-shaped area, edged with buxus around an unknown pale-pink old-fashioned rose in the centre, underplanted with pink forget-me-nots. A stone courtyard surrounds a waterlily pond, enclosed by a low curving stone wall beneath a pink cherry tree. A touch of blue completes the scene, with lithospermum behind the pool-side seat.

275

CLACHANBURN
Ranfurly

Owners:
Jane and Charles Falconer

Address: Puketoi Runs Rd, Patearoa;
Postal: Patearoa, R D 4, Ranfurly
Directions: From Ranfurly, travel
18km south to Patearoa. Cross
Sowburn Bridge, continue 0.5km,
then turn first right. After 200m take
first turn left. Cross Taieri River and
continue to T intersection. Turn left
into Puketoi Runs Rd. Continue 3km
to Clachanburn garden on right
Phone: 0-3-444 7501
Fax: 0-3-444 7044
Open: October to March, groups only
Groups: By appointment
Fee: $3 per person
Size: Medium – 1.2ha (3 acres)
Terrain: Flat to undulating
Nursery: Plants from garden eg buxus,
roses, ericas, lavenders, & perennials
Cottage: Clachanburn produce & craft

🚶 🐴 👫 ♿ mostly
⛩ 🍵 🍽 by arrangement

Clachanburn is Gaelic for the "Stoney Creek", which flows through the property. Poplars, pines, willows, prunus and an *Acer negundo* were the original plantings in the 1920s, but Charles and Jane have extended the garden since 1977, when they moved into the homestead, designing a new area each year. Despite the harsh Maniototo climate, with its hot, dry summers and freezing winters, Jane manages to plant for seasonal colour. Spring blossom is accompanied by drifts of daffodils, primulas, trilliums, fritillarias, aquilegias, forget-me-nots and hellebores. Then wisteria, clematis and peonies bloom, followed in summer by roses and perennials. A large formal rose garden of old-fashioned and modern roses is bordered by a low hedge of *Buxus sempervirens*. The deciduous trees provide the rich autumn colours of Central Otago, and its schist stone features in walls throughout the garden. White Pekin ducks swim in a natural stream-fed pond edged with water irises, hostas and astilbes and featuring a curved stone bridge and waterfalls created by boulders lining the stream. Jane is developing the orchard vista, being careful to retain the northern vista of the vast Maniototo plains to the hills beyond. The cottage provides refreshments, incorporates the nursery and sells Clachanburn produce and craft, including gardening clothing and accessories.

HEREWEKA GARDEN AND NURSERY
Portobello

Owners:
Dr Peter Cooke and Anna Moore

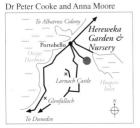

Address: Hereweka St, Portobello
Directions: From Portobello, turn
right into Hereweka St. Continue
500m then follow steep gravel road
1.4km through bush to garden
Phone: 0-3-478 0165 or
0-3-478 0880 (work)
Open: All year, most weekends or by
appointment
Groups: By appointment
Fee: $5 per adult; refund on purchase
from nursery
Size: Large – 2ha (2 acres garden and
3 acres bush walks)
Terrain: Hilly
Nursery: Rare old perennials eg
Barnhaven double primulas, "Pink
Sensation" delphiniums, *Gladiolus
tristis*, species aquilegias, irises,
penstemons, campanulas, heliotropes,
meconopsis, choice dwarf bulbs

Hidden in a valley of native bush, including the only extant stand of mature rimu trees on the peninsula, Hereweka looks out to hills and the inlet beyond. A decade ago, the steep slope in front of the house was bulldozed into two levels, dry stone walls built, herbaceous borders planted and ponds established. Peter's walls overflow with blues and yellows – a favourite colour combination of Anna's – such as weeping rosemary, blue aquilegias, purple aubrietia, and lilac *Thalictrum aquilegifolium* contrasting with drifts of lemon *Gladiolus tristis*. A bed of creamy rhododendrons underplanted with daffodils is shaded by a kanuka tree, with a rare native *Clematis foetida* climbing to a tiny rifleman bird-box. Anna prefers scented species in soft muted lemons, yellows and creams, rather than hot colours. Early spring begins in September with flowering cherries and bulbs including miniature narcissi and a bed of pink tulips. *Convolvulus mauritanicus* adds to the blues in summer, when the perennial bed peaks with delphiniums, drifts of gypsophila, peonies, old roses and lilies. The sloping lawn leads to a recent stone and kanuka arbour, to be draped with white wisteria and old roses. Peter has planted the largest southern collection of over 25 bamboo species.

  pending

277

LARNACH CASTLE GARDEN
Otago Peninsula

Owner:
Margaret Barker

Address: Camp Rd, Otago Peninsula
Postal: P O Box 1350, Dunedin
Directions: From the city, take
Highcliff Rd along the top of Otago
peninsula. Turn left into Camp Rd.
Castle on left
Phone: 0-3-476 1616
Fax: 0-3-476 1574
Open: All year, daily, 9am–5pm;
during daylight saving 9am–7pm
Groups: Guided tours by arrangement
Fee: $5 per adult, $1 per child
Size: Large – 5ha (12½ acres)
Terrain: Mostly flat
Nursery: Rhododendron species and
hybrids, perennials, woodland plants,
alpines, damp-loving plants
Tearooms: 9.30am–4.30pm daily
Accommodation: 12 rooms with
private bathrooms; meals in castle

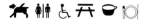

The gardens surrounding Larnach Castle have been recreated from 1967, incorporating 120-year-old trees. An expansive lawn in front of the castle is formally designed, with conifers symmetrically placed on the perimeter around the central focal point of a marble fountain from Pisa. A great laburnum arch underplanted with spring bulbs leads to a square pool with a view between immense conifers over the harbour 300 metres below. Alice in Wonderland figurines by Tenniel adorn the lawn border, with the Cheshire cat in the boughs of the original old cedar encircled with daffodils next to the historic glass cupola. A rhododendron dell features beyond the original holly hedge and on the opposite side of the castle is the restored rock garden. Azalea and heather gardens in front of the ballroom provide spring and autumn colour. The alpine garden also features in spring and the lath-enclosed perennial garden peaks in summer, when the damp garden near the driveway entrance flowers. Behind the ballroom, a box walk leads to an original copper beech by the wishing well. Beyond, Margaret's rainforest garden of native ponga, beech, kauri, rimu, totara, rewarewa and cabbage trees is interplanted with species rhododendrons, the colourful flame creeper *Tropaeolum speciosum*, and cardiocrinums. Accommodation is available in the adjacent Lodge.

GLENFALLOCH WOODLAND GARDEN
Otago Peninsula

Owner:
Otago Peninsula Trust
Manager: Alan Gilbert

Address: 430 Portobello Rd, Otago Peninsula
Postal: P O Box 492, Dunedin
Directions: Travel from city to Otago Peninsula. Follow Portobello Rd for 11km to Glenfalloch on the right, just before Macandrew Bay township
Phone: 0-3-476 1775
Fax: 0-3-476 1137
Restaurant phone: 0 3 476 1006
Open: All year, daily, dawn to dusk and evening meals
Groups: Book dinners
Fee: By donation
Size: Large – 9.8ha (24 acres)
Terrain: Flat and steep
Restaurant: Licensed; restricted hours in winter
Restrictions: Consideration to be shown for other visitors

♦♦ 🥢 ♿ to lower flat garden

Gaelic for "Hidden Glen", Glenfalloch is situated in a coastal valley overlooking the harbour. Developed as a private garden by Phillip Barling in 1917, Glenfalloch was bought by the Otago Peninsula Trust in 1968 to ensure public access. Sheltered by a ring of pines and eucalypts, Glenfalloch features original European trees from 1872, underplanted with sizeable azaleas and rhododendrons, including many unique hybrids and large-leafed species. Daffodils announce the arrival of spring, followed by tulips blooming beneath flowering cherries, magnolias and chestnuts. Native clematis climb the trees under which peonies and lilies flower in summer. Mature maples and silver birches provide spectacular colour in autumn. Then the early camellias bloom, including a Women's Year planting of white camellias, established in 1993 and interspersed with native hebes. A 45-minute bush walk leads past an ancient matai where birdlife includes tui, bellbirds and native pigeons. Russell Creek runs through the garden, bordered by massed azaleas under a woodland canopy. Perennials and moisture-loving plants include gunneras, hellebores, aquilegias, Solomon's seal, bergenias and hostas. Drifts of bluebells, ajuga and cerise primulas carpet the stream-banks in spring. Other features include a 1945 "Peace Arch", Otago Herb Society Herb Garden, and a studio selling pottery.

279

JOY'S BONSAI STUDIO
Abbotsford

Owners:
Joy and Colin Morton

Address: 6 Torquay St, Abbotsford, Dunedin
Directions: Take motorway south-west of city to Abbotsford. Turn right into Abbotsford Rd, then third right crossing over the railway line into North Taieri Rd. Take second right into Exmouth St, then fourth left into Torquay. Garden first on left
Phone: 0-3-488 4592
Fax: 0-3-488 4224
Open: All year, daily, by appointment
Groups: By appointment, as above
Fee: No charge
Size: Small – 1,200 sq metres
Terrain: Flat
Nursery: 450 bonsai trees; $10–$500
Tuition: 5-week courses available
For sale: Bonsai kits, pots, soil mix, wire, tools
Services: Bonsai sitting, re-designing, re-potting services available

Joy's specialist bonsai nursery has over three thousand trees in various stages of development into bonsai. Some are 40 years old, with bonsai for sale up to more than 20 years old. The predominant species are larches, cedars and maples, although Joy's private collection of about 70 trees includes some very rare species such as the white needle pine. Her oldest bonsai is a *Cryptomeria japonica* "Elegans" and her favourites include the native kowhai which flower in spring. Other flowering species are the azaleas, rhododendrons and wisterias. The leaves of maples and zelkovas turn a beautiful red in autumn and drop in winter. The larches display gold foliage in autumn, while the beeches turn bronze throughout winter and hold their leaf. Joy makes *penjin* or Chinese landscapes with tall, sharp peaks and Japanese *saikei* in softer lines. Special trees create a driftwood effect with *jins* or *sharis* on them, as if they have been through a forest fire or are struggling to recover from a strong wind. Joy instructs customers on general care and provides an information sheet about potting up, trimming, watering and feeding. Bonsai need re-potting every two years or so, depending on their age, and branches trimmed in the growing season. Joy can provide these services or teach beginners the skills needed.

GARVAN HOMESTEAD
Milton

Owners:
Joy and David McDonald

Address: SH 1, Lovells Flat, R D 2,
Milton
Directions: 45 minutes south of
Dunedin. Take SH 1 to Milton.
Continue another 12km. Garden on
right. 12.5km north of Balclutha.
Phone: 0-3-417 8407
Fax: 0-3-417 8407
Open: All year, daily
Fee: No charge
Size: Large – 2ha (5 acres)
Terrain: Flat and slightly rolling
Accommodation: Luxury B&B with
à la carte dinner available; licensed bar

Garvan Homestead is set in an historic Buxton garden, designed and constructed by the well-known Christchurch landscape gardener, Alfred Buxton, 80 years ago. This English-style woodland garden has been restored since 1987. The original rhododendron plantings are still the predominant species, underplanted with huge drifts of violets, lily-of-the-valley and hellebores, and set amid a large collection of mature trees, mainly English oaks, elms and birches. Other Buxton features that are still apparent include the sweeping drive lined with assorted hollies and *Crataegus* (hawthorn), the tennis court, hazelnut walk, pond and the weeping trees that Buxton so often used. The pond was rediscovered and planted round with multiplying white and pink primulas, silver astelias and deep blue *Iris sibirica,* in Monet-like effect. Primulas were also used with ligularias, gunneras and other bog plants to beautify the bog garden created from a boggy part of the front lawn. Camellias and spring bulbs accompany the spring blossom, followed by colourful perennial borders and old English roses that adorn the garden and house. The roses continue into autumn when the maples and English trees colour up, in contrast with the conifers and evergreens, and the Virginia creeper turns scarlet.

SOUTH AND CENTRAL OTAGO, SOUTHLAND AND INVERCARGILL

Inland from Dunedin is Central Otago with its cold winters and hot, dry summers producing wonderful stone-fruit. The three beautiful glacial lakes backed by Aspiring National Park make this a favourite area for winter sports and summer sightseeing. At Lawrence is The Ark with its cottage garden, then near Beaumont are the Craigellachie Downs Rockery Gardens selling alpine plants. Inland at Tapanui are two nurseries: Crystal Brook Nurseries with trees, shrubs and perennials, and Blue Mountain Nurseries, specialising in double azaleas, with a range of hardy trees and plants. En route to the vast rocky landscape of Alexandra is Millers Flat where two gardens at Avenel Station incorporate valleys with a series of ponds, one with established rare conifers and the other with rockeries. Nearby at Ettrick are three more gardens: Joals Nursery Garden specialising in perennials, Lammerview Orchard and Nursery with mature trees framing mountain views, and the Seedfarm Eating House and Garden, where a formal colonial-style garden surrounds historic buildings.

There are three gardens at Wanaka, with views out to the lake and mountains beyond. Wanaka Floral Studio Gardens are planted round streams. Ashdon Garden, although small, features many rhododendrons, and Motatapu Station, set high above the lake, incorporates two massive rocks. At Lake Hawea, Nook Road Nursery specialises in hardy plants, and on the high-country road towards the Lindis Pass at Tarras is The Timburn Garden, a woodland garden surrounding the historic house. At Queenstown beside Lake Wakatipu and the Remarkables, Garden Tours travel out to Lake Hayes and Arrowtown and include the formal park-like Speight Gardens.

Southland is a rich farming region at the southern tip of New Zealand. To the west is the extensive Fiordland National Park and south, across Foveaux Strait, is Stewart Island. Invercargill, the southernmost city in New Zealand, is sited on open plains at the centre of the Southland grasslands. Like Dunedin, it was settled by Scots and the speech of locals incorporates the Scottish burr, undampened by the cooler temperatures experienced at such a southerly latitude. Many of the regional names and garden names also reflect this origin. Three gardens feature in the Balclutha area: Glenory with its island beds and roses, and at Clifton, two gardens in farm settings – Dawson Downs, a floral artist's garden, and Clifton Downs, a summer garden. Just west of Gore is Hokonui Alpines with its extensive alpine nursery. There are three more gardens west towards Lumsden. The first is Elm-Lea, south of Balfour, incorporating mature trees in a garden of perennials and roses. Pahiwi Perennials, closer to Balfour, is an immaculate garden with a perennial nursery. Josephville Gardens are nearer Lumsden, with roses, alpines and bulbs in an established woodland setting.

North-east of Invercargill are three gardens in the Wyndham area. Just south of Glenham are Winfield Nurseries with certified Bio-Gro perennials and a view to Stewart Island on a clear day. Nearby is Maple Glen with its birdlife, series of ponds and mature trees. A little further south at Mataura Island are Hillside Gardens with rhododendrons predominating and a view up Mataura River. Further inland, just north of Glencoe, is the Hosta Garden with over 150 varieties for sale and hostas planted throughout the woodland garden. Just north of Invercargill is Myross Bush Rhododendrons, with 250 different rhododendrons for sale, displayed in the garden of 900 varieties under a canopy of flowering cherries and magnolias. North-west of Invercargill, at Northope, is Belle Fleur, specialists in dahlias featuring in summer. And, finally, at West Plains just west of Invercargill is Marshwood, specialists in lavender, salvia, euphorbia and nepeta and selling a wide range of perennials

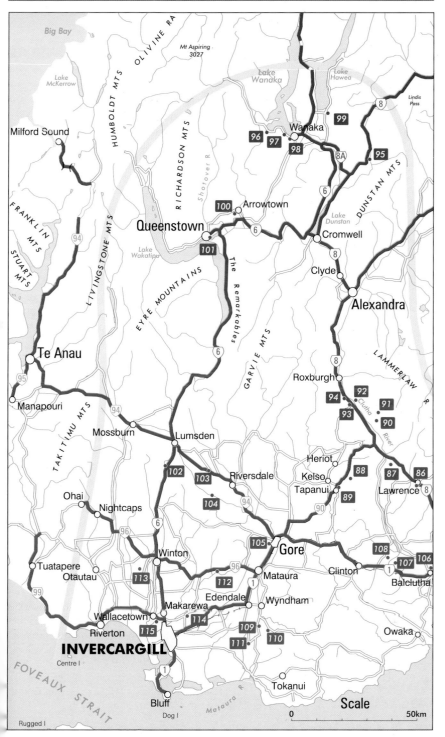

THE ARK
Lawrence

Owner:
Frieda Betman

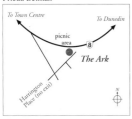

Address: 8 Harrington Pl, Lawrence
Directions: From Dunedin, take SH 8
towards Lawrence. Just at the
"Welcome to Lawrence" sign, garden
immediately on left. Parking in
No Exit road, Harrington Place,
behind The Ark
Phone: 0-3-485 9328
Open: November to March, daily,
preferably by appointment
Groups: As above
Fee: Gold coin
Size: Small – 0.2ha (½ acre)
Terrain: Flat
Nursery: Some perennials from
garden for sale
Accommodation: Available

 in park across road

by arrangement

Frieda has created a florist's cottage garden as a setting
for her restored turn-of-the-century house dubbed "The
Ark", situated in the old gold-mining town of Lawrence.
Frieda's favourites are cottage perennials such as phloxes,
bergamots and penstemons. She worked with the contours
of the garden, planting in whites through to pinks, lavenders
and blues, with a touch of yellow such as the primulas with
the deciduous azaleas by the bridge which crosses the pond.
A stick bridge and curved brick wall provide further
structure and a pergola is engulfed in blue wisteria in
spring. Blossom trees include "Mt Fuji" cherry, "Eddie's
Wonder" dogwood, *Magnolia stellata* and viburnums.
White daisy-like *Anthemis cupaniana* begin flowering in
October and continue through to March, and rhododendrons
start blooming in November. These are followed by
peonies, summer perennials and a few roses. Catmint and
Lady's mantle (*Alchemilla mollis*) make wonderful borders
and the ponga edging is sprouting in damp areas that
favour Solomon's seal, hostas, Auricula primulas, astilbes,
phlox, filipendulas and astrantia. A huge weeping willow
on the fenceline provides shade, other trees including eight
maples, a walnut, beech, golden ash, four claret ashes,
silver birches and a medlar tree. Frieda's inseparable fox
terrier, Holly, is an added attraction.

CRAIGELLACHIE DOWNS ROCKERY GARDENS
Lawrence

Owners:
Anne and John Benington

Address: Beaumont, R D 1, Lawrence
Directions: Take SH 8 north of
Lawrence for 14km. Turn left at
Athenaeum Rd. Craigellachie Garden
immediately on right, in sight of SH 8
Phone: 0-3-485 9447
Open: August to April, daily,
by appointment
Groups: By appointment, as above,
but call a couple of days prior
Fee: $2 per adult or purchase from
nursery
Size: Medium – 0.8ha (2 acres)
Terrain: Flat
Nursery: A comprehensive selection
of plants grown in garden

    by arrangement

Craigellachie hills are reminiscent of their namesakes in Scotland. Anne started her garden here 16 years ago, expanding it to accommodate new bulbs and alpines, limited only by local weather conditions. Fences were moved repeatedly, and green beds raised for drainage. A magnificent oak tree is the only original remnant, an extensive rock garden formed with mossed local stones now being the main feature, creating a tapestry of colour in contrast to the green lawns. Anne's favourites are the miniature rockery bulbs and plants that feature in her alpine gardens. Brick-edged gravel paths weave throughout the rockeries, among treasures including hellebores, fritillaria, pulsatillas, gentians, crocuses, mini narcissi, trilliums and specialist miniature bulbs. A silver birch in the centre provides shade for hostas, interplanted with aquilegias, ericas, bluebells and dwarf conifers. Wider grassy paths, bordered with catmint, lead past a silver garden to rhododendrons underplanted with ajuga and phlox. Masses of spring bulbs complement the flowering prunus, then peony beds bloom in November, with old roses. Miniature roses and clematis flower in summer when the large perennial border peaks, then the ericas and callunas accompany the colourful autumn foliage. Groups of conifers shelter and frame the garden. New pergolas and archways frame views to the hills beyond.

285

CRYSTAL BROOK NURSERIES
Tapanui

Owner:
Colin Beattie

Address: Sheddan Rd, Tapanui, R D 1
Directions: Take SH 90 south from
Raes Junction to signpost at Brooks
Dale Rd. Turn left, then right into
Sheddan Rd. Nurseries on left. From
Tapanui, turn right off SH 90 into
Cameron Rd. Turn left into Sheddan
Rd. Nurseries on right
Phone: 0-3-204 8782
Fax: 0-3-204 8782
Open: All year, daily, 9am–5pm
Groups: By appointment
Fee: No charge
Size: Large – 6ha (2 acres garden;
14 acres nursery)
Terrain: Mainly flat
Nursery: Conifers, deciduous trees,
ornamental trees & shrubs, perennials

The display garden at Crystal Brook Nurseries has been intensively planted over the past 15 years, but is blessed with a century-old oak tree. The predominant species to be seen now growing in the garden are *Camellia japonica*, 300 to 400 varieties of rhododendrons and over 40 different hostas. A hidden garden is edged with daffodils in spring and features camellias, rhododendrons and white lilac. A dwarf garden is moon-shaped and a circular garden is formed by wisteria-covered pergolas. Quite a few magnolias and native kowhai trees contribute to the spring colour. Then the laburnums and azaleas flower, followed by the summer perennials that line the driveway. The creek is crossed by a bridge and has been closely planted. An added water attraction is the water wheel on the stream that falls into a pond. A range of young deciduous trees down the paddock provide autumn colour as they mature, together with the oaks and maple collection. Native trees include *Nothofagus* or New Zealand beech, white pines or kahikatea and cabbage trees under which the eight peacocks like to shelter. Two hectares (ten acres) of native bush below the nursery create a wonderful setting and add character to Crystal Brook.

BLUE MOUNTAIN NURSERIES
Tapanui

Owners:
Denis and Margaret Hughes

Blue Mountain Nurseries

Address: 99 Bushy Hill St, Tapanui
Directions: Take SH 90 south from
Raes Junction or north-east from
Gore, to Tapanui. Where highway
turns, take Bushy Hill St east to
Nurseries on right
Phone: 0-3-204 8250
Fax: 0-3-204 8278
Open: All year, Mondays to Saturdays,
9am–5pm
Closed. Sundays
Groups: By appointment
Fee: No charge
Size: Large – over 6ha (16 acres)
Terrain: Flat
Nursery: Hardy trees & shrubs, alpines,
perennials, climbers, rhododendrons
& azaleas, specialising in double
azaleas; catalogues available

hot water available

Denis' father began the bulb and perennial nursery in 1943, then Denis and Margaret developed the trees and shrub side of the business in 1966. Denis' favourites include the deciduous azaleas that he began in 1972, raising his own double hybrids, with the fragrant white "Pavlova" the first to be released, and apricot "Sunray" available this year. Next to appear will be the creamy pink "Softlights". The azalea beds also provide lovely autumn colour, along with the maples and over 20 different fragrant viburnums. The nursery features an extensive rhododendron shade house, where Margaret breeds the compact "yak" hybrids, and ivy cultivars climb the poles, the Hughes being registered as national ivy collectors. A glass house displays the extensive collection of pleione orchids that Denis loves, in whites, yellows and cerise, including rare varieties selling for $200 per bulb! Denis is also keen on tree peonies, and other spring highlights include a bed of trilliums with three main varieties for sale. In summertime the 15 *Eucryphia* trees bear white and pink flowers. A comprehensive range of conifers provide winter colour, as do the berries on the rowan trees, until the snowdrops emerge. Other interesting features include variegated yuccas and native flax-like astelias.

287

AVENEL STATION GARDENS
Millers Flat

Owners:
Noeline and Eoin Garden

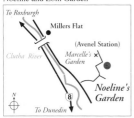

Address: Millers Flat, R D 2,
Roxburgh
Directions: At Millers Flat, cross
bridge, then turn right and continue
3km. Turn left, travel uphill 9km,
then left at intersection. Travel 3km
to Avenel Station. Noeline's garden
on right
Phone: 0-3-446 6560
Fax: 0-3-446 6744
Open: Late October to April, daily,
by appointment
Groups: By appointment, as above
Fee: $3 per adult; discounts for group
garden & farm tour with afternoon tea
Size: Large – 2ha (5 acres)
Terrain: Hilly
Nursery: Plants from garden
Tours: Farm tours of Station available
Accommodation: B&B with dinner

 partly
by arrangement

Over the past two decades Noeline and Eoin have established five acres of woodland gardens on their high-country station, framing panoramic views of sheep grazing golden tussock pastureland. Broad steps curve down the terraced gully, past a series of water gardens to a lake on the valley floor. Large block plantings have understoreys of rhododendrons, azaleas and spring bulbs, while an extensive collection of rare conifers provides structure and year-round colour. Silver firs and cypresses are predominant, and a pair of blue weeping Atlas cedars flank an archway. Pathways disappear into a cool larch grove which turns brilliant gold in autumn, merging into Douglas firs thinned to provide shelter for large-leafed rhododendron species, underplanted with trilliums and fritillarias. Warm sunset colours include a red blaze of deciduous azaleas and pockets of apricot-pink lewisias in rock walls. Elsewhere Noeline chooses more restful greys and pinks, and mauve wisteria climbs verandah columns around the house. Noeline loves the flowering dogwoods in spring and gentians which feature around the ponds and pathways until autumn, when her favourite medlar displays reds, oranges and yellows. Maples too provide intense autumn colour, along with the azaleas, claret ash and *Sorbus* varieties with their red berries. Accommodation is available, with dinner included.

AVENEL STATION GARDENS
Millers Flat

Owners:
Marcelle and Pat Garden

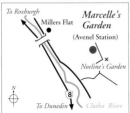

Address: Millers Flat, R D 2, Roxburgh
Directions: Take SH 8 south of Roxburgh to Millers Flat. Turn across bridge, then turn right and continue 3km. Turn left, travel uphill 9km, then left again at intersection. Travel 3km to Avenel Station. Marcelle's garden on left, 600m past Noeline's garden
Phone: 0-3-446 6532
Fax: 0-3-446 6625
Open: October to end April, daily, by appointment
Groups: By appointment, as above
Fee: $3 per adult
Size: Medium – 1.6ha (4 acres)
Terrain: Flat and hilly
Nursery: Some alpines and small bulbs from garden

top garden
by arrangement

After establishing shelter, 14 years ago Marcelle began developing her high-country garden. First she planted a small rockery around her new house, then as a micro-climate developed, so did the rockeries, featuring the early bulbs, irises and alpines that she loves. In front of the house, a recent L-shaped pergola, to be clad in roses, forms a trellised outdoor room with seating, overlooking a sheltered south-facing gully planted in maples and rhododendrons. Silver birches shade beds of pompon *Primula denticulata*, irises, daffodils and purple pansies, while a patch of natives includes the Mt Cook lily.

A hornbeam copse is underplanted with drifts of bluebells, meconopsis and trilliums, followed by azaleas and further rhododendrons and hostas beneath silver birches.

A honeysuckle hedge screens a cottage garden, and massed conifers of different shapes and sizes merge together, separating off the vegetable garden. A series of ponds and a small stream sheltered by willows and underplanted with irises, gunneras, hostas, ligularias, primulas and *Euphorbia griffithii* "Fireglow" lead down to a newly developed dam. A bog garden is surrounded by masses of white daisies. Colourful perennials in the summer garden and many trees and shrubs planted for their autumn display provide interest until April.

JOALS NURSERY GARDEN
Ettrick

Owners:
John Tomkin and Alan Garthwaite

Address: Clutha Rd, Ettrick
Directions: Take SH 8 south of
Roxburgh to Ettrick. Continue to
Clutha Rd on left. Follow road for
1.5km to Joals Nursery on banks of
Clutha River
Phone: 0-3-446 6785
Open: All year, daily
Groups: As above
Fee: No charge
Size: Medium – 1ha (2½ acres)
Terrain: Flat with a bank
Nursery: Perennial specialist;
wide selection of trees, shrubs, and
over 100 different perennials for sale

   limited

Named from a combination of the first letters of John and Alan, Joals Nursery is only six years old, yet already includes an extensive display garden. This consists of both cottage and woodland areas, featuring John's favourite dogwoods, old-fashioned roses and perennials. Fifteen different dogwoods, such as "Eddie's White Wonder", pink "Spring Song" and "Rainbow" with a variegated leaf blossom in spring with the early roses and *Viburnum xanthcarpum* attracts red admiral butterflies. Peonies, romneyas and lilies accompany the 250 roses which bloom throughout the garden in summer in the perennial borders, as well as the formal box-edged rose garden set off with a two-metre-high statue of David. Two large goldfish ponds are planted with waterlilies, and bordered with flaxes, water irises and conifers. Nearby, a weeping silver pear shades Auricula primulas, and double azaleas contrast colourfully with fragrant lilacs in spring. Stone paving is a special feature and white river stone makes an attractive pathway around ranunculus encircling a clematis-clad ponga tree-stump. Walkways meander through the wooded bank, with strong autumn colour provided by the collection of deciduous trees which include oaks, sorbus, ashes, alders, birches and cornus. Lewisias create a bright border beneath the luminescent pale-leafed *Sorbus aria* "Lutescens" in spring.

LAMMERVIEW ORCHARD AND NURSERY
Ettrick

Owners: ·
Judith Hunter and Alistair Stevenson

Address: Dalmuir Rd, Ettrick
Directions: Take SH 8 to Ettrick.
Turn west into Moa Flat Rd, then
right into Dalmuir Rd, garden second
drive on right
Phone: 0-3-446 6887
Fax: 0-3-446 6887
Open: All year, unless "closed"
Groups: By appointment
Fee: No charge
Size: Medium – 0.6ha (1½ acres)
Terrain: Flat
Nursery: Hanging baskets of fuchsias;
old roses; hydrangeas; aquatic, bog
and marginal plants
For sale: The "Secure Plant Hanger"
and the "Melbourne Garden Frame"
Accommodation: Self-contained
cottage with breakfast

& access to drive around garden

With a view to the Lammerlaw and Lammermoor mountains beyond, the garden and home orchard block at Lammerview are sheltered by a hedge of walnut trees that were planted in 1912. Alistair's father added oaks, birches and fir trees in the fifties, then Judith and Alistair established the present garden around the house in the early 1980s. Other mature trees include a large lacebark, dogwoods, flowering cherries, malus, magnolias, catalpas and lindens. The design takes seasonal colour into account, with an outer "Ring-of-fire" walk featuring a blaze of rhododendrons and deciduous azaleas, surrounding an inner summer perennial garden. A secret garden to the side of the house features more perennials shaded by a tall *Prunus yedoensis*. A patio area is softened by potted plants and camellias and hydrangeas in tubs, with clematis, roses and campsis climbing the walls of the house and pergolas. An original irrigation pond, now a waterlily pond, is home to brilliant red goldfish and countless frogs and attracts the abundant birdlife that features in the garden. The pond is surrounded by a hedge of the single white *Rosa multiflora*. Extensive plantings of deciduous trees and shrubs provide a brilliant display of autumn colour through April and May. A self-contained cottage for two, in the garden, provides quality accommodation.

291

THE SEEDFARM EATING HOUSE AND GARDEN
Roxburgh

Owners:
John and Raewyn Lane

Address: SH 8 Dumbarton, Roxburgh
Directions: Equidistant from
Queenstown and Dunedin. Take SH 8
south of Roxburgh for 9km towards
Ettrick. Seedfarm on right
Phone: 0-3-446 6824
Open: Groups only; December to
Easter, daily, 10.30am–5pm;
other times Friday to Sunday
Groups: As above
Fee: No charge
Size: Medium – 0.7ha (1¼ acres)
Terrain: Flat
Accommodation: B&B and dinner
Restaurant: Home-made fare for teas,
lunches, dinners;
dinners by reservation

The Seedfarm was a training farm which experimented with vegetable seed after World War I. Now the 125-year-old stone building has been transformed into a restaurant, with the adjacent barn offering deluxe accommodation. Over the past six years, a colonial garden has been developed in keeping with the era of the buildings, incorporating original trees such as the huge old oak, planted around the 1920s, on the lawn by the carpark. Rows of English beech form unusual hedges throughout the garden, turning copper in autumn, but holding their leaves. Curving low schist walls also structure the garden, which is formally designed with old-fashioned roses featuring throughout, mostly in pinks. Raewyn likes to keep the colours soft and muted, although a hot garden features under the trees bordering the roadside. A triangular bed edged with schist rock is planted in apricots, purples and whites with perennials such as geums and lychnis. An outdoor eating area is shaded by a pergola, with ivy climbing the rustic poles, and seating beneath a "tortured" willow. A circular stone-edged bed in the lawn features blue and way into a lavender and box-edged potager laid out formally in triangular beds with rustic arches.

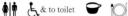 & to toilet

THE TIMBURN GARDEN
Tarras

Owners:
Anny and John Lucas

Address: Timburn Station, Tarras
Directions: Take SH 8 north of Tarras
for 13.3 km. Timburn Garden on right
Phone: 0-3-445 2877
Fax: 0-3-445 2877
Open: October to April, daily,
by appointment
Groups: By appointment, as above
Fee: $2 per adult
Size: Medium – 0.8ha (2 acres)
Terrain: Flat
Nursery: A few plants from the
garden
Shop: Lindis Country Shoppe selling
garden accessories and country
collectables, just north on SH 8

 by river

 by arrangement

Anny's garden surrounds a 1912 block house constructed from riverbed shingle. A large scarlet oak was originally planted when the garden was laid out in a very formal English design with box hedges and roses. As the garden matured and roses struggled for light, it changed into a woodland-style park with underplantings. In very early spring, chionodoxa bulbs form a carpet of blue beneath the established English trees framing views to the mountains and hills of Lindis Valley beyond. Then masses of violets, bluebells and primroses follow, with azaleas and rhododendrons which Anny loves, constant watering enabling them to withstand the high-country summer. The shrubbery features viburnums, and purple wisteria forms a canopy over the courtyard. The varied foliage of the copper beeches, maples and oaks make lovely colour combinations, especially in autumn, and provide welcome shade in the summer when the peonies, roses and perennials flower, including the many irises and renowned Otago lupins. Anny likes reds and yellows which glow in the Central Otago sun, and plans a "hot" orange, yellow and cream area. The original fences are adorned with ivy, and an old grapevine still bears fruit. An aviary featuring canaries, doves and turquoisines adds interest.

MOTATAPU STATION
Wanaka

Owners:
Sally and Don Mackay

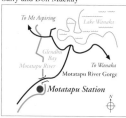

Address: Motatapu Station Rd,
Wanaka
Directions: 25 mins from Wanaka.
Take the Mt Aspiring Rd to Glendhu.
Continue on to gravel and take next
turn left into Motatapu River Gorge
Rd. Continue 6km over the bridge to
the garden
Phone: 0-3-443 7051
Open: Mid October to end February,
Wednesday to Friday, by appointment
Groups: By appointment, as above
Fee: $4 per adult; buses $3 per person
Size: Medium – 0.8ha (2 acres)
Terrain: Flat and hilly

 at gorge, hot water available

Motatapu, meaning "sacred river" is a high-country
garden situated above a spectacular river gorge,
with backdrops of snow-covered mountains. Sally began
planting in 1980 on a site bereft of all vegetation. Two
enormous rocks are natural architectural features, one the
focal point of a conifer bed and the other planted with
a white garden. Nearby roses climb a cabbage tree underplanted with white honesty. Anthemis and white buddleias
echo the snowline beyond the top of the rock, contrasting
with a weeping yellow deodar. Elsewhere, Sally chooses
lively colour, grouping hot reds, oranges and yellows
together. The view is unimpeded by the single weeping
silver pear and a new honeysuckle arch frames the
mountains. A rose garden is underplanted with pinks,
purples and blues and a bank of lupins, down the steep
driveway, erupts into colour each spring. Rhododendrons,
underplanted with forget-me-nots and aquilegias, include
Sally's favourite lilac-pink "Irene Stead". The double white
azalea "Pavlova" and heart-shaped epimedium break up
the colour bands of blues and yellows merging into peaches
then pinks. Sally is keen on foliage, using soft-green
Alchemilla mollis for groundcover. Her white romneya
have seeded beneath the white chestnut which colours
up well in autumn, a favourite season now the deciduous
trees are maturing.

ASHDON GARDEN
Wanaka

Owners:
Ashlea and Don King

Address: 8 Tapley Paddock, Wanaka
Directions: From Wanaka, take the lakeside road, Ardmore St, into Mt Aspiring Rd. Turn right into Tapley Paddock. Garden at end of road on right
Phone: 0-3-443 8067
Fax: 0-3-443 7885
Open: September to April, daily, by appointment
Groups: By appointment, as above
Fee: $4 per adult
Size: Small – 0.08ha (⅕ acre)
Terrain: Flat

Ashdon Garden, its name a combination of Ashlea and Don's names, has been developed over the past 16 years, adjacent to a bush reserve leading down to Lake Wanaka and Wanaka Station Park. This was part of the original Wanaka Station homestead, featuring historic oaks and cedars and provides a borrowed view for the Kings, making their garden appear much larger than its fifth of an acre. Rhododendrons are Ashlea's favourite species, over 100 featuring in the garden, such as "Sarita Loder" beneath the montana clematis cascading from a sycamore tree. Camellias beside the house colour the early spring, and a white wisteria drips from the verandah. Further spring features include tulips, the cornus "Eddie's White Wonder" and several species of crab-apple that provide spring blossom, summer fruit and autumn colour, as well as attracting the birdlife. A rosebed features old roses with climbers and ramblers on the fence-line accompanied by lots of summer perennials. Don constructed a rockery and stone walls which form low terraces planted with ferns, ericas, pieris and weigela. The path to the front door is bordered by malus, pink azaleas and white camellias underplanted with lush bergenias. A pieris and rhododendrons shade peonies and drifts of blue forget-me-nots.

WANAKA FLORAL STUDIO GARDENS
Wanaka

Owners:
Pat and Keith Stuart

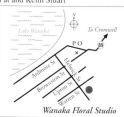

Wanaka Floral Studio

Address: 32 Warren St, Wanaka
Directions: Take SH 89 from
Cromwell to Wanaka. Turn left into
Helwick St. Continue past Warren St.
Garden entrance on left. (Nursery
entrance from Warren St)
Phone: 0-3-443 8866
Fax: 0-3-443 7846
Open: September to May, daily,
by appointment
Groups: By appointment, as above
Fee: No charge
Size: Medium – 0.4ha (1 acre)
Terrain: Gently sloping
Nursery: Specialists in rare and
unusual plants
Accommodation: B&B by
arrangement; not school holidays

  by arrangement

A decade ago the Stuarts converted an acre of peat
bog into garden, diverting springs to form streams
meandering through a series of waterfalls into Bullock
Creek. The creek-banks have been landscaped with blossom
trees, cornus, maples, gunneras, rodgersias and *Peltiphyllum*.
Drifts of phlox, Japanese irises, astilbes and azaleas tumble
over rocks, which also edge the clear water, enhancing the
plantings of hostas and primulas. Bridges cross the waterways to paths edged with purple violas, leading past red
native astelia and peonies canopied by dogwoods, parrotia
and maples. Early spring features a collection of hellebores
with carpets of *H.* "White Magic" and many new hybrids.
These are followed by primulas, meconopsis, alpines and
bulbs. A woodland path leads to an azalea bed with bright-
coloured companion plants. Further spring highlights
include groups of rhododendrons, camellias, and enkianthus
underplanted with trilliums, wood anemones, primroses
and Auriculas. White wisteria hangs from the house
balcony, while another climbs high into a red silver birch.
Summer and autumn feature herbaceous gardens and
a rosebed punctuated by schist rock columns. Maples,
stuartia, cornus and other deciduous trees display brilliant
autumn colour. A New Zealand cedar gazebo provides
a lake view with a backdrop of snow-capped mountains.

NOOK ROAD NURSERY
Lake Hawea

Owners:
Jamie and Vicky Urquhart

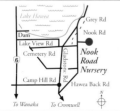

Address: Nook Rd, Lake Hawea
Directions: 20 minutes from Wanaka.
Either take Camp Hill Rd to Hawea
Flat, turn left into Gladstone Rd, right
into Grey Rd, left into Hawea Back
Rd, and right into Nook Rd. Or take
SH 6 to dam at Lake Hawea, cross
dam, veer left along lake front, left
into Cemetery Rd, into Grey Rd, left
into Hawea Back Rd, and right into
Nook Rd. Garden at end
Phone: 0-3-443 1495
Fax: 0-3-443 1555
Open: All year, daily, 9am–5pm
Groups: By appointment
Fee: No charge
Size: Medium – 0.8ha (2 acres)
Terrain: Flat
Nursery: Range of specimen trees,
rhododendrons, old roses, natives,
perennials

This nursery is a continuation of a family business established originally over 30 years ago as Maryeds Garden. In 1989 it became Nook Road Nursery, nestled in a sheltered nook under the mountains on the eastern side of Lake Hawea, with views to the snow-capped peaks of the Southern Alps beyond. Jamie's mother specialised in perennials, now Vicky's favourite plants. Jamie has developed the native plants, foliage and tree side of the enterprise, his favourites being viburnums. The Urquharts specialise in plants that flourish in the Central Otago climatic conditions of very cold winters and hot summers. All plants are grown outside, not in glass house conditions, making them already hardy and suitable for planting in similar situations. Spring fare includes the viburnums, flowering cherries, hybrid and native clematis, ceanothus, lots of rhododendrons and the spring-flowering philadelphus that Jamie is fond of. His mother's collection of old peonies (which are not for sale) bloom with the old-fashioned roses in summer. Autumn colours the foliage of the deciduous trees, including the maples and pear trees. Gums and ponderosa pines also feature, with many natives including New Zealand beech, manuka, kanuka, hoheria or lacebark, *Cordyline australis* or cabbage trees, pittosporum, flaxes, grasses, and hebes. New improvements include sealed paths throughout.

SPEIGHT GARDENS
Queenstown

Owners:
Mairi and David Speight

Address: Speargrass Flat Rd, R D 1, Queenstown
Directions: From Queenstown, take SH 6 to Lake Hayes. Continue towards Arrowtown, then turn left into Speargrass Flat Rd. Travel 2km to garden on left
Phone: 0-3-442 1520
Fax: 0-3-442 1520
Open: All year, 9.30am till evening
Groups: As above, or included in Queenstown Garden Tours (see over, page 300)
Fee: $5 per adult
Size: Large – 3.2ha (8 acres)
Terrain: Flat with hillocks
Nursery: Perennials from garden; plants that grow in extreme conditions
Toilets: At Arrowtown, 5 minutes away

These park-like gardens incorporate formal areas planted since 1986. From the pergola entrance, a long axis separates a roadside shrubbery from daffodils that drift in spring through oaks in the parkland. Beyond a circle of *Cupressus glabra* "Blue Ice" is Thyme Hill and an area of ericas, callunas and pernettya. A yellow summer border lines the Long Walk to a gate into the Strawberry Walk. A stone pathway extends from a horseshoe-shaped native garden to a sunken garden, where a dry river-bed serpentines through creek-side plantings of shade-loving plants to a folly as focal point. An arboretum on the slope above provides rich autumn colour and overlooks an island planting of grey foliage. Eight formal lavender-edged beds of 1000 old roses are backed by pergolas with a canopy of climbing roses, wisteria and clematis providing shade for camellias. A native bank, including a chess set of wooden pieces, provides a vista through to the cloistered garden, deliberately green in contrast to the adjacent colour wheel where 14 segments of perennials in graduated colour surround central white valerian. *Robinia* "Mop Tops" enhance two symmetrical formal ponds and, finally, an intimate terraced cottage garden leads to a hot bed of intense oranges and golds.

QUEENSTOWN GARDEN TOURS
Queenstown

Operator:
Barry Dolman

Address: Queenstown Information
Centre, corner Shotover and Camp
Streets, Queenstown
Postal: P O Box 780, Queenstown
Directions: Book at Information
Centre. Mini-bus will collect you
from your accommodation 10 mins
prior to departure time
Phone: 0-3-442 7319
Fax: 0-3-442 6749
Open: Tours depart daily, October to
mid-April. Allow 4 hours per tour
Groups: Book as above
Fee: $48 per adult; discount for
groups
Size: 4 gardens of varying sizes
selected out of a total of 7 gardens
Terrain: Varied – wear sensible
footwear

🧍🏃 👫 🚻 ⚰ ☕ Devonshire

(included half-way, at Stone Cottage)

Dramatic mountain scenery is included in this tour of
four rural gardens, with white hawthorn blossom
adorning the fields and hills of Queenstown in spring,
followed by red berries. The owners show the tour group
around their varied gardens in a friendly personal way.
A 12-year-old alpine garden, on a plateau of less than an
acre overlooking the Wakatipu basin, features all sorts of
treasures including trilliums, fritillaria, pulsatillas and bulbs,
with mounds of ericas, hebes and conifers among local
schist rock. A flat garden overlooking the Lower Shotover
River, with snow-capped peaks beyond, displays weeping
cherries above colourful beds, with roses, a sumac tree
and a remarkably southern paulownia tree. Jerusalem
donkeys, goats and hens are added attractions in this
garden that covers almost an acre. A large 11-year-old
garden at Arrow Junction has many old roses, rugosas and
rose pergolas accompanied by peonies, perennials,
rhododendrons and maples, including sugar maples. This
garden extends even to the top of a huge schist rock.
A 13-year-old half-acre garden overlooking Lake Hayes
features a massive rock face and is planted with a bank of
rhododendrons, masses of irises and a silver birch grove
underplanted with woodland species. Speight Gardens
(see page 299) are included in summer.

JOSEPHVILLE GARDENS
Lumsden

Owners:
Annette and Bob Menlove

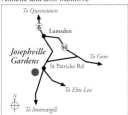

Address: SH 6, R D 4, Lumsden
Directions: From Lumsden, take SH 6
south towards Invercargill. Travel
9km to Josephville. Garden on right
at foot of hill
Phone: 0-3-248 7114
Fax: 0-3-248 7114
Open: October to Easter, Friday and
Saturday, 10am–5pm, other times
by appointment
Groups: By appointment
Fee: No charge
Size: Medium – 1ha (2½ acres)
Terrain: Terraced
Nursery: Rhododendrons, perennials,
& specimen tree selection eg maples
Accommodation: Homestays –
1 double and 1 twin with shared guest
bathroom; self-contained unit

This garden in a woodland setting among the hills has been developed over the past 24 years from a paddock edged with pine trees. Rhododendrons and maples are the predominant species, with peonies and over 70 heritage roses Annette's favourites in summer. Bob likes the maples and conifers which suit the Southland climate, especially abies and the row of blue atlas cedars along the roadside. Annette colour-coordinates the garden with drifts of pinks, lemons and reds, such as the pink primulas in spring, and she is developing an apricot area. A rockery is full of miniature rock plants including daffodils, trilliums, fritillarias and early primulas with a small waterfall spouting from an urn. Daffodils spread through the top garden followed in late spring by Chatham Island forget-me-nots, rhododendrons and a large selection of peonies. Roses include both old-fashioned varieties and hybrid teas, with the old apricot "Albertine" rambling on the far side of the creek. A pond at the bottom of the garden is being planted with trees such as alders, poplars and birches underplanted with patches of various-coloured primulas. Hostas and further primulas flourish in a wet area at the end of the tennis court.

PAHIWI PERENNIALS
Balfour

Owners:
Fiona and Ken Drysdale

Address: Pahiwi Rd, R D 6, Gore
Directions: Take SH 94 east from Lumsden or west from Gore, to Balfour. Turn south at crossroads into Queen St, and continue into Glenure Rd. Travel 4km, then turn into first sealed road on left, Pahiwi Rd. Turn left again at first mailbox and travel 1km. Turn right across cattle-stop and follow drive another 1km to garden
Phone: 0-3-201 6122
Fax: 0-3-201 6122
Open: 1 October to 31 March, daily, by appointment
Groups: By appointment, as above
Fee: No charge
Size: Small – 0.35ha (⅞ acre)
Terrain: Flat
Nursery: Wide range of perennials from garden, eg pulsatillas, gentians
Accommodation: B&B by arrangement

This is an immaculate garden of serpentine beds carving into the lawn with clean-cut edges. Over the past six years Fiona has designed and developed these sweeping beds, with an equally immaculate nursery blended into the overall design. Fiona loves building up collections of perennial plant families, favourites including pulsatillas, gentians, centaurea, meconopsis, dianthus, campanulas, veronicas, polemoniums, pulmonarias and some hard-to-find species. These provide year-round colour accompanied by blossom, rhododendrons and azaleas in spring, then peonies and roses in summer. A rose pergola with a trellised walkway beside the house adds structure, and a sunken courtyard of hexagonal stones changes the contour. Blue *Moltkia* (formerly *Lithospermum*) spills over a raised bed of miniature roses, and a trellised walkway leads to rock-edged beds of violets, delicate saxifraga and rock irises. A lavender-edged bed connects to a tiered bed, terraced with sleepers, featuring groundcover clematis and primulas, with climbing roses against the garage. A maple is reflected in a small kidney-shaped lily pond edged with stones. A formal rock garden features gentians, cyclamens, succulents, alpine daisies, with a tall clematis-covered rock and potted conifer providing vertical accent. Views extend to the snow-capped peaks in the distance.

ELM-LEA
Gore

Owners:
Gail and Geoff Dickie

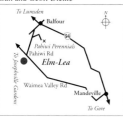

Address: Waimea Valley Rd, R D 6, Gore
Directions: From Gore, take SH 94 towards Lumsden. Turn left at Mandeville School into Waimea Valley Rd. Travel 27km to Elm-Lea, last property on tar-seal on left
Phone: 0-3-201 6072
Open: October to April, daily, by appointment
Groups: By appointment, as above
Fee: $3 per adult
Size: Medium – 0.6ha (1½ acres)
Terrain: Gently sloping
Nursery: Old roses, herbs, lavenders and perennials from garden

Elm-Lea, meaning "elms in a meadow", is a romantic name for the original sheep paddock with two elms in it. The garden has been developed in the past three years around mature trees planted in the 1950s, although the Dickies have lived at Elm-Lea for 14 years. Gail's favourites are the old roses which bloom with a cottage blend of perennials including aquilegias, dianthus and mallows. Gail likes bold splashes of colour against the green foliage, although she keeps the sun-dial garden pastel beyond the clematis archway. The driveway is a glorious sight in spring with forsythias underplanted with 3,000 daffodils which also drift through the woodland area intermingled with over 4,000 blue muscari. Camellias feature by the summer house which is adorned with Virginia creeper turning scarlet in autumn along with the deciduous foliage of maples, oaks and cotinus. Other introduced trees include liriodendrons, birches, prunus and pussy willow, accompanying a native hoheria that flowers into winter. A small pond is planted with Spanish bluebells, rhododendrons, lily of the valley bushes and maples. Other points of interest include dry stone walling between the drive and the house, roses climbing a domed gazebo over a brick rondel, and panoramic views towards the Garvie Mountains.

HOKONUI ALPINES
Gore

Owners:
Peter Salmond and Louise Salmond

Address: Croydon Siding, R D 6, Gore
Directions: From Gore, take Hokonui
Drive towards Queenstown. Travel
6km, then turn into Croydon Siding
Rd on left. Garden 1km on right
Phone: 0-3-208 9609
Open: August to May, 9am–5pm, daily
Closed: Sundays & public holidays
Groups: Buses by appointment
Fee: No charge
Size: Medium – 0.8ha (2 acres)
Terrain: Hilly
Nursery: Specialist in NZ alpines,
hardy small flowering perennials,
miniature bulbs, dwarf shrubs, ground-
covers, woodland plants, new releases;
for mail-order catalogue, send five
45-cent stamps
For sale: Salmonds' Tufa Tubs eg
garden pots, bird-baths, water bowls

🚶🐕 ⚓ partly & to nursery
👫 🍽 🥄 by arrangement

Peter and Louise are a brother-and-sister team who took over the alpine nursery their mother, Dorothy, established over 30 years ago. Set in the Hokonui hills, a bare paddock was transformed into the nursery and display garden with rockeries bordering neatly sloping lawns. Large rock gardens edged with stone and sleeper walls provide views to the Tapanui Blue Mountains. One thousand stock varieties cover everything that grows in rock gardens from over 20 genera, including difficult, unusual and rare alpines, such as *Paraquilegia* and *Dionysia*, as well as a native alpine section. Cushions of colour are punctuated by dwarf conifers and irises for vertical accent. August features miniature daffodils, trilliums, adonis, choice primroses and woodland plants such as blue *Corydalis cashmeriana* particularly suited to the South Island. Then in summer, rockery phloxes, irises, dianthus, campanulas, alyssum and rock roses flower. Hanging baskets of lobelias and geraniums add interest and popular buys are the blue gentians and colourful lewisias. In autumn, berry trees such as the miniature rowans provide colour. Other dwarf trees include 30-centimetre-high elms, willows and ericaceae such as *Andromedas* and *Cassiopes*. In late winter, choice saxifrages flower in the Salmonds' hypertufa tubs. Classic Tufa Tubs of original designs are for sale.

GLENORY
Balclutha

Owners:
Lorraine and Graham Ramsay

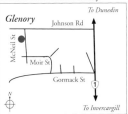

Address: 37 McNeil St, Balclutha
Directions: Take SH 1 south towards Balclutha. Turn right into Johnson Rd (unsealed), then first left into McNeil St. Garden on right. Or continue past Johnson Rd and turn right into Gormack St, then right again into Moir St. Take second left into McNeil St. Garden last on left
Phone: 0-3-418 2759
Open: October to April, daily, by appointment
Groups: By appointment, as above
Fee: $2 per adult
Size: Medium – 0.45ha (1⅛ acres)
Terrain: Flat

by arrangement

Situated on the edge of Balclutha with a rural backdrop, the garden at Glenory is eight years old. Lorraine has developed it into island beds, moving the fences out and incorporating existing conifers in boundary shrubbery. She has added a conservatory linking house and garden, and plans to extend brick paths and erect trellis to separate the garden into rooms. Lorraine's favourite plants are roses, with the miniatures predominating, but she is increasing the David Austins, as she enjoys the repeat flowering. The rock garden features spring bulbs including daffodils, tulips, "April Tears" narcissi and alpines. These are followed by camellias, rhododendrons and miniatures irises interplanted with the miniature roses. Perennials are used extensively in the island beds which are sheltered by exotics such as a Chilean firebush contrasting with the blue conifer, *Atlantica glauca,* a snow gum, viburnums, calico bushes, banksia and wattles. Autumn colour is provided by oaks, birches, a walnut, chestnut and fasciated willow, with flowering cherries including four *Prunus* "Accolade" along the front fence underplanted with spring bulbs, and two *P. subhirtella* "Autumnalis" for year-round interest. Native kowhai trees feature in the garden in spring and in the native area at the gateway which also includes hebes, pseudopanax, cabbage trees, lacebark and lancewoods.

DAWSON DOWNS
Clifton

Managers:
Helen and Peter Gilder

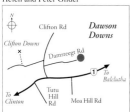

Address: Damsteegt Rd, R D 3, Clifton
Directions: From Balclutha, travel
about 15km west, then turn right into
Clifton Rd. Continue 2km, then turn
right into Damsteegt Rd. Travel to
end of this gravel road (no exit) to
garden. From Clinton, travel 15km
east to Clifton Rd. Then as above
Phone: 0-3-415 7244
Fax: 0-3-415 7244
Open: October to April, daily,
by appointment
Groups: By appointment, as above
Fee: $2 per adult
Size: Medium – 0.4ha (1 acre)
Terrain: Flat
Farm tour: By arrangement with Peter
Campervans: Welcome

  by arrangement

Bought by Landcorp in 1990, Dawson Downs is a
finishing farm, where Peter fattens up lambs, cattle
and deer. The first year, Helen brought a few plants and
trees over from West Otago. Then in 1992 the major
structure work of the garden began. The fence came out
next as the garden took shape and developed. The Gilders'
son, who was studying architecture in the seventh form,
drew up the garden plan. Helen is a floral artist, so she
plants for colour, form and texture. The predominant species
at present are the birches, rhododendrons and roses, but
natives are to come, especially those with bold foliage,
to provide strong structure on the east side. Helen plans
to plant ponga tree ferns when the garden becomes shady
enough. Ashes and maples are maturing and she'd like
to spot plant the paddocks in front of the house with
English trees for added autumn colour. She thinks in terms
of the colour wheel as she plants, one colour flowing into
the next. Yellow conifers in one corner dictate the nearby
planting of red roses, while the silver birches call for an
accompaniment of simple white, grey and blue. The birches
are limbed up above the low planting of echiums, catmint,
rhododendrons, hellebores and hostas, to reveal the sheep
and cattle in the paddocks beyond. Alpines in tufa pots
decorate the courtyard area, with larger specimens in the
rockery and pond area.

CLIFTON DOWNS
Clifton

Clifton Downs

Owners:
Cindy and Russell Liggett

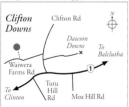

Address: Waiwera Farms Rd, R D 3, Clifton, Balclutha
Directions: From Balclutha, travel about 15km west, then turn right into Clifton Rd. Continue 3km, then turn left into Waiwera Farms Rd. Garden is first house on right. From Clinton, travel 15km east to Clifton Rd
Phone: 0-3-415 7211
Fax: 0-3-415 7211
Open: October to April, Fridays and Saturdays, 10am–5pm, or by appointment
Groups: As above, buses welcome
Fee: $2 per adult
Size: Small – 0.2ha (½ acre)
Terrain: Flat
Shop: Antique & country decorating
Nursery: Perennials & old roses
Accommodation: B&B farmstays

 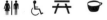

by arrangement

Cindy began the garden 20 years ago, but the main development has been since 1990, with a new area opened up last year. This is a circular lawn bordered with old roses and perennials planted according to a colour wheel. A new goldfish pond is overlooked by a gazebo, and newly planted woodland area of copper beeches, pin oaks and maples will provide autumn colour. An area of pin oaks and silver birches is used as the family's pet cemetery and there is an alpine playhut for children. The garden is popular for wedding photography, especially the old stone house ruins and the bride's walkway of crab apples that blossom in spring, along with the camellia hedge "Donation" and hundreds of spring bulbs. Another photogenic area is the fountain under the silver birches. Cherry trees blossoming above the peonies are pretty in December and a bed of "Sexy Rexy" roses continues the pink colourings. Cindy has planted one area in soft pink, white and blue, another in purples and her wild seed area is in more vibrant Monet-style colours. Cindy's favourites include old roses that climb the ponga archways, the deciduous trees, rhododendrons and azaleas, peonies, irises, aquilegias and catmint. A birds' area and farmyard animals add interest. Clifton Downs is also an Arabian horse and angora goat stud. The peak time to visit this garden is from Christmas to the end of January.

MAPLE GLEN
Wyndham

Owners:
Muriel, Bob and Rob Davison

Address: Glenham, R D 1, Wyndham
Directions: Take SH 1 north from
Invercargill or south from Gore, to
Edendale. Turn east and travel 5km to
Wyndham, then continue 11km to
Glenham. Travel another 2.4km to
Maple Glen on left. (18.4km from
Edendale)
Phone: 0-3-206 4983
Fax: 0-3-206 4983
Open: All year, weekdays 2pm–4pm,
Saturdays 9am–5pm
Closed: Sundays
Groups: As above; northern visitors
other times by appointment
Fee: No charge
Size: Large – 4ha (10 acres)
Terrain: Hilly to steep
Nursery: Wide range of flowering
shrubs, bulbs, rhododendrons,
perennials, etc

This woodland garden has been developed since 1970 as a "Home for Plants" and also a home for birds, with many lovebirds, exotic parrots, and waterfowl. Muriel's love of acers is seen in the maples flanking the house and throughout the garden. The terraced slope below the house is an extensive alpine rockery, with patches of bright blue gentians and splashes of red Mollis azaleas punctuated by conifers. Creepers tumble from sweeping balconies and clematis climbs white stuccoed pillars. Looking down from the house, the valley resembles an intricate tapestry with pockets of colour amid green grass. Sculptured cushions of ericas and geometrically shaped conifers create winter interest, structure and form. Massed hostas line the intersecting grassy avenues that lead past the extensive pond system, alive with ducks, swans and Canada geese. Gunnera foliage provides shade for astilbes, bog primulas and a ribbon border of new Siberian irises. Muriel is continually planting trees around the distant ponds, while selectively culling out others to create windows for vistas. Snowdrops emerge in July, joined by thousands of bluebells and daffodils in late September carpeting the laburnum and silver birch grove. *Magnolia campbellii*, dogwoods and cherry blossom are underplanted with rhododendrons, including the elegant *R. yakushimanum* species.

WINFIELD NURSERIES
Wyndham

Owners:
Jenny and Ian Sloan

Address: Glenham, R D 1, Wyndham
Directions: Take SH 1 north from
Invercargill or south from Gore, to
Edendale. Turn east and travel 5km to
Wyndham, then continue 11km to
Glenham. Take first left into
Mitchells Rd, then first right into
Owen Rd. Winfield first on right
Phone: 0-3-206 4907
Open: All year, Saturdays or
by appointment
Groups: As above
Fee: No charge
Size: Medium – 1.2ha (3 acres)
Terrain: Rolling
Nursery: Mainly perennials, a few
alpines and bulbs

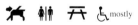

Originally part of the Winfield estate, this garden has been established over the past six to 19 years on paddock which was bare except for a macrocarpa hedge. Jenny planted English trees including limes, silver birches and the rowans which seed everywhere, followed by the rhododendrons which are now the predominant species, including "Kaponga" with its red blooms reflecting in the pond and "Hawkscrest" with yellow trusses glowing in the early morning and evening light. In spring, cornus and prunus blossom such as "Mt Fuji", "Accolade" and "Ukon" complements pink and white rhododendrons including "Van Nes Sensation" and "Pink Pearl" and a raised alpine bed features. Jenny is developing the water garden with hostas, astilbes and her favourite irises, contrasting with giant-foliaged gunneras, and is planning another pond and bog garden. Long curving beds of perennials with cranesbill geraniums and many different iris species feature through summer and autumn. The deciduous trees, especially the maples and beeches, colour up well in autumn, then the bare limbs and conifers feature in winter, when the ericas and callunas provide colour. The view across rolling farmland right down to Stewart Island on a clear day is a special feature of this certified organic Bio-Gro Garden.

HILLSIDE GARDENS
Mataura Island

Owners:
Eileen and David McKenzie

Address: Mataura Island, R D 1,
Wyndham
Directions: From Edendale, take road
to Seaward Downs. Turn left at
school and continue to Mataura
Island. Turn right and travel to
Hillside Gardens on left. (17km from
Edendale)
Phone: 0-3-246 9545
Open: Early August to Christmas,
Saturdays or by appointment
Groups: By appointment
Fee: No charge
Size: Medium – 1ha (2½ acres)
Terrain: Slightly sloping
Nursery: Rhododendron specialist,
bulbs and perennials

Eileen has planted her hillside garden in the last decade from bare paddocks with only a few original trees. These include the pair of old English beeches that form an archway over the drive. Once shelter trees such as limes, oaks, eucalypts, poplars and David's favourite maples had been planted, Eileen began the garden beneath, establishing her favourite rhododendrons, with a collection now of over a thousand. Most of her time these days is taken up with the several hundred show daffodils that look stunning in early spring. Following the rhododendrons, the lilies emerge, but the roses have been curtailed by the possums. A special feature is the bricked courtyard, where seats and tables are sheltered by a central silver birch. Rhododendrons and azaleas surround this area, creating a colourful spring garden. Conifers and shrubs, including ericas and callunas, are underplanted with daffodils, hostas, primulas and Chatham Island forget-me-nots, with grassy pathways separating the beds of perennials. Eileen plans to establish walking tracks through a stand of native bush to the side of the garden, and develop a pond on the edge. Sited on a hillside, this terraced garden overlooks the river valley with a panoramic view up the Mataura River.

311

HOSTA GARDEN
Glencoe

Owners:
Gaynor and Chris Miller

Address: Roslyn Downs, R D 2,
Glencoe, Invercargill
Directions: From Invercargill take
SH 6 to Lorneville. Turn right and
continue to T intersection at
Hedgehope. Turn right into SH 96
and travel to Glencoe. Continue to
McDonald Rd on right. Take first left
to Hosta Garden
Phone: 0-3-230 6144
Fax: 0-3-230 6144
Open: Labour weekend (end October)
to end November, Wednesdays to
Saturdays, or by appointment
Groups: By appointment
Fee: $3 per adult
Size: Large – 2ha (5 acres)
Terrain: Undulating with levels
Nursery: Hosta specialists; over 150
varieties for sale; new releases from
America; mail-order catalogue

mostly

This 30 year-old woodland garden is heavily
underplanted with hostas which thrive in the sheltered
moist conditions. A wide range of hosta species features,
with many new cultivars and hybrids mainly derived from
H. fortunei, H. montana and the blue-leafed *H. sieboldiana*.
Structure is provided by brick pathways, rocks, retaining
walls and steps Chris made from sleepers, creating various
levels and heights. A bog garden is planted with ligularia,
primulas and gunneras complementing the hostas, and
a bridge crosses a rock-edged creek planted with further
hostas, which will run into a large pond. A belvedere will
overlook the Douglas firs, gums, native ponga and
deciduous oaks, ashes, prunus, birches and maples,
including some new and rare varieties. Gaynor uses white
and blue with the bright spring colours of rhododendrons,
edged with large drifts of unfurling hostas. The texture
and form of hosta foliage cools the summer, when peonies
and roses provide splashes of colour. Gaynor is using
natives increasingly, with kauri, totara, indigenous cedars,
pittosporums, pseudopanax, ponga ferns, grasses and
some native groundcovers. She has developed a rustic
shade arbour, with species clematis climbing over it and
a hosta display around a central urn. The Hosta Hut sells
hand-made crafts including designer rabbits and terracotta
earth-mothers.

BELLE FLEUR GARDENS
Northope

Belle Fleur

Owners:
Walter and Kathleen Jack

Address: Northope, R D 4, Invercargill
Directions: From Invercargill, take
SH 99 for 13km to Wallacetown.
Continue 5km, turn right into Oporo-
Northope Flat Rd. Travel 15km, then
turn left into Drain Rd. Garden
second on left. From Lumsden, take
SH 6 towards Invercargill. Turn right
into SH 96 before Winton. Take first
left, then turn right into Drain Rd
Phone: 0-3-236 8523
Fax: 0-3-236 0594
Open: First weekend in February to
late April, daily, daylight to dark
Groups: By appointment
Fee: No charge
Size: Medium – 1ha (over 2 acres)
Terrain: Flat
Nursery: Dahlia specialist; hardy
pot-grown tubers @ $4.50 – $7.50

hot water available

Belle Fleur, French for "beautiful flower", is the home of Oreti dahlias which the Jacks breed. Begun in 1976, when gums, silver birches and rhododendrons were planted for shelter, the dahlia garden now features over 700 different varieties. The shaped display beds are arranged in different types; some are colour coordinated and others feature companion planting. Dahlia sizes range from the tiny dwarfs which are ideal for border displays, to the giant 40-centimetre dahlias planted in exhibition beds. The Jacks find that red, lavender and purple dahlias sell well, while the yellows, oranges and whites are not as popular, so they have a demonstration bed of red dahlias interplanted with yellow and white to show how these colours bring the red out. Colour combinations change each year, with many of the beds edged in annuals such as the fluffy blue ageratum bordering lemon and yellow dahlias in one plot, and pink dahlias in another. Dahlia foliage varies from green to a rich black, with one plot devoted to the black leafed varieties. Lavenders and ageratum edge the garden by the bridge which leads to a trial garden, where new dahlias are assessed by the National Dahlia Society, along with a public voting system. The Jacks' dahlia video, selling for $17.50, features over 150 dahlias. A mail-order catalogue is available for $2.50.

MYROSS BUSH RHODODENDRONS
Myross Bush

Owners:
Frances and Alan Wise

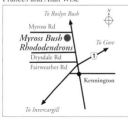

Address: R D 6, Myross Bush,
Invercargill
Directions: From Invercargill, take
SH 1 towards Kennington. Turn left
towards Roslyn Bush. Take third on
left into Myross Rd, garden first on
left
Phone: 0-3-230 4407
Fax: 0-3-230 4407
Open: All spring, weekends, or
by appointment
Groups: By appointment
Fee: No charge
Size: Medium – 0.4ha (1 acre)
Terrain: Flat
Nursery: 250 rhododendron varieties
grown in garden; limited range of
evergreen and deciduous azaleas;
good range of perennials

This is a formal rhododendron display garden established 13 years ago. Frances has added more of her favourite "yak" species and hybrids recently. These *Rhododendron yakushimanum* have become increasingly popular in modern gardens because of their compact shapes, attractive deep-green shiny foliage and elegant trusses. Apart from the house garden featuring a rockery, the main areas are Margaret's Maze and Charlie's Woodland, named after the previous owners. A pair of conifers flank the entrance to the "maze" where about 900 different rhododendrons are arranged in beds sheltered by a canopy of flowering cherries and magnolias, which provide dappled shade. The prunus flower throughout the peak of the rhododendron season, in October and November, complementing each other beautifully. Underplanting includes heaths and evergreen azaleas, although the rhododendrons are widely spaced to allow visitors to walk across to them and read their names. New and rare rhododendrons such as apricot "Donald Palmer" feature, with a good selection of the pale-pink "Loderi" group, many dwarf varieties, yellow *R. macabeanum* and other large-leafed species. A few deciduous Mollis azaleas are included and Frances is experimenting with vireyas in the tunnel house. She is finding the orange spectrum is becoming more popular and reds less in favour.

MARSHWOOD
West Plains

Owners:
Geoff and Adair Genge

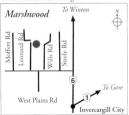

Address: Leonard Rd, West Plains,
R D 4, Invercargill
Directions: From Invercargill, take
SH 6 north towards Winton. Turn left
into West Plains Rd & continue 4km.
Turn right into Leonard Rd (no exit)
Phone: 0-3-215 7672
Fax: 0-3-215 7672
Open: All year except Christmas,
Boxing, New Year's, & Easter Days
and Good Friday; open Wednesdays
to Saturdays 10am–5pm, Sundays
1pm–5pm; Mondays & Tuesdays in
summer holidays
Groups: By appointment
Fee: $2 per adult
Size: Large – 2.8ha (6 acres)
Terrain: Flat
Nursery: Wide range of perennials;
specialists in lavenders, salvias, nepeta,
euphorbias; mail-order catalogue

Named after Geoff's family home in Dorset, Marshwood has been developed from a bare windy paddock over the past 16 years. The hedges, planted for shelter, now form a sculpted structural framework for the garden, creating vistas and dividing the garden into rooms. Marshwood is known for the hybrid stoechas lavender of that name, with its outstanding long, mauve bracts. Another is "Helmsdale", with deep purple bracts, and the Genges are breeding new varieties. Various lavenders feature as low hedges and clumps throughout the garden, as do many salvias, the Genges holding a New Zealand Herb Federation National Collection. Other predominant perennials include nepeta and euphorbias, accompanied by rhododendrons in spring, followed by *Lilium auratum* and old roses in summer, with a large rose pergola providing a new attraction. Sweeping lawns and grassy walkways are edged with lavender, salvia and catmint, beneath a spring cascade of cherry blossom such as the chartreuse "Ukon". The rhododendrons bloom above a carpet of ajuga and other groundcovers. Massed hostas edge perennial borders featuring Siberian irises and trilliums, contrasting with architectural-leafed rheums and gunneras. English lavender lines a pathway with a sun-dial focal point, leading to an archway into a white garden enclosed within clipped macrocarpa hedges.

NORTH ISLAND GARDENS INDEX

North Island Owners Index

SOUTH ISLAND GARDENS INDEX

SOUTH ISLAND OWNERS INDEX

Jillian and Denis Friar have the following books published:
New Zealand Gardens Open to Visit – North Island
New Zealand Gardens Open to Visit – South Island
Private Gardens of New Zealand – Wellington, Wairarapa & Kapiti Coast
Private Gardens of New Zealand – South Island
Friars' Guide to New Zealand Accommodation for the Discerning Traveller – 1996
Friars' Guide to New Zealand Accommodation for the Discerning Traveller – 1997